The sociology of literature

Longman
London and New York

The sociology of literature

John Hall

Longman
London and New York

Longman Group Limited London

Associated companies, branches and representatives
throughout the world

Published in the United States of America
by Longman Inc., New York

© Longman Group Limited 1979

First published 1979

British Library Cataloguing in Publication Data

Hall, John
   The sociology of literature.
   1. Literature and society
   I. Title
   809   PN51   79-40138

   ISBN 0 582 48590 8

Printed in Great Britain by McCorquodale (Newton) Limited, Newton-le-Willows, Lancashire

Contents

Preface

This book was designed with two aims in mind. First, the book should serve as a textbook for students taking courses in the sociology of literature and culture. This apparently innocent aim necessitated undertaking a second, more general task. It is well known that the sociology of literature is not one of the more high-powered areas of sociology. Part of the reason for this is surely that the field of the subject has not been systematically defined: this book attempts to remedy this deficiency. More particularly, the great traditional weakness of the sociology of literature has been its refusal to progress beyond a type of superior cultural criticism based upon often dubious readings of literary classics. The most obvious criticism to be made of this is that it ignores the insistence of Wimsatt and Beardsley (1949) that it is an 'affective fallacy' to presume that the actual meaning of the text is the one that the reader eventually makes his own. Once, however, this argument is accepted it becomes necessary to rigorously distinguish matters of 'consumption' from those of 'production'. And I have tried to nudge the sociology of literature in a more empirical direction by considering 'popular' as well as 'high' literature.

During the course of writing the book a third theme thrust itself forward. Discussions of literature in this book are typically drawn from Europe in the last few centuries. This literature has, of course, been considered frequently and forcefully by Marxists, and it was thus perhaps only natural that some dialogue with the Marxist position would result. This dialogue centres on a disagreement over the character of the European bourgeoisie. It seems to me that the Marxists, given the social background of authors and the composition of the reading public, are right to consider the literature mentioned as bourgeois. But the Marxist concept of 'Bourgeois Literature' is nevertheless of very strictly limited utility: at its worst it seems to consider the recent European novel as the transposition into a literary plane of the demands and interests of a strictly economic class. In reaction to this narrowness I have preferred a neo-Weberian concept of 'Bourgeois Literacy' which emphasises the role of the bourgeoisie as the carrier of values of discipline and literacy that proved of great importance in creating a powerful literary culture. The informed reader will be able to note that the dialogue with Marxism in fact runs throughout the book, but it may be of some use to indicate the two areas where the discussion is most pointed. In Chapter 4 a description of the novel in realist and modernist form is proposed that goes some way beyond both the traditional Marxism of Lukács and the more radical positions favoured by members of the Frankfurt School. In Chapter 8 more recent Marxist attempts to discuss the political functions of literature are critically reviewed. The concept of 'Bourgeois Literacy' is most fully outlined in the latter chapter.

My intellectual debt to the work of Lionel Trilling and Ernest Gellner is obvious. It is a pleasure to be able to record help and advice from Denis McQuail who first suggested I write this book. Various chapters were improved by comments received from Jacques Berthoud and Strix O'Brien. Graham Allan and Tony Rees were a constant source of encouragement. Michael Lane kindly let me make use of unpublished work on publishers, whilst David Musselwhite and Peter Mann helped to obtain other unpublished material. John Rule provided the information about wife sales. Herculean labours were performed on the typescript by Karen Fulbrook to whom I am very grateful. An earlier version of Chapter 8 appeared in *Lo Spettacolo* in 1979.

We are grateful to New York Public Library for permission to adapt tables after Altick from 'The sociology of authorship' in *New York Public Library Bulletin*, 1962 edn.

Chapter 1

Theoretical traditions

One way in which any subject may be approached is by considering the various theoretical strands involved in its development. There are advantages and disadvantages in the application of this method to the sociology of literature in this chapter. The reader convinced of the disadvantages can proceed directly to the next chapter in which the alternative approach of outlining a view of the actual state of affairs in the sociology of literature is adopted.

It may be said at once that sympathy can easily be extended to the reader who chooses to avoid a consideration of the intellectual constituents of the sociology of literature. The great disadvantage of outlining these constituents is that they are sometimes mutually contradictory, rarely in mutual contact or dialogue and quite often of rather limited quality. Indeed, a type of theoretical exuberance plagues the subject so that for example, too great a proportion of recent effort has centred on attempts to unravel the intellectual debris offered by recently hailed luminaries such as Derrida, Lacan, Adorno and Althusser. There are so many possible intellectual constituents of the subject that it has seemed necessary, in the interest of clarity, to limit our discussion to six. This in itself might seem overly generous; consequently, it is instructive to note one reason why such diversity is at present unavoidable. Beneath most of the traditions to be considered lies some conception of 'the beautiful'. Unfortunately, aesthetic philosophy is in such a poorly developed condition that the proliferation of approaches can be explained by the ease with which exceptions can be found to every generalisation about 'the beautiful'. In this book some attempt will be made to chart a *via media* between conflicting positions. But exceptions will doubtless be found to this too, and it is thus probably necessary to conclude that, in the absence of a better developed aesthetic theory, all that can be hoped for is interesting but slightly flawed generalisations.

The advantage of studying these diverse intellectual traditions is simple, namely that this approach alone can show the problems that a synthesis must resolve. And it is only fair to admit that the problems emphasised in this chapter dovetail neatly with the particular synthesis offered in the next chapter.

For the sake of convenience the principal problems have been emphasised on their first appearance. Some of these issues can be clarified in the course of this chapter, but others provide the material for the next chapter. The position reached on the various issues is described in the conclusion to this chapter.

1. Marxism

Marxism, of various kinds, has dominated sociological discussions of literature. This is in one sense peculiar as a reading of, say, *Capital* would not make one expect that such an obviously political theory would lead to such keen interest in aesthetic matters. That this is so is perhaps the product of an accident, namely the incredible fertility of Marx's mind. And in Marx's own early but unsystematic observations can be seen the two issues raised by the Marxist approach to literature.

The first of these comprises the promise of the Marxist approach, and is simply the insistence that literature can only be understood in its social context, or that an **external** referent is necessary for the full comprehension of any text. This point could be put in many other ways. Most importantly, it is stressed that literature is part of society and can offer social content that will serve as information about society. Marx himself produced interesting comments on very varied texts, and at one time planned a book on Balzac whose portrait of industrialising France he much admired. But for all this, Marx never systematically worked out any theory specifying the exact links between literature and society. All that can be said is that these relations were not seen in a crude way. In a celebrated letter, Engels argued that mere socialist commitment was no guarantee of meritorious art. This view was defended with reference to Balzac:

> Well, Balzac was politically a Legitimist ... his sympathies are with the class that is doomed to destruction. But for all that, his satire is never keener, his irony never more bitter, than when he sets in motion the very men and women with whom he sympathises most deeply – the nobles. And the only men of whom he speaks with undisguised admiration are his bitterest antagonists, the republican heroes ... (Marx and Engels, 1947, p. 38).

This argument has since become something of a critical orthodoxy enshrined in the insistence of the American 'New Critics' that one commits an 'intentional fallacy' if (to use D. H. Lawrence's famous phrase) one trusts the teller rather than the tale (Wimsatt and Beardsley, 1946). Whilst it is, of course, much to the credit of the Marxist founding fathers to have realised that the role of the critic is, in Chesterton's words, to make the writer jump out of his skin by showing him what he is really up to, two general weaknesses of this position should be noted. First, it too often encouraged rank ignoring of authors. This was a pity since it tended to turn the process of creation into something unduly mystical. In Balzac's case, for example, it is less the case that he was able to gain a critical perspective on his society in spite of his values but rather that such values, as was the case with Eliot and Yeats, gave him the distance from his society that his work needed. Secondly, the displacing of the author led inevitably to critical licence. Authors became fodder for critical schemes, and in the process even the supposedly sacred respect for the text became somewhat sullied.

The second issue that Marx raised showed his own intellectual open-mindedness. Marx's thought was deeply marked by the nineteenth-century belief in social evolution; consequently one of its central points is the emphasis on a series of historical stages. When applied to literature, this approach led to the inevitable question as to why, to use Marx's own example, the literature of the Greeks should be of interest in the entirely different circumstances of capitalism. Marx suggested that the explanation for this lay in the nostalgia exhibited by men of later 'stages' for their childhood. What characterises this rather weak explanation is a fundamental open-mindedness; for what Marx is implicitly recognising is that great art could be produced at a relatively 'low' stage of the historical process. Marx, in other words, preferred to place his conviction of the merit of Greek art above a strict interpretation of his theory of stages. Marx's tolerance in this matter contrasts with two recent attempts to solve the problem in strictly Marxist terms. The first attempted solution, that of Macherey and Balibar (1974), offers an amusing intellectual sleight-of-hand whereby it is suggested that there is not really any 'problem' of Greek art. They suggest that Greek art was not truly 'art', and that it only came to be seen as such when the bourgeoisie chose to so elevate it – seemingly in order to enhance their position by posing as protectors of culture. Eagleton's (1976b) solution is based on the argument that nostalgia is a characteristic lapse only of men living under the fragmenting experience of capitalism. Insofar as these positions suggest that the future will be different they are hard to criticise – although a future in which we would be freed from the regrettable nostalgia of appreciating Homer may not be such as to be too profoundly desired. However, rank suspicion should be accorded to the common characteristic of the two arguments, namely that literature is the passive reflector of particular historical circumstances without interest for later cultures. It will prove fairly easy to find some solution to this problem of **historicism**. But what is more worrying in the long run is the ease with which a scheme can be used for reductionist purposes. The ghost of reductionism will haunt us in the next chapter.

Where Marx offers only the barest but most exciting of insights, Lukács, the greatest Marxist critic, offers much system but rather few literary insights. Lukács' main work is initially but a gloss on that of Marx. He follows Marx in admiring Balzac, but goes further in suggesting that Balzac's achievement is made possible by his ability to depict 'types':

The central category and criterion of realistic literature is the type, a particular synthesis which organically binds together the general and the particular both in characters and in situations. What makes a type a type is not its average quality, nor its mere individual being, however profoundly conceived; what makes it a type is that in it all humanity and socially essential determinations are present at their highest level of development, in the ultimate unfolding of the possibilities latent in them, in extreme presentation of their extremes – rendering concrete the peaks and limits of men and epochs (Lukács, 1950, p. 6).

Lukács insists that only the use of types allows social reality to be properly described. Consequently he condemns as mere 'naturalism' the novels of Zola which he considers to accumulate social detail without the ability to create types.

Three comments need to be made about Lukács' theory of the realism of the early nineteenth-century novel. First, Lukács is so concerned with the social content or external dimension of literature that, particularly in comparison with Marx himself, his sympathies prove to be rather narrow. More particularly, his analysis of realism moves quickly from a descriptive to a normative state which is used to condemn other modes. It will be seen later that this adulation of realism is unfortunate. A second point related to the concern to draw out social content can be raised by asking how Lukács in fact distinguishes true realism from naturalism, or accurate social content from subtle distortion. The answer is disconcertingly simple, and has been well described by Lerner writing about Lukács'

> ... discussion of Balzac's *Les Paysans*. After describing the attempt of the landowner Montcornet to do away with the traditional rights of the poor, and so assist the move from feudalism to capitalism on the land (a description that certainly misrepresents the novel), Lukács remarks that 'this presents in literary form the same essential development of the post-revolutionary smallholding that Marx described in *The Eighteenth Brumaire*' ... [Lukács seems] to be measuring Balzac against Marx and Engels, and judging him by how well he attains to their insight (Lerner, 1977, pp. 48–9).

Put more bluntly, the conviction of some Marxist critics that they already possess the truth can prove debilitating to their literary sensitivity. Thirdly, Lukács bases his work on the best literature of the age which is capable of summing up conflicts most profoundly. The weakness of this position is that it assumes too easily that popular literature is not a worthy receptacle of 'social content'. But this point should not, at least in Lukács' case, be overstressed since there is a little truth to the argument that his defence of realism against modernism is the defence of a popular form against an elitist one.

Nevertheless, if Lukács' interpretation of the social content of literature is generally unsubtle, the historicism involved in his theory about the development of the European novel after Balzac is disastrously crude. Lukács follows the Marxist belief that the mechanism of historical change is class conflict, and he suggests that the defeat of the 'revolutions' of 1848 marks the moment when the bourgeoisie moves from its progressive period as destroyer of feudalism to its reactionary period as opponent of the proletariat, the next and indeed the last historical class. Lukács' theory of the novel follows this scheme very closely. He argues that progressive values allowed for the great novels of Balzac and Stendhal, while the reactionary values dominant since 1848 have caused the deterioration of modern European literature. This deterioration is a consequence of the character of realism. Realism, in Lukács' opinion, is a mode that can only be used when the world is, precisely, worth describing. Lukács considers that the world after 1848 was so little worth describing that other inferior symbolic and subjectivist modes naturally took its place. The worm in the bud of the European novel was first planted by Flaubert, developed in the naturalism of Zola, and reaches for Lukács a peak in the subjectivist and pessimist vision of Kafka. In a celebrated essay Lukács argued that it is necessary to choose between the pessimistic and enclosed world of Kafka and that created (apparently as the result of a vigorous adherence to bourgeois values) by Thomas Mann (Lukács, 1963).

Such a schematisation is brutal and deserves to be since it is clear that Lukács' theory has had a very wide reception. The classic criticism to be made against Lukács comes as a reaction to the melancholy sight of a critic deliberately detracting from the obvious power of some modernist writers in the interests of his own critical scheme. This criticism was made very early on by members of the Frankfurt School who consciously championed Proust and Kafka against Lukács. Nevertheless, it should be noted that even the Frankfurt School accepted the theory that 1848 marked a turning-point since they argued that modernism was to be seen as a cryptic and complex style appropriate to the post-1848 world. Both Lukács' attack on modernism and this particular defence of it are open to criticism, as will be seen in Chapter 4. But Lukács may be criticised on other, more obvious grounds. His own theory has at least one striking ambiguity. His criticism of Zola depends upon a committed writer being unable to transcend the objective circumstances of his time (i.e. the inability of the reactionary 'late' bourgeoisie to foster progressive values); but this does not prevent him suggesting that Thomas Mann was a great bourgeois writer in, presumably, worse objective circumstances, as a result of *his* adoption of progressive values. Usually, in other words, writers are conceived as passive reflectors of historical circumstances, but this mechanistic model is occasionally abandoned without real justification. And finally little real agreement can be discovered among Marxists about the actual effects of 1848. John Berger, for example, has argued that Millet developed his characteristic style after these events, albeit the radical intention of his work could not be perfectly carried out in the post-1848 world (Berger, 1976). Whatever the truth of the matter in Millet's case, it is quite certain that the clear triumph of realism in the visual arts post-1848 presents problems for Lukács' general theory.

Lukács in effect made rather poor use of the two issues raised by Marx. In doing so he gave Marxist literary criticism a justified reputation for insensitivity to literary qualities. Lucien Goldmann's work has been given a good reception as a result, for his approach seemed initially to be far subtler. Goldmann had been influenced by the neo-Hegelian Lukács of *The Theory of the Novel* as well as by structuralism: both of these traditions encouraged him to declare that he would pay far more attention to texts. Thus in his celebrated *The Hidden God* (1970) he argued for a continual movement from text to society and vice versa. In this particular case he felt able to suggest that a 'homology' (along with resonance and mediation a much weaker metaphor than the idea of reflection that usually underlay Lukács' work) of structures of thought existed between the works of Pascal and Racine and the *noblesse de robe* of seventeenth-century France. The homology occurred in the following manner. The *noblesse de robe* lost their effective function as a result of Louis XIV's policy of imposing civil servants (*intendants*) as provincial governors; they thus remained bound to the king but bereft of social function. Goldmann suggests that this position of tied impotence is seen at work in Racine and Pascal whose universe is one in which the individual cannot save himself but is forced to acknowledge a supreme God. Thus Pascal and Racine were able to give literary form to the 'world view' of a particular social class.

There is no question but that *The Hidden God* is one of the few really significant sociological works that illuminate particular authors. But it is worth noting that Goldmann's argument depends on a rather narrow definition of tragedy, namely that tragedy results from a refusal to compromise on the part of an individual who is placed in a situation from which he cannot escape without compromise. Such a definition would not be applicable to Sophocles or to Shakespeare, and raises the worrying spectre of Goldmann having defined a literary mode in such a way as to make it amenable to social treatment (Thody, 1977, pp. 74–5). Such worries become more pressing when considering Goldmann's work on the novel. For Goldmann's actual definition of the novel as a literary form ('The transposition on the literary plane of daily life in the individualistic society born from production for the market') is, as Caute observes (1972, p. 211), a definition which is oriented to social content at the expense of the close textual analysis that Goldmann formally espoused.

Goldmann's theory of the genesis and fall of the novel shows, moreover, an historicism as brutal as that of Lukács. The crux of the novel is, according to Goldmann, the manner in which a 'problematic hero' tries to make sense of liberal values in a world which frequently denies them. The hero slowly disappears from the novel as a result of changes in capitalism: cartel capitalism (1880–1914) lessens the importance of the hero, crisis capitalism (1918–39) effectively destroys him, and consumer capitalism (post-1945) only allows for the portrayal of alienated heroes. This is schematism gone wild, all the more so in that no attempt is even made to explain how reputed authors would fit into it. Goldmann justifies the scheme by an analysis of Malraux's novels, but this justification is extremely questionable. Malraux is allowed to have written a good novel (*La Condition Humaine*) at a time when he was an advocate of progressive values; such advocacy apparently allowed him to transcend the material conditions of crisis capitalism (although this does not stop Goldmann claiming that the objective conditions of consumer capitalism are such as to have stopped him writing altogether). However, Malraux's later novels, notably *L'Espoir*, are judged to be flawed by Malraux's adoption of a non-progressive Communist Party line. This is quite false: Malraux was no stooge of the communists in Spain and was in fact an active member of many leftist writers' organisations. The style of *L'Espoir* is to be explained far less by a change in values than by the rush involved in publishing a novel concerned to comment on contemporary events (Caute, 1972, p. 209). Far more worrying, however, than the apparent belief that writers can suddenly shed their skins according to social circumstances is the complete misreading of Malraux. Malraux's novels all centre on the romantic and Nietzschean desire to live heroically in order to defy the ravages of death and aging; these novels are in virtually no way representative of larger historical patterns, although they provide fascinating insight into the quirks of a particular variant on rather well-known ideas of French intellectuals.

In the final analysis the work of both Lukács and Goldmann suffers from historicism and an overzealous attempt to pull out of particular texts requisite meanings. That these weaknesses are not likely to have escaped the notice of anyone working in this tradition is indicated by the work of Swingewood. After noting the traditional Marxist literary insensitivity to texts, Swingewood fails to transcend it as the following two examples demonstrate. First, his concern to schematise leads him to spend some considerable effort explaining away an author otherwise widely hailed. Swingewood follows Goldmann in arguing that modern capitalism outlaws all progressive world views, unless they are Marxist: and he argues that a good novel must be progressive by definition. Swingewood attempts to prove his case by showing how poor a novelist D. H. Lawrence was forced to be as the result of his reactionary views. This absurdly partial view takes no cognizance of Steiner's wry realisation that artistic achievement has no absolute connection with political progressiveness. Unless very constricting definitions are to be used, Céline must be considered a significant writer; and the same is surely true of Beckett, Lawrence and, as Steiner notes, Lucien Rebatet who went so far as to approve the fate of the Jews (Steiner, 1972, p. 54). Secondly, the concern with social content, recognised as a result of the possession of Marxism, leads to a distortion in the reading of particular texts. Swingewood's discussion of Conrad suggests that his work was flawed by his failure to recognise the future of socialism. All his characters are thus mere individuals rather than types, with the single exception, in Swingewood's view, of Nostromo whose 'organic' relation to history makes him Conrad's single 'successful' character (Laurenson and Swingewood, 1972). Once again, it is alarming to see how much of an author's actual achievement is ignored; and it is not necessary to accept all of Leavis's reading of *Nostromo* to realise that Nostromo himself is one of the least successfully realised characters in the novel of that name (Leavis, 1972). One rather similarly baulks at the grounds of Swingewood's defence of Grassic Gibbon's 'proletarian novel' in comparison with those of Tressell and Greenwood:

> At first [the hero] despises and remains apart from his fellow workers,
> but unlike the other intellectual ascetic heroes of Tressell's and
> Greenwood's novels, Grassic Gibbon's hero has the enormous advantage
> that the distance between himself and the masses is necessarily bridged
> by the knowledge that the working class and the Communist Party
> embody the sole hope for social change (Swingewood, 1977, p. 65).

This is, of course, a vast step backwards from the position advocated by Engels in the letter cited above.

This discussion of traditional Marxist approaches to literature can be summarised simply. The promise of Marxism to place literature in its social context has not been redeemed. Instead literature has been pressed into historicist schemes without due regard to its inherent qualities.

2. The English School

The failure of Marxism to fulfil its promise makes the approach to literature and society contained in the English School seem the more impressive. By the English School is meant that approach deriving from Matthew Arnold, and having as a late and fierce champion F. R. Leavis. This approach has had considerable influence on a number of eminent writers who do not always share Leavis's political views, notably on Richard Hoggart and Raymond Williams. There are two reasons for examining this school, further to their obvious interest in the relations of literature and society. Firstly, this school, and especially Leavis, has a reputation for close textual scrutiny. Secondly, this has resulted in very striking readings of the English literary tradition; this is important insofar as the Marxist tradition has developed its method on European material in a way that often makes it inapplicable to other circumstances (Lerner, 1977).

Superficially, it might be thought that the interest of this school in the relations of literature and society in combination with their literary sensitivity might, as it were, make them better Marxists. Such a view would be mistaken since there are fundamental differences between this approach and Marxism. The first area of difference concerns what may be called the **truth** of literature. Broadly speaking, where Marxists are prone to measure the success or failure of an author by reference to the Marxist classics, the English School in comparison suggests that a complex literary achievement is likely to be better than any sociological theory, and clearly better than Marxism. This very high valuation of literature can be seen when Hoggart insists that the literary imagination is essentially at odds with sociology:

> Ideal type analysis abstracts from the detail of society so as to make a usable theoretic design; creative writing recognizes 'significant detail' whilst at the same time recognizing and recreating the flux of untypical life (1973, Vol. 2, p. 249).

In a recent statement Leavis went further in seeming to suggest that the very nature of language means that only the literary imagination can fully comprehend social experience:

> ... a language is more than a means of expression; it is the heuristic conquest won out of representative experience, the upshot or precipitate of immemorial human living, and embodies values, distinctions, identifications, conclusions, promptings, cartographical hints and tested potentialities. It exemplifies the truth that life is growth and growth change, and that the condition of these is continuity (1975, p. 44).

Whilst this concern with the power and capacity of literature is refreshing, it is only fair to say that the general argument is so vague as to solve few problems. Most obviously, the English School has a tendency to make the opposite error to that of the Marxists. Where the latter ignore or explain away literature that does not fit their schemes, the English School tends to ignore or explain away independent social evidence. This can lead to the error wittily observed by John Gross:

> This [concern with the social context] might seem too obvious to need saying, to anyone who hadn't seen what actually goes on, to anyone who hadn't, for example, come across students praising *Hard Times* for the deadly accuracy of its satire on Utilitarianism, a subject on which it turned out most of their ideas derived from – *Hard Times* (1973, p. 321).

What is missing from both Marxism and the English School is an ability to hold social and literary modes in tension. And it must be noted that the pose of some members of the English School as critics whose faithfulness to the text is enhanced by their repudiation of social theory is exaggerated. It can in fact easily be seen that both Leavis and Williams choose novelists for inclusion in their different versions of the tradition of the English novel on the grounds of different philosophies of history. It is as well to discuss these philosophies of history openly since the alternative is to smuggle them in through the use of emotionally loaded words. Philip Abrams has seen this problem and has argued that there is more to be said in favour of the style of argument of sociology than some literary critics allow:

> ... if assent is withheld from the commentary of a literary critic on a work such as *Little Dorrit*, the response tends to be a matter of difficult and increasingly opaque reiterations, the invocation of elusive notions such as 'life', 'community', 'nisus', '*ahnung*', demands for an honest response to 'experience', ... When assent is withheld from the sociologist's account of capitalism, on the other hand, reference is made not to such mystifications or unexplorable tenets but to a body of information that can be directly scrutinised and to the scholarship, care and integrity with which the account has been assembled ... (1976, p. 353).

The second area in which the English School tends to differ from Marxism is that of the nature of artistic activity. Where the Marxist view has traditionally been that of the artist passively reflecting social circumstances, the English School, in line with its high valuation of the literary imagination, tends to emphasise the ability of the creative artist to describe things not generally understood and as a result to alter social life itself. This emphasis on the artist as creator rather than reflector can be seen in Williams' recent and interesting development of a theory of language. Williams argues that language is not something static that pictures the world; rather it allows for flexibility and creativity and itself plays a part in the creation of new social meanings. Language is thus not just a tool to describe a pre-existent reality, but a 'constitutive' and 'material' part of reality itself. This theory of language serves as the basis of Williams' attack on the idea of reflection:

> ... the underlying problem is obvious. If 'reality' and 'speaking about reality' (the 'material social process' and 'language') are taken as categorically distinct, concepts such as 'reflection' and 'mediation' are inevitable. The same pressure can be observed in attempts to interpret the Marxist phrase 'the production and reproduction of real life' as if production were the primary social (economic) process and 'reproduction' its 'symbolic' or 'signifying' or 'cultural' counterpart. Such attempts are either alternative to the Marxist emphasis on an inherent constitutive 'practical consciousness', or, at their best, ways of specifying its actual operations. The problem is different, from the beginning, if we see language and signification as indissoluble elements of the material social process itself, involved all the time both in production and reproduction (1977, p. 99).

Williams' position is refreshing insofar as it escapes from rather simplistic Marxism, but it is highly idiosyncratic and raises two objections. First, his description of language as a material force, despite the worthiness of its attempt to preserve art from dogmatic schema, raises problems of its own. In particular, Williams' appreciation of art at times runs over into the rather questionable assertion that, as material and constitutive, art must be a social force in its own right. This rather sweeping position probably has justification in some circumstances, but it may be compared unfavourably as an analysis of the present position of art with the more temperate position of Leavis who combines the necessary respect for art with an awareness of the fragility of its social position. Secondly, Williams seems on occasion to jump too far towards dogmatisms the opposite of those of crude Marxism. In particular, his argument about the creative author at times gives the impression that art cannot be explained in social terms at all. This impression is basically the result of the way in which Williams moves from a criticism of the failure of the metaphor of reflection to the unwarranted assertion that no means of explaining creative powers, however subtle, can possibly work. A middle way between the extremes is needed.

In summary, it may be said that the English School stands as a corrective to some of the crudities of traditional Marxism. But its own stress on the ability of literature to provide the truth about society is of rather little use since it is so undifferentiated. And at times the stress on the independence of the creative mind seems to be such as to remove any link between art and society. But the insights of this school are too valuable to ignore, and much effort will be expended in Chapter 2 in an attempt to systematise and integrate them.

3. Popular art

The previous discussion mentioning Leavis and Williams provides a suitable moment to raise the question of popular literature since both authors have made some contribution to the debate over the relationship between mass society, **popular** art and the quality of literature.

In the 1930s the Leavises worked out a striking theory about the effect of industrialisation on literature. It was suggested that mass society led to the isolation of the minority from the rest of society. This isolation could be seen in the use of the word 'high-brow':

> 'High-brow' is an ominous addition to the English language. I have said earlier that culture has always been in minority keeping. But the minority now is made conscious, not merely of an uncongenial but of a hostile environment. 'Shakespeare', I once heard Mr Dover Wilson say, 'was not a high-brow'. True: there were no high-brows in Shakespeare's time. It was possible for Shakespeare to write plays that were at once popular drama and poetry that could be appreciated only by an educated minority ... The same is not true ... of *The Waste Land, Hugh Selwyn Mauberley, Ulysses,* or *To the Lighthouse.* These works are only read by a very small specialised public and are beyond the reach of those who consider themselves educated. The age in which the finest creative talent tends to be employed in works of this kind is the age that has given currency to the term 'high-brow'. But it would be as true to say that the

attitude implicit in 'high-brow' causes the use of talent as the converse. The minority is being cut off as never before from the powers that rule the world ... (F. R. Leavis, 1930, p. 25).

The contrast between the current isolation of the minority and its ability to lead popular taste is even more clearly exhibited in Q. D. Leavis's important *Fiction and the Reading Public* (1938). In this book Mrs Leavis suggests that in the eighteenth century authors such as Fielding and Richardson were very widely read, but that sensibilities declined thereafter with the brutalisation endemic to industrialisation. For Mrs Leavis, this brutalisation could be exhibited by reference to the low quality of the modern best-seller.

The Leavisite argument is but one representative of the attack on the new mass society created by industrialism. Many intellectuals felt that their social position (and particularly their monopoly on literacy) was being eroded by the new society, and most reacted by arguing that the new society would lower standards. Another classic theory along the same lines was produced by leading members of the Frankfurt School. In a celebrated essay on 'The Culture Industry', Adorno and Horkheimer argued that popular art was merely designed to provide sufficient escapism to keep the population in a drugged state. Adorno and Horkheimer even felt that the culture industry would debase high art which had hitherto held out the possibility of a better society:

... the culture industry dresses works of art like political slogans and forces them upon a resistant public at reduced prices; they are as accessible for public enjoyment as a park. But the disappearance of their genuine commodity character does not mean that they have been abolished in the life of a free society, but that the last defense against their reduction to culture goods has fallen. The abolition of educational privilege by the device of clearance sales does not open for the masses the spheres from which they were formerly excluded, but, given existing social conditions, contributes directly to the decay of education and the progress of barbaric meaninglessness (1977, p. 378).

This debasement of great art was referred to as the ending of the 'aura' that had previously given a work of art its character and ability to shock. It was this view of the culture industry that led to Adorno's praise for the very difficulties of modernist art as a sophisticated way of retaining 'oppositional' thought.

This theory of mass society with its concomitant distrust of popular literature has obvious weaknesses. Edward Shils has argued convincingly that the organic community of the past may well have been more cohesive but was certainly, on the basis of popular entertainments such as bear-baiting and public executions, no more civilised (1957). Williams has sensibly observed that certain types of reading either have a use or are made necessary by particular social conditions:

Reading as this kind of easy drug is the permanent condition of a great bulk of ephemeral writing. But the question still is one of the circumstances in which the drug becomes necessary. I think there are certain circumstances – times of illness, tension, disturbing growth as in adolescence, and simple fatigue after work – which are much too easily overlooked in sweeping condemnations of 'reading as addiction' (Williams, 1971, p. 193).

Williams's own neo-populist radicalism naturally makes him opposed to Leavis over a wide range of matters. He has quite justly criticised the accuracy of the Leavisite picture of the eighteenth century, and has placed a much greater emphasis on the importance of popular culture. Nevertheless, this emphasis on the 'ordinariness' of culture should not hide the rather striking similarity between Leavis and Williams. Where Leavis sees certain pre-industrial situations as ones of organic community, Williams tends to suggest that such community may be achieved in the future. In this way they are both representatives of the 'English Dream' of small-scale, artistic and organic community life (Filmer, 1969).

This brief discussion is essentially one of different interpretations of popular art. This is appropriate in that few empirical studies have been made. This is, given actual reading patterns, essential. But in the absence of such empirical work we are left with questions which will concern us later. Is the function of popular literature escapism that people want, escapism that the 'Culture Industry' thinks they should have, or is its function something altogether different? Equally important, especially bearing in mind Williams' theory of a possible future common culture of high standard, is to make some attempt to establish the exact connections between high and low literature. More particularly, to what extent and in what way does high literature depend on popular literature?

4. Structuralism

Both the English School and Marxism think that literature can give information about society. Structuralism is in large part an attack on this view. It concentrates on the **internal** qualities of literature – occasionally in the open belief that literature has nothing to say about the larger society. The intellectual origins of structuralism are extremely complex and certainly include the very different milieux of Moscow, Prague, Copenhagen and Paris as well as diverse intellectual currents such as semiology, French anthropology and modern American syntactical linguistics. However, these important difficulties may here be skirted over due to the excellence of Jonathan Culler's *Structuralist Poetics* which allows concentration on the basic charge – that literature is something in itself with its own qualities and not merely sociology. The argument of this section is that structuralism has made a considerable contribution but that its occasional claim to be free from any concern with society can be taken with a pinch of salt – for the merit of structuralism is to encourage us to ask more interesting questions about literature and society.

Culler has argued (following Barthes) that structuralism is to be understood as an approach to the 'literariness' of the text based upon linguistics:

> The notion that linguistics may be useful in studying other cultural phenomena is based on two fundamental insights: first, that social and cultural phenomena are not simply material objects or events but objects or events with meaning, and hence signs; and second, that they do not have essences but are defined by a network of relations, both internal and external (Culler, 1975, p. 4).

If this is the justification for the linguistic underpinning of structuralism, it is equally important to stress its ambition. This is to provide hard, scientific knowledge to replace the impressionistic affair that has been literary criticism hitherto. This can be clearly seen in the distinction basic to all structuralism, that between language as *parole* and *langue*. The former of these refers to daily utterances, but the latter refers to the system of rules which allow such utterances to be made. The linguistic basis thus encourages structuralism in its desire to understand the rules of literary discourse.

Culler further helps us in pointing out that two models of language have hitherto been at work in structuralism. The first of these is associated with Roman Jakobson and Lévi-Strauss and argued that language can best be understood as the opposition of binary pairs; in Lévi-Strauss's view, at least, the human mind itself is structured in terms of binary oppositions. Culler is quite certain that binary oppositions are not of great help in analysing literature – in large part since fertile minds seem to be able to find pairs at work in virtually anything (1975, Ch. 3). He argues strongly in favour of adopting the more recent Chomskian stress on linguistic competence as the most sensible basic model. Chomsky is not wedded to any necessary notion of binary pairing, and is able to offer some closure on investigation by asking social actors whether a particular sentence makes sense to them. Similarly Culler feels that the actual meaning of a text can be established with reference to the standards of literary competence that readers may be expected to attain.

The power of this approach may be seen when Culler discusses the question of realism. Unlike both Marxism and the English School he is quite free from the illusion that realism is in some sense real. Realism is but one literary **convention** amongst others. This case has been put with vigour by Kermode whose *The Sense of an Ending* demonstrates that literature cannot be reality since it must be ordered especially in having an ending. No attempt to escape this is possible; even Sartre's *Nausea*, for all its attempt to escape convention, remains clearly a fiction above all else (Kermode, 1967, especially Ch. 5). This is not, of course, to deny that there are discrete conventions of realism. Culler's discussion of the conventions of what he terms *vraisemblance* may usefully be abbreviated. He distinguishes five such conventions:

(a) The first convention is one which simply presumes the correctness of its observations. This is obviously the most widespread since no novelist spends much time establishing such well-found conventions as those asserting that individuals, not collectivities, have minds and emotions.

(b) Secondly, there is a more narrow range of cultural stereotypes which can be more clearly recognised as such. Thus it is culturally accepted and therefore informative for Balzac to describe a character as 'as gloomy as a Spaniard' – there would be something peculiar about the perfectly linguistically correct 'as gloomy as an Italian' (Culler, 1975, pp. 141–2).

(c) Culler's third convention refers to the world that groups of novelists or even single novelists impose. Thus, famously, it was at one time not acceptable, at least for Monsignor Ronald Knox, for a detective story to be solved by discovery that the detective had 'done it', or that the supernatural was to blame – nor should the detective work on the basis of revelatory intuition (Symons, 1974, p. 7). Less obviously, a reader of Proust soon becomes aware that he must expect any instability or surprise from the principal characters; the convention is that of arbitrariness.

(d) The fourth convention is that in which open acknowledgement is made of the character of fiction with the usual rider that the novel or poem concerned is an exception. Thus Proust's *À la recherche du temps perdu* ends in the explanation of how the novel we have just read was born. In Culler's words:

> The text finds its coherence by being interpreted as a narrator's exercise of language and production of meaning. To naturalise it at this level is to read it as a statement about the writing of novels, a critique of mimetic fiction, an illustration of the production of a world by language (1975, p. 150).

It would, however, be a grave mistake to take the author at his word even here. Proust's life, despite the disclaimers of the end of his masterpiece, was quite different from that of his main protagonist Marcel; this can easily be seen by comparing *À la recherche* with the far more autobiographical *Jean Santeuil*.

(e) A final convention relates to those works which are concerned to parody a single work. The greatest individual instance of such parody is that of Cervantes on courtly and chivalric tales, but a recent master of the art has undoubtedly been Borges.

A few final comments may be made about structuralism. It has, firstly, no concern with the author as such since it tends to be argued that the language is put into operation by an author rather than that the author controls the language. This approach has been sanctified by

Barthes (1977a) whose proclamation of the death of the author shows the extent to which he has accepted the dictum of Proust (his favourite author) that 'a book is the product of a different self from the one we exhibit in our habits, in society, in our vices'. There is something of an irony here in that Barthes, the castigator of all those who believe and accept the reality of realism, seems prepared to accept the work of Proust. Moreover, it is quite certain that a knowledge of the author need not be equivalent to acceptance of the truth of his statements, and Barthes himself has failed to live up to his self-denying ordinances in this matter (Thody, 1977). However, despite this the structuralist stress on competence does have one obvious advantage. The emphasis on literary competence of the reader is such as to avoid the division between 'high' and 'low' culture to some extent; for whilst there are variations along these lines, the more significant emphasis is on the skill required by all readers necessary to 'naturalise' or make sense of a text. Secondly, Culler's account of realism encourages the view that literature is, as it were, an institution in its own right with its own internal laws: (d) and (e) clearly refer to a growth of sophistication dependent upon the initial conquests made by (a) and (b). This internal dynamic is referred to in Kristeva's concept of 'intertextuality' which argues simply that literature is best read as a comment on other texts, rather than on society. There is an obvious truth to this; Proust, for example, cannot be understood without reference to his knowledge of Balzac. But it is worth stressing that this concept when rigorously applied is designed to rule out any concern with society at all. Nobody has expressed this better than Oscar Wilde in his characteristically brilliant essay on 'The Decay of Lying':

> Art never expresses anything but itself. It has an independent life, just as Thought has, and develops purely on its own lines. It is not necessarily realistic in an age of realism, nor spiritual in an age of faith. So far from being the creation of its time, it is usually in direct opposition to it, and the only history that it preserves for us is the history of its own progress (1973, p. 86).

The concern with the absolute autonomy of art, even if absolutely true, does not outlaw the possibilities of sociological approaches to literature. It does, however, encourage us to ask new questions. Typically, the approaches so far noted have been concerned with the genesis of works of art, but the structuralist stress on the autonomy of art encourages us to ask about the effects of literature. This is in itself a favourite literary theme. Both *Madame Bovary* and *Don Quixote* are best read as warnings about the overly powerful effect that too much uncritical reading can have. Similarly, Barthes himself as a follower of Proust is keen to point to characters in real life who model themselves after literary characters. And such modelling is perfectly open to sociological investigation. Barthes himself argued that those involved in the trial of a provincial hill farmer named Dominici in 1955 were typically bourgeois in modelling their behaviour on nineteenth-century realist novelists such as Zola, Maupassant and Daudet; such modelling, of course, only confused the less well educated Dominici (Thody, 1977, pp. 91–2). More importantly, the full potential of this approach can be seen in the work of Lionel Trilling who has argued that modern literature has become sufficiently isolated from the larger society to form an 'adversary culture'. As developed by Daniel Bell in his *The Cultural Contradictions of Capitalism* (1976), these views lead to the possibility of asking most interesting questions (the answers are not entirely satisfactory) about the potential impact of art.

It is indeed the case that literary development can occur in the internal manner observed by the structuralists. A clear example of this seems to be Flaubert whose fascination (for Barthes as well as for a traditional critic such as Turnell) depends upon his technical artistry and invention in fact outrunning any notable themes, social or otherwise. Nevertheless, it is essential to be somewhat sceptical about the excessive claims implicit in the concept of intertextuality. For most of the literary codes described by structuralists can best be understood as social codes. Thus, for example, it is clear that different social codes are involved in the portraying of violence: senseless violence is indeed 'read' as dangerous and anarchic but this is clearly not the response usually accorded violence exerted by heroes in the service of socially acceptable causes. Moreover, changes in such codes seem to tell us a very great deal about society. Thus Gombrich (1963) has argued that the rise of realism in the visual arts can only be understood in terms of a new society's desire to portray sacred images accurately. Peter Burke, in part following some hints of Gombrich, has argued that there exists some link between the growth of 'realism' in the arts (defined simply as the amount of treatment accorded to secular as compared to religious subjects) and social factors. More precisely, he suggests that in Renaissance Italy there was a link between the merchant classes and the new secular realism, and he has further argued that some such link probably holds true for the cultural flowerings of the Netherlands in the fifteenth and Japan in the seventeenth centuries (Burke, 1974, especially pp. 338–48). The birth of *vraisemblance* can thus be socially located. We are learning, in other words, less about the structure of the human mind than about the appropriateness of certain codes to certain social conditions.

The structuralist approach is of great merit in its insistence on the 'conventional' quality of art. This corrective to the rather crude Marxist views already noted has been accepted by a significant school of Marxist Structuralists whose work is currently under discussion. The founding father of this approach is undoubtedly Louis Althusser. In an important 'Letter of Art' Althusser argues:

> Art (I mean authentic art, not works of average or mediocre level) does not give us *knowledge* in the *strict sense*, it therefore does not replace knowledge (in the modern sense: scientific knowledge), but what it gives

us does nevertheless maintain a certain *specific relationship* with knowledge. This relationship is not one of identity but one of difference. Let me explain. I believe that the peculiarity of art is to 'make us see', 'make us perceive', 'make us feel' something which *alludes* to reality ... What art makes us *see*, and therefore gives to us in the form of '*seeing*', '*perceiving*' and '*feeling*' (which is not the form of *knowing*) is the ideology from which it is born, in which it bathes, from which it detaches itself as art, and to which *alludes* ... Balzac and Solzhenitsyn ... make us 'perceive' (but not know) in some sense *from the inside*, by an *internal distance*, the very ideology in which they are held (1977, p. 204).

This rather arcane statement needs some explanation. Althusser is suggesting that the world is made up of separate realms, namely the economic, the ideological, the scientific and the artistic. His novelty as a Marxist seems to lie in his two arguments: that the latter three realms have a measure of autonomy (although there are confusing and ritual pronouncements about 'determination in the last instance') and that science (i.e. Marxism) provides us with the truth. The rigidity of this latter insistence is perhaps ultimately the true characteristic of Althusser, but it is the insistence that art has some autonomy that has been developed. Althusser himself seems to suggest that art is not, as it were, as bad as pure ideology since its very use of ideological concepts allows the reader to stand at some distance from absolute immersion in socially accepted habits.

Althusser's difficult comments have been translated into literary theory by Macherey (1968) and Eagleton (1976a). Macherey has argued that the proper manner of interpreting literature depends upon realising that the text is 'decentred'. All that is meant by this is that different elements of various ideologies are likely to be in conflict with one another and that the manner of such conflict will provide information, but only, as it were, at second hand, about society. Added to this is the belief that in certain circumstances 'determinate' absences will be observed in the text; the state of the society will, in other words, prevent certain types of resolution being made. Eagleton's *Criticism and Ideology* is essentially at one with Macherey's views, but has the advantage of additional clarity. Eagleton first stresses that literature is to be seen as a play on ideology, and is in no sense real:

... Dickens deploys particular modes of signification (realism) which entail a greater foregrounding of the 'pseudo-real'; but we should not be led by this to make direct comparisons between the imaginary London novel and the real London. The imaginary London of his *Bleak House* exists as the product of a representational process which signifies, not 'Victorian England' as such, but certain of Victorian England's ways of signifying itself. Fiction does not trade in imaginary history as a way of presenting real history; its 'history' is imaginary because it negotiates a particular ideological *experience* of real history (1976a, p. 77).

Secondly, however, Eagleton is keen to insist that the occupation of literature of an area of autonomy inside the ideological realm does not mean that it is in any sense as correct as science:

> It is not, however, a question of 'degrees of knowledge', in the sense that the more 'knowledgeable' text (let us say, *Caleb Williams*) necessarily achieves the more valuable perceptions. On the contrary, the value of Austen's fiction thrives quite as much on its ignorance as on its insight: it is because there is so much the novels cannot possibly know that they know what they do, and in the *form* they do. It is true that Austen, because she does not *know*, only 'knows' ... (1976a, p. 71).

It is important to stress that Eagleton's use of the word 'value' is mistaken; he is really expressing an interest in Austen because her work is symptomatic of the ideological stresses he would expect to find as a result of capitalism. This treatment is not so different from that offered by the Marxists already examined.

The Marxist structuralists have, however, made a significant advance in one way beyond the position of their Marxist colleagues. The emphasis on literature as often a discussion of theories about reality rather than reality itself is a useful distinction. But this gain does not mean that the programme need be accepted wholesale. For one thing it is by no means as original as advertised. Thus Macherey's insistence on the 'decentred' nature of the text reads like nothing so much as the traditional English literary critical maxim that ambiguity will character-ise literary work. And there is much to fear in the notion of determinate absences. Whilst this is a useful concept in itself, one fears what could happen if it was placed in the hands of a hack: at the worst such tools provide excuses for failing to examine determinate presences. And most importantly, it is very doubtful whether the whole approach should be seen as anything other than an additional one. Eagleton's stress on 'valuable' literature being that which puts 'ideology into motion' is of rather limited use. It is a clear and lucid guide to, say, Bernard Shaw whose ceaseless ideology critique would seem to make his work the exemplar of literary achievement for Eagleton. But, as we shall see, some literature is, *pace* Eagleton, precisely concerned to penetrate behind ideologies. Insofar as this is true of, say, Eliot, Eagleton's reading of his avant garde experiments as the appropriate analogue to the con-servatism of a ruling minority does not generate much confidence (1976a, p. 150). Finally it must be noted that Eagleton is unconcerned with the audience as a result of the naive belief that the writer actually succeeds in his attempt to make his own audience.

5. Hermeneutics

In the previous section it has been argued that structuralism is at its most exciting when it turns its attention from analysing the structures of the human mind to an analysis of social codes. This could be put more technically by saying that structuralism is at its best when it accepts the hermeneutic insistence that men are not dead atoms, but sentient beings whose creation of meanings should provide the centre of investigation for sociological knowledge. Therefore the position is best called structuralist-hermeneutic, except when clear reference is made to the scientific desire (which I by no means reject out of hand) to understand the structures of the human mind. Hermeneutics makes its own contribution to this mixture, as can be seen once its characteristic ideas are briefly elaborated.

The hermeneutic tradition so ably outlined by Wolff (1975) runs from Schleiermacher, via Heidegger to Gadamer and Derrida. The stress on different civilisations being based upon independent unities of meaning leads to the insistence that social investigation be concerned to elucidate such 'circles' of meaning rather than attempt to set up some impossible and reductive social science. This position raises the problem of relativism. For the meanings of the past will be approached by an investigator himself caught in the circle of meaning of his own civilisation: therefore objective knowledge is inherently impossible. Such difficulties of objective appreciation have been positively welcomed by recent members of the Tel Quel Group who have seen it as a way of creating multiple readings of a text in defiance of the habitual and limiting 'logocentrism' of the West (Culler, 1975, Ch. 10).

Although the Tel Quel Group is prepared to welcome this situation, its anarchy seems to me to remain a problem. And it is a problem which can rather easily be solved in two ways that have some importance here. The first of these has been put forward by Daniel Bell in a recent lecture in which he offers a new definition of culture:

> I would define culture as the modalities of response by sentient men to the core questions that confront all human groups in the consciousness of existence: how one meets death, the meaning of tragedy, the nature of obligation, the character of love – these *recurrent* questions which are, I believe, cultural universals, to be found in all societies where men have become conscious of the finiteness of existence.
>
> Culture, thus, is always a *ricorso*. Men may expand their technical powers. Nature may be mastered by scientific knowledge. There may be progress in the instrumental realms. But the existential questions remain. The answers may vary – and do . . .
>
> All cultures, thus, 'understand' each other, because they arise in response to common predicaments (Bell, 1977a, p. 428).

This is an escape from relativism insofar as it is indeed true that different cultures have to find answers to common predicaments. But the importance of Bell's argument for our purpose is that it provides a way in which historicism can be avoided. Bell's position allows for a theory of literary value in that men will remain interested in differing attempts to solve the fundamental questions he refers to. There is no reason, *pace*

Marx, why we should expect a diminishing of interest in Greek art.

Secondly, however, some solution to the problem of relativism raised by more extreme hermeneutic theorists may be found via a logical distinction introduced by Hirsch (1975). Hirsch suggests that texts may be examined in terms of their meaning and significance. The latter of these is easy to place. The significance of a work refers to the use made of it by later generations who approach it with different meanings of their own. The classic example of such a difference was the re-writing of Shakespearian tragedy in the eighteenth century to give it proper and happier endings. However, a concern with the uses made of a text would not detract from studying the meaning that it must have had in the world or social circle in which it was produced. Such a distinction is perhaps difficult to rigorously uphold, but John Shearman's *Mannerism* shows that it can be managed. Mannerism was rediscovered in this century. It was judged (in the light of early twentieth-century concerns) to be preoccupied with aggression, instability and anxiety. There is, of course, nothing wrong with an age seeking to discover spiritual predecessors. But this history of significance should not be allowed to detract from the realisation that, in historical terms, these qualities were not constitutive of Mannerism. The contortions of Mannerist figures are, in Shearman's eyes, better explained by reference to new aesthetic standards consequent on the position of artist and patron (1967, Ch. 1). The newly valued status of genius encouraged courtly patrons to ask for an art work exhibiting genius. This quality could best be conveyed when the artists' powers were fully stretched when dealing with difficult problems. Hence the contortions of Mannerist figures represent the demands made by patrons on a newly self-confident generation of artists much more than they represent instability or anxiety.

Relativism need not pose too serious a problem to the hermeneutic approach. A more serious threat comes from idealism. It is all too easy to move from the insistence that human affairs are conducted via social meanings to the argument that meaning itself as embodied in ideas or ideologies is itself a significant social force. This idea has already been encountered and criticised in the work of Raymond Williams. It is essential to keep an open mind on the question of the **social force** of literature and not to so define things that only single conclusions are possible.

6. Mass communications

Mass communications sociology has not, strictly speaking, been much involved in the sociology of literature but its development highlights one particular issue and points to a moral that the sociology of literature would do well to follow.

The sociology of mass communications has its intellectual roots in the mass society theory examined above. Early arguments in the field

suggested that mass media would be extremely powerful, and would
have the ability to manipulate whole populations. The result of such
fears led to the amusing contrast whereby in America broadcasting was
decentralised (too dangerous to be allowed to fall into the hands of any
one group) whilst in England it was centralised (the governing elite had
sufficient cohesion not to fear any other group being able to control the
new media) (Smith, 1976). But, however the institutionalisation
proceeded, little attempt was made to question the belief that the
audience was passive, and thus prone to swallow uncritically all that was
put before them. Denis McQuail (1972) has argued that this
presumption delayed the actual development of mass communications
sociology: in particular it allowed social criticism to be rather naively
read off the content of particular programmes.

This view has been largely exploded by the work done on the **audience**
since the 1940s. The research carried out by Lazarsfeld, Berelson and
Gaudet (1944) on American elections discovered that very few voters
changed their minds as a result of being exposed to party election
material, that influence, such as it was, tended to be mediated by local
opinion leaders, and that the audience in general used the media
actively. This research has since burgeoned, particularly under the title
of 'uses and gratifications' research which has tried to systematise the
ways in which the audience makes active use of the media. It is thus
utterly and completely invalid to presume that the mere analysis of a
literary text tells us about the whole condition of a society. Audiences
can use, or give a false significance to, the literary material they
encounter.

The immediate lesson to be learnt from the development of mass
communications is that no excuses should be accepted for not doing
empirical work. This is especially important in the sociology of
literature where the habit of reading cultural criticism of the whole
society off a few classic texts is responsible for the rather limited
development of the subject to date.

Conclusion

The discussion of these different schools may be made a little less
confusing by examining the state of play with the issues raised. This will
enable the problem to be faced in the next chapter to be described
exactly.

Two issues raised need trouble us no longer. The structuralist-
hermeneutic position has made it clear that art proceeds by way of
convention, and that the traditional preference for realism was naive
and regrettable. In a sense, this point is so obvious that it is surprising
that it ever had to be spelt out. Nobody, for example, doubts that *The
Time Machine* is not a piece of realism: but its allegorical status does not,
of course, prevent it from containing rather interesting social evidence.

Secondly, historicism need no longer bother us since Bell's argument about the common existential predicaments facing all cultures explains why literature of other cultures and ages retains its interest.

Three other issues have been clarified. These issues call for investigation, but the need for such investigations does not in itself pose conceptual problems. The first issue is that of the actual social force exhibited by art in different cultures. The second issue is the nature of the dependency of high upon popular literature. Finally, research into the uses and gratifications accorded by literature is sorely needed.

Three final issues raised come together in such a way as to create the problem of the next chapter. The external referent of Marxism was seen to be promising, but in reality turned out to be either vague or brutalising. The internal referent of structuralism is a necessary corrective to this, but it has been seen that interest rapidly developed in a sociological direction. What exactly is the relationship between internal and external dimensions? This in turn raises the question of the ways and extent to which literature may be seen as telling us the truth about man's life in society. We can now turn to an attempted answer to the ways in which the issues of external referent, internal referent and truth relate to each other.

Chapter 2

The sociology of literature

This chapter is concerned to outline the particular areas of interest and to describe the general character of the sociology of literature. We may start by asking what it means to have a sociology of some facet of social life. The confusion in the matter can be illustrated most clearly by looking at the sociology of religion. Bluntly, is it the case that being a sociologist of religion also prevents one being religious? This is a vexed question but it points to two different kinds of question conflated under the single heading 'sociology of religion'. First and most obviously, there is a concern to investigate the forms that religious belief takes in particular circumstances. The effect on belief of such investigation is obviously complex. But if the discovery, say, that the congregation of a particular American sect is wealthy and white might disenchant more evangelical members of the sect, it is perhaps equally the case that the very variety of the forms in which 'the religious impulse' occurs offers some comfort to those who consider a belief a universal human attribute. Second, however, is the attempt to understand the religious impulse as such. Undoubtedly, were they true, the theories offered by Frazer, Feuerbach or Durkheim would seriously undermine religious belief, for in each instance what was originally religious is shown to be something else (primitive science, false alienation, the worship of society). The thesis of this chapter is that no such analogous attempt to explain away the 'literary impulse' or 'literary imagination' has been successful. Several consequences follow from this: that the disenchanting or, as it were, the atheist-inducing effect of the sociology of literature need at present not be feared; that the spectre of reductionism is as yet but a spectre; that further attempts to explain the literary impulse should not be ruled out of court; and that there are good reasons for sociologists choosing to investigate larger questions of genre and convention.

Understanding texts

One of the greatest weaknesses of the traditional sociology of literature has been its inability to specify the exact links between literature and society. In Sartre's celebrated formulation about Marxist aesthetics: 'Valéry is a petit bourgeois intellectual, no doubt about it. But not every petit bourgeois intellectual is Valéry. The heuristic inadequacy of contemporary Marxism is contained in these two sentences' (1963, p. 56). Nor is everything perfect in traditional literary criticism where some influential schools, notably the American 'New Critics', have deliberately chosen to ignore any social referent. Moreover, much literary criticism is still of the rather arid sort that suggests that an author is but the product of his literary predecessors. This view has been rightly criticised in Hill's *Milton and the English Revolution* (1977) which sees Milton as an active social being reacting to certain predecessors on the basis of his own needs. Hill's book is important in suggesting that some middle way can be found in which text and society can be properly interrelated. Broadly speaking, we can expect two benefits from such a dialogue. Firstly – and this is a point against the most ardent of the structuralists – it is possible to see the manner in which literature refers to society and so enable us to regard it as legitimate social evidence. It is not strictly possible to separate this from the second benefit, namely that knowledge of the social context may serve as an aid in understanding the text itself. The examples which follow (designed to provide evidence for later theoretical comments) tend to move from the first to the second of these considerations. But before embarking on these examples and the attempt to combine internal textual sensitivity with the external social context, it is as well to offer a general example which exhibits the attitude typically taken here towards the 'truth' provided by literature. *The Crossman Diaries* have been hailed in various quarters as an accurate portrayal of the Labour Party; some have argued that this portrait was made possible by the 'literary' nature of the enterprise. It is in fact already clear that *The Crossman Diaries* should not be accepted as the unadulterated truth – but this does not mean that they provide no social evidence. Detailed social reading would insist that these diaries do tell the truth about, say, the Labour Party *as it seemed to a gifted, journalistically–minded intellectual of a rather particular social background.* The book provides the most reliable historical evidence about, precisely, Crossman, and therefore to a lesser extent about the Party 'intellectuals' in general. However, something can be learnt about the Party itself when we remember the way in which he approached it; and certain details of his account (especially when he dropped his pose of latter-day Bagehot) ring true. But what is clearly needed to discover the 'truth', or actual social content, is to investigate the actual representativeness of a particular text – general theories about the superior truth of literature are too vague to be useful.

1. My first example suggests that literature can even, or perhaps especially, when 'wrong' still provide evidence about the society.

The first chapter of Thomas Hardy's *Mayor of Casterbridge* describes the arrival at a small fair of a labourer named Michael Henchard who is accompanied by his wife and child. Under the influence of drink and of long-standing exasperation at being 'tied down', Henchard sells his wife to a sailor who offers a considerable sum of money for her. The rest of the novel has often been seen as concerned with the consequences of this initial act. It must be made clear immediately that all that is at issue here is the accuracy of the first scene as a description of Dorset local custom. As a description of local custom, Hardy's scene is inaccurate. This does not mean, however, that what he describes could not have occurred, nor does it make the story any less powerful – indeed it could be argued that the slight distortion he imposed enabled him to investigate much greater issues than those of local custom. Nevertheless, some consequences do follow from the inaccuracy of Hardy's accounts.

The sale of wives is best seen as a local custom that took the place of formal, and expensive, divorce proceedings. The very nub of the matter was likely to rest on the parties knowing each other well. The money involved tended to be purely nominal. What counted was that the local society could witness the proceedings. This familiarity between parties explains why they would often go off after the sale and take drinks together; this was not the result of callousness, only the natural consequence of the only proceedings the poor had available instead of formal divorce. A final support to this theory of wife-sales is found in the fact that their number rose in the years after the Napoleonic Wars. As soldiers returned home, it was only natural that many were put in a position where new relationships had to be formalised.

Hardy's mistake in understanding wife-sales does perhaps suggest something about him. At one time the accepted picture of Hardy was of the chronicler of Wessex life offering a faithful account of that life as a result of his proximity to it. More recently, however, critics have begun to realise that Hardy's relations with Wessex were complex; as Raymond Williams has suggested, it seems clear that, in social terms, he stood above most of those whose life he described (Williams, 1973, Ch. 4). In other words, Hardy was more of an outsider in Wessex than is often allowed. And this discovery is of considerable interest in that it makes it necessary to examine the ways in which Hardy approached rural life, rather than to merely presume that his account is itself historically accurate.

2. The same necessity of considering the social context and the possibility of discovering the social reference through careful reading can be illustrated with reference to an exemplary essay by Chesterton on 'Slum Novelists and the Slum' (1905). This example refers less to the outright falsehood that literature can engender than to the selective truths therein to be discovered.

Chesterton begins his discussion of the slum novels of Edwardian England by noting that the genre grew out of the awareness of 'the social problem'. This awareness is itself in his opinion biased:

> But the modern laws are almost always laws made to affect the governed classes, but not the governing. We have public house licensing laws, but

not sumptuary laws. That is to say, we have laws against the festivity and hospitality of the poor, but no laws against the festivity and hospitality of the rich (1905, p. 275).

On the basis of this observation and with the dictum in mind that a 'poor man is a man who has not got much money', Chesterton turned to an analysis of the slum novelists' investigation of the psychology and social conditions of the poor. He argued that novels such as Maugham's *Liza of Lambeth*, whatever their aesthetic merit, are useless as social description. They are sensationalist since they see events from the outside; the interior of a pub may be squalid to someone of middle class sensibility but may be a haven of warmth and cosiness (qualities that Chesterton as a populist admired) to others after hard work. But although Chesterton thinks that the portrait of the slums is socially inaccurate, he marvellously captures the social world to which they do refer: 'In short, these books are not a record of the psychology of poverty. They are a record of the psychology of wealth and culture when brought in contact with poverty' (1905, p. 281). Chesterton concludes his piece with a final observation which is probably as true now as it was then: that these novels must be middle class in nature since the poor prefer romance to realistic description of what they cannot anyway escape.

Chesterton's essay on the slum novelists is an apposite example of what Laslett (1976) would surely refer to as looking at literature through the right end of the telescope. Laslett argues that literature as historical evidence is of little use since literature has, in any case, to be checked against the documents. But when more detailed questions are asked about the manner in which an author comes to see a situation and society this is no longer the case. However, it is worth remembering that the evidence gathered in this manner is likely to be rather more limited than the traditional Marxist preference for social realism allowed. This can be exhibited by cursory examination of some Edwardians.

3. On the surface it might seem as if Wells and Shaw, because of their openly committed stance, are likely to tell us more about society than their contemporaries. This commitment was classically expressed in the celebrated quarrel between Wells and James, and the received wisdom thereafter has been that commitment, whatever its moral value, is hostile to 'art'. The position is slightly more complex than this, as we shall see in a moment when leaving Wells and Shaw for Conrad.

Shaw and Wells were products of the extremely high social mobility that characterised late-Victorian England and which was associated above all with Board Schools, expanding suburbs and the growth in administrative work of a more centralised state. They were representative of all those provincial intellectuals who conquered the capital with vigour but also with uncertainty. They were a curious case of what might be called social dislocation rather than absolute alienation; for they were essentially members of the lower middle class striving for a place in a society which had tended to ignore this status group. Their troubles were thus limited, but nonetheless deeply felt (Hobsbawm, 1964).

This background helps us understand their work for it makes us realise that political commitment was rather limited and idiosyncratic, being markedly concerned to make the world safe for the *'nouvelle couche sociale'* they represented. Moreover, such political interest was not always long-lived. It is clear that it is a dreadful mistake to consider, say, Shaw a 'socialist' dramatist throughout his career. This epithet might well be applied to his first two plays, but does not fit his neo-Nietzschean, supermen figures at all. Thus it is possible to distinguish three separate 'levels' of their work:

(a) The first level does concern the obviously 'social' world from which they came. This can most clearly be seen in Wells's neo-Dickensian novels of social manners, most notably *Kipps* and *Love and Mr Lewisham*. The heroes of these novels, red-tied and rubber-collared, undergo all the agonies of social manners in hotels and interview rooms that Wells had obviously experienced himself.

(b) More important to Wells and Shaw, however, than the social world from which they came were their theories about where it should go. Commitment to them means a commitment to abstract ideas; their work becomes in large part a vehicle for such ideas. These ideas are very peculiar. Wells's heroes – whether scientific, industrial or military – are all tough-minded, blue-eyed heroes whose discipline (as Wells admitted) is the mirror image of his own intemperate brashness; the plans for reforming the world proposed by this elite are terrifyingly authoritarian. Shaw's supermen are similar fantasy-type figures, superior in wisdom and knowledge to the stupid masses below; such heroes represented Shaw's shell against the world which he found so painful. A number of things are of note about this second level. First, such elitist heroes are very natural for the socially isolated and it is not surprising to find that they are modelled on their authors' imagined characteristics. Second, these figures usually fail to convince. I am not suggesting that elitist or authoritarian figures cannot be realised in fictional terms or that they are incapable of receiving artistic support. But Wells and Shaw offer us heroes who are too obviously theoretical homunculi: they do not convince because they are made to talk too much and because they are so obviously concocted rather than realised.

(c) The third level of their work is that in which Wells and Shaw do convince us; these are the areas in which we are moved to more than intellectual consent. In Wells this happens whenever he addresses what Weeks has called his 'disentanglement' theme (1954). The desire to escape from a social situation and from social responsibility clearly dominated Wells's deepest feelings and when he addressed it artistically it gave new powers to his work. Thus Mr Polly's desire for escape is better articulated than anything in the other Edwardian novels. Shaw's case is somewhat the same. His saintly characters find themselves isolated because of their superior wisdom and kindness. This can be seen most clearly in one of Shaw's most forceful scenes, that of the elderly gentleman in *Back to Methuselah*, who refuses to return to the asinine world with his fellow ambassadors, and is killed all too kindly by the oracle. Some of Wells's and Shaw's highest artistic achievement is thus concerned with a rejection of or escape from the world.

Before going on to speculate further about the reason for the higher quality of the third level, it is worth briefly digressing to consider their contemporary Conrad. Conrad knew Wells rather well, and had a passing and disastrous encounter with Shaw. I like to think that he was aware of the theme of social rejection in his contemporaries (who were gaining far more praise, publicity and money than he was). Certainly he was aware of the weakness of Wells's whole approach and made this clear to Wells in a letter of 1903:

> For this is what in the last and most general pronouncement the book amounts to. It is – and as a matter of fact the whole tone of it implies that – it is a *move*. Where the move to my apprehension seems unsound is in this, that it seems to presuppose . . . a sort of select circle to which you address yourself, leaving the rest of the world outside the pale. It seems as if they had to *come into* a rigid system, whereas I submit that Wells should *go forth*, not dropping fishing lines for particular trout but casting a wide and generous net, where there would be room for everybody; where indeed every sort of fish would be welcome, appreciated and made use of . . . (H. and J. MacKenzie, 1973, p. 167).

Conrad showed himself, along with Chesterton, the most perceptive of Edwardian critics. He realised that the authoritarianism and elitism of Shaw and Wells, both personally kindly men, came from their social isolation.

It is possible to go further than Conrad's criticism in order to suggest that Conrad's insistence on the necessity of a social location for the individual acts as a basic principle of his own work. A reading of Conrad's fiction on these lines would certainly be able to point to its centrality in early novels such as *The Nigger of the Narcissus* as well as in particular characters such as Decoud in *Nostromo*. However, the undoubted advantage of this approach would be to save *Victory* from the critical disfavour into which it has fallen. In this novel Conrad is in a sense arguing against the escapism of Shaw and Wells. Heyst is indeed a man who has tried to 'disentangle' himself; but he finds himself and his humanity in his relations with Lena; and this new-found self is contrasted strongly with his earlier neutered complacency. It is, of course, characteristic of Conrad's vision that the moment of self-discovery should also effectively be the moment of death, for Conrad's world is ultimately one of tragedy. This does not, however, in any way detract from the force and power of Conrad's vision. There is irony in such a vision being produced by an exile.

This discussion of the three Edwardians suggests a number of points. First, support has been given for the claim that a social referent can be distinguished in literature. In particular, the rather peculiar heroes of Wells and Shaw are shown to be representative of their social position. Secondly, it can be seen that there is no automatic and easy relationship between political commitment and literary quality. The open commitment of Shaw and Wells did not prevent them for much of the time failing to have the courage of Conrad in addressing their most deeply felt experience. Thirdly, it is worth showing briefly how the interpretation of the work of Shaw and Wells in comparison to that of Conrad goes against the tenor of the recent argument concerning the relations of literature and society advanced by Terry Eagleton (1976a). His argument that literature is best seen as a discussion of ideology has some use; it is helpful, for example, in understanding the second level of the work of Wells and Shaw, and slum novelists analysed by Chesterton. But the insistence that literature cannot touch the real (the realm of science, i.e. Marxism) is contradicted by Conrad's treatment of the theme of the isolated individual. Conrad's insistence in this matter is, to put it simply, correct, as any sociologist familiar with Durkheim's *Moral Education* will surely testify. So in this case it may be claimed that Conrad has told us something that is sociologically true. This is not, of course, to argue that only 'sociologically true' literature can be good literature. The point made above (that quality ultimately depends on imaginatively facing actual experience) rules out such a conclusion. And indeed the third level of Wells's and Shaw's work reminds us of the limits to any general theory since they successfully realised exactly the opposite point to that endorsed by Conrad. But the question whether there are inherent limits to the type of experience capable of engaging a writer's attention and the reader's respect is extremely complex and cannot be adequately treated here.

4. A final example concerns the helpfulness of a knowledge of society in understanding the work of Marcel Proust. One immediate way in which this is clearly the case concerns Proust's portrait of the position of Jews in fashionable French society before the First World War. Hannah Arendt has convincingly argued (1968, pp. 80–88) that Proust alone realised the hideous paradox of the Jewish position in the period of the Dreyfus case, that Jews were welcomed socially at their time of supposed notoriety but dropped as quickly once it was realised that Dreyfus had been the victim of a common frame-up. This history is important in Arendt's view since it helps explain why the upper orders were thereafter so opposed to the Jews.

All this, of course, again goes against any application of Eagleton's view that literature can only concern itself with the ideological. But there is something else to note in Proust's novel, which, for all its extreme brilliance, verve and insight, is one which is hard to come to terms with. Even as good a critic as Turnell (1950) ends rather disapprovingly with the view that Proust's portrait of man's instabilities somehow shows a lessening of moral confidence in comparison to Stendhal. This is a misreading of the novel based upon a lack of awareness of the changed social reality that Proust describes. And as was the case with Conrad, part of Proust's value lies in the fact that his description of, above all, the nature of the self in the modern world is so very plausible. Marxists have ignored this (some of them have paid attention, however, to his condemnation of the aristocracy) because their philosophy of history is one that envisages the re-blending of private and public man; it is exactly this which Proust suggests is, in a complex society, impossible.

The difficulty of understanding the novel comes about as a result of the conflict between its recognition of the 'intermittences of the heart' (seen in the instabilities of nearly all the leading characters) and its remorseless demand (exemplified in Proust's own tireless search for hard explanations of conduct) for a solid set of ethics to guide behaviour. Proust is often disliked because his characters are so unstable and seem, like Marcel, to be all layers without any centre. It is a mistake to criticise them on this ground for Proust is trying to portray the difficulties of personality in the modern world, and in so doing he comes to conclusions that are by no means pessimistic.

Proust's argument is, in a sense, simple. In a complex society (i.e. Paris rather than Combray, or, city not country) the self is presented with the opportunity of assuming many roles. The world is indeed complex, for it offers the possibility of some freedom from the neatly ascribed roles of the past. Proust is not a pessimist about this. Marcel in *À la recherche du temps perdu* is indeed confused and lost but he does eventually find some identity in the famous last volume concerned with *Time Regained.* In the modern world, the openness of a complex society means that identity is no longer something given but something which, with time, luck and perseverance, can be found or created. Those critics who lambast Proust for the instability of his characters fail to realise that this is the modern condition and that, since it does offer an increase of certain types of freedom, it is a condition in many ways to be valued.

Proust's paradox is now easily explained. Respect must be given to the roles that people play in order that behind these masks they may develop their identities. Characters in the novel who do respect social fronts (notably Baron Charlus) are highly admired by Marcel, whatever he may think of them in other matters (Deleuze, 1973). This ability to respect fronts comprises a key element in Durkheim's 'cult of the individual' (his creed for modern society); and its workings have been examined with tireless efficiency by Goffman. Ethics, in other words, are important although they are likely in these personal matters to concern the surface of activity and prevent the actor from saying what he really thinks. It is clear, however, that Proust's superb analysis of the instability of character endemic in complex society is such as to rule out any easy Marxist assumption of any spontaneous and liberating fusion of the private and public realms. This is perhaps especially the case with the Marxism of Jean Paul Sartre (Hall, 1977). Where Sartre calls for authentic openness, Proust demands a respect for people's appearances; he is aware that an attempt to anchor human individuality at any particular moment (by a vow in Sartre's case) is bound to lead to authoritarianism since it will prevent the instability of character necessary if the individual is to make his own identity.

Social referent or reflector, or What is literature?

What are the implications of saying that it is possible to gain certain insights into the social world through a careful reading of literary texts? Implications in fact abound since the question quite properly being raised is that of the nature of literature, and they may best be drawn out by starting with some comments on the use that has been made here of the concept of 'social referent'. I have preferred this concept to the more traditional one of literature as reflector of social reality, and it is now time to explain why this is the case.

The great weakness of the idea of reflection can be seen by briefly looking at the epistemology advanced by Karl Popper (1972). Popper has argued that the traditional theory of how the human mind obtained knowledge was that the mind was a receiver of sense impressions. This theory suggests that the mind is some sort of bucket which will give a true picture of reality provided that something (class prejudice, Freudian obsession, etc.) does not prevent the mind from seeing 'the facts as they really are'. This epistemology is false. In Gombrich's words:

> We can focus on *something* in our field of vision, but never on *everything*. ... A heightened awareness of reality as such is something mystics may dream about, but cannot realise. The number of stimuli that impinge upon us at every moment – if they were countable – would be astronomical. To see at all, we must isolate and select (1965).

Popper suggests that the mind must be seen as a searchlight which actively seeks out some things rather than others. The concept of literature as reflection of society will no longer do as it suggests that the artist is a passive agent opening himself manfully to the bombardment of social stimuli; the concept of literature containing a social referent is, however, perfectly viable since it takes into account the writer's active concern to understand his society.

Gombrich's argument that the realism of Western visual arts is but a convention requiring the 'matching' and 'making' that he examines so well (1963, *passim*), may also be applied to literature. Realism in literature is thus one of several possible conventions, and is not, as the Marxists tend to believe, somehow sacrosanct. And three possible avenues of investigation follow from this. First, saying that an author approaches reality through a convention does not explain why he should want to do so at all. The literary impulse that is so clearly active remains unexplained by this approach; an examination of the problems of explanation in this matter will be offered in the next section. Secondly, the remaining avenues of investigation follow from the realisation that a convention can be seen either as a device enabling investigation of reality or as a subject of inquiry in its own right insofar as it places boundaries upon what can be said at all. The former of these possibilities stresses the freedom that conventions give the artist and will occupy us in the rest of this section. The latter, stressing the restraining quality of particular conventions, has already been noted in the discussion of realism, but will be taken up again later. This distinction about conventions could be put another way. Analysis of the 'codes' of the convention is obviously indebted to the structuralist-hermeneutic position outlined above. But the insistence that actual reality can be seen via these conventions is indebted to the Marxist belief that social content may be contained in literature – albeit that it is here being argued that the manner in which this social content is contained in literature is problematic.

The primary point to be made about the idea of reflection is then that it is based on a faulty conception of mind. However, the concept of reflection is at once descriptive and prescriptive; and although it is useless as a description, this by no means deals with the prescriptive injunction that the artist should, even if he be seen as an active agent, concern himself with describing social reality. And any discussion of why literature should (indeed must if it is to be of high quality) concern itself with society naturally raises the central question as to the relation between literature and society.

It is remarkable that few explicit attempts have been made, even by sociologists of literature, to characterise the nature of literature as such. R. Williams (1977) begins his discussion in a very helpful manner by noting that 'literature' has changed its meaning historically. What was once a term that covered all printed books came, in his view via principled opposition to the industrial revolution, to take on the meaning of creative and imaginative literature only. Williams in effect suggests that it is a mistake to seek too insistently for essentialist definitions of literature. Some such tolerance is probably necessary insofar as literature is seen in society to include both Barbara Cartland and Conrad. But it is worth seeing whether something useful may be said in a rather more ideal-typical manner about the character of the literary imagination. David Lodge (1977) has suggested that it is indeed possible to talk sensibly about an essentialist conception of literature. Whilst there may be difficulty and dissension about particular works, there is not in his opinion likely to be any doubt about the fact that certain works – *The Divine Comedy, King Lear, Ulysses* and so on – must always be considered to be literature. Furthermore he suggests that the very possibility of talking about giving, say, *Capital*, a literary reading means that we do have a conception of literature that is worth exploring.

Lodge argues that the most striking characteristic of literature is its very high level of formal organisation. Literature, in other words, is language at its fullest stretch. This formulation raises more problems than it solves, and it is to the credit of Lodge that he tries to confront them openly. He notes that there have been two aesthetic demands that above all others (perhaps most notably ideas of expression and of pleasing the audience) have been at the centre of controversy. These are the demand that art should have a content and the demand that art should be something which is in itself of great beauty; these positions are familiar to us as they have been advocated respectively by Marxists and structuralists. Lodge is insistent that the truth must lie somewhere in between. He defends the idea of social content when criticising 'post-modernism' (1977, p. 245), but equally insists that literature can only be judged in terms of the words on the page (1977, p. xii). Much the same confusion can be seen in a sophisticated critic such as John Gross who criticises those who think literature can be understood without a knowledge of society, but nevertheless insists that literature must be studied only for its own sake (1973, pp. 321-2).

The question is one that has generated so much heat that it is not open to easy solution; indeed, it is perhaps what one philosopher refers to as an 'essentially contested' notion. Nevertheless, it is worth making some statement about the matter, if only to make clear the position that is being posited in this book. Both Lodge and Gross are perfectly right to insist that the truth lies somewhere between the poles of content and form, but they are not much use in specifying exactly where. However, they still retain at the back of their minds the notion that language and life are somehow in different camps. Whatever the difficulties of Williams's recent position there can be no doubt of his courage in trying to escape this dualism. His work encourages us to say that *language is pushed to its full stretch in order to capture social experience*. A number of aestheticians and artists have argued along these lines. T. E. Hulme insisted that language had to renew itself if it were to capture experiences that would otherwise prove evanescent. In his *Time Regained* Proust speaks of the power of the artist to 'translate' his experience; and insofar as this urge to capture experience is known to all societies Williams's insistence that it is a 'material' part of life may be accepted. The great merit of this position is that it allows for, and indeed refuses to countenance an alternative to, the unity of form and content. Consequently it is not possible to rewrite without loss of meaning this comment of Swift's: 'I saw a Woman flayed, and you will hardly believe how much it altered her Person for the worse'.

The central consequence of this position can be brought about by asking 'what is the "truth-status" of the literary imagination?' The argument I am making here is that literature in its ideal-typical form must tell the truth about social experience, although this truth is sometimes hard to untangle. This conception of the truth of the literary imagination does not deny that information about all sorts of fantasies and ambitions, as in the case of Wellsian and Shavian heroes, can be discovered from books which do not fully engage the literary imagination; nor is it designed to suggest that some popular literary genres cannot engage the imagination fully. The term truth, however, is meant to refer to those successful attempts to discover or uncover the meaning of social experience. Proust describes the matter thus:

> ... that reality which there is grave danger we might die without ever having known and yet which is simply our life, life as it really is, life disclosed at last and made clear, consequently the only life that is really lived, is literature; that life which in one sense is to be found at every moment in every man, as well as in the artist (cited in Shattuck, 1964, pp. 118–19).

And of course it must be admitted that the discovery of the meaning of social experience may be at the expense of some literal facts; just as a painter misses out some things, so Proust himself changed the names of people and places in order, as Painter (1959 and 1965) has shown, to lay the skeleton of his experience free of cloying flesh. The view of literary truth can be specified in two particular ways. First, literature is as it were a different form of discourse from formal sociology. Where the latter is open to disproof by evidence, literature is not. Mayhew's account of London may or may not be correct; if it is not it can presumably be replaced by better research. The same is not true of Dickens's vision of London. It is quite conceivable that, as Eagleton has argued, Dickens's image of the city tells us more about the middle-class image of the city than about the city itself; but as such an image the vision of Dickens cannot be disproved or abandoned. The difference is close to that between a photograph and a picture; whilst the former includes everything, the latter has the power to heighten appreciation by missing some things out. The second point follows naturally from this. The characteristic of the literary mode is that it is, as it were, self-authenticating. It is a document of how human beings feel and its singleness of vision is capable of moving human feelings in a uniquely powerful way. This point was made with characteristic forthrightness by Orwell when writing about *Gulliver's Travels.* Orwell argued that Swift's vision lacks balance and that his conception of reason was potentially capable of generating vicious political practice. Nevertheless, Orwell admits that the book moves him as few others:

> The views that a writer holds must be compatible with sanity, in the medical sense, and with the power of continuous thought: beyond that what we ask of him is talent, which is probably another name for conviction. Swift did not possess ordinary wisdom, but he did possess a

terrible intensity of vision, capable of picking out a single hidden truth
and then magnifying it and distorting it. The durability of *Gulliver's
Travels* goes to show that if the force of belief is behind it, a world view
which only just passes the test of sanity is sufficient to produce a great
work of art (1970, Vol. 4, p. 261).

Orwell's argument can be put in a different way. Literature is an attempt
made by men to understand their social experience; it is thus more of a
witness to that particular experience than illuminating a fully balanced
account of the complete social scene. Consequently, it is necessary to
take the self-advertisement of writers with a pinch of salt; they may write
about something other than they themselves realise. If, for example, the
argument made above about Conrad is correct, then his work in one
significant part must be read as a witness to the condition of exile. There
are two corollaries that follow from this. First, the insistence on reading
backwards until the real subject is discovered is one that presumes that
what might be called the 'unit of account' is not necessarily the whole
literary text but rather those parts of it that engage the writer's
imagination. This emphasis does not of course imply that there is no
point to analysing the structural principles of whole texts; such analysis
will indeed tell us something about the author's mind and perhaps even
more about the rules of particular conventions. Nevertheless, the
structuring principles or design of the author himself are unlikely to tell
us as much as a study of the smaller unit of account in which his
imagination is fully engaged; general designs are likely to be more or less
socially shared, whilst the unit of account alone will reveal the
particularity of experience. Secondly, it is as well to admit openly that
the concept of social experience being utilised here is one that is designed
to allow both belief (or ideology) and social fact as the necessary
constituents from which, in varying proportions, men try to make sense
of the world.

An insistence on the power of literature to testify to social experience
leads to certain obvious questions. First, is it the consequence of this
view that sociology is, as the English School often presumes,
unnecessary?That this is not the case can be seen when it is remembered
that the very concept of the social referent encourages us to ask how
representative the social experience described might be. Some sociologists of literature seem to imagine that literature itself provides
automatic sociology. This position leads to the dreadful mistake of
treating Malraux as representative of the problems of late capitalism.
The examples earlier in this chapter imply that literature has a degree of
freedom with which to investigate the social world; the social experience
described may then be idiosyncratic and ideologically discomfiting.
Consequently, sociology is obviously needed to portray general social
processes left unexamined by literature; and this sociological awareness
can, as argued, be of use in helping to determine the true character of the
text's social referent. The position argued for then is one that allows that

literature may describe social experience that is not generally representative. Thus there is much to be said for a sociology of literature concerning itself with general patterns of literary development rather than only with particular authors; the analysis of particular authors may tell us about particular social experiences, but an understanding of, say, the social origins of realism and modernism may allow rather more general conclusions.

A second question concerns the view of the imagination implied here. Lionel Trilling is but one of many critics to argue that the imagination can create in totally novel ways; thus he argues reluctantly and courageously that: '. . . art does not always tell the truth or the best kind of truth and does not always point the right way . . . it can even generate falsehood and habituate us to it . . .' (1967, p. 15). Trilling's fear stems from his belief that modern art has gone so far as to attack the very basis of social relations. This view is open to criticism, as we shall see in Chapter 4, insofar as it ignores the social experience, however unrepresentative, that modernism records. But the weakness follows the presumption that the imagination can dream up something without a basis in experience. This belief underlies many well-known aesthetic clichés such as that of the independence of the 'creative mind', the ability of art to 'transcend' experience, and probably the currently popular but resoundingly vague idea of art as a 'praxis'. This belief has already been implicitly criticised in the discussion of Conrad in which it was claimed that literary quality resided in the ability to face experience.

Finally, two theories claiming that literature has but a single character may be examined. The first of these is that of Eagleton who suggests that literature is but a play on ideology. This view has some use, as the discussion of the slum novelists has established. But it is as well to bear in mind the constant warnings of Saul Bellow that literature which rests at this level can become very sterile. As Bellow has often noted, most modern authors are capable of reeling off philosophies of history at the drop of a hat; these theories have, after all, become common property. Bellow's insistence that literature tests such theories against the feelings of actual human beings is one that has guided his own fiction; but, more importantly, it suggests that literature can delve below the realm of ideology. The discussion of Conrad has tried to argue that this possibility is a real one. A second theory suggesting a uniform content for all literature is that offered by Joan Rockwell. She argues that literature is concerned with the enforcement of moral standards:

> Literature [is] . . . an essential part of the social machinery, as much an institution as any other, and to have been so from the very earliest times when human beings were human and in possession of language. For language . . . does very greatly extend the possibility of communication and it is thus possible to *tell* something to another without acting it out. This is of course very important in the socialisation of infants, and in human society, unlike animal society, they are indoctrinated into the

behaviour and norms of their society not only through the exemplary
behaviour of their elders but also, and very largely, through language.
And not only through language, but especially through narrative fiction
(1977, pp. 35–6).

Rockwell is able to give interesting readings of the 'social control' and
'transmission of norms' aspects of both Greek tragedy and Icelandic
sagas on the basis of this approach (1974). However, as a general theory
it is not successful. Its greatest weakness lies in its presuming that there
are a set of codified social norms to be passed on so that social cohesion
will be assured. Some literature is of this variety and it includes works of
the greatest merit, perhaps most obviously *Anna Karenin*. However,
some literature is clearly not designed to enforce social norms but to
serve as social criticism. What possible Russian social norms could
Solzhenitsyn have been trying to preserve when he was writing *Cancer
Ward*? We must content ourselves with the general approach insisting
that literature is not bound to be socially representative, politically
balanced or functional to the larger set of social norms.

For all the relative modesty of the position being argued for, there
remain good reasons why sociology should interest itself in literature. A
straightforward one is that sociology might be of help in understanding
the texts themselves. More important, however, are those reasons which
suggest that sociology itself will have something to gain from literature.
First, sociology has no monopoly of discovery techniques that will
guarantee finding out the truth about society. Literature is of use in
making sociology more sensitive to society in general and to the reaction
of individuals to their society in particular. Secondly, it may be fairly
argued that the literary imagination deserves to be paid particular
attention. The reason for this can be discerned from a comment by
Philip Roth to the effect that, for him, the pleasure of writing lay in
sorting through his collection of beliefs in order to find out what he
really believed in. The literary imagination, in other words, is able to
investigate actual feelings; it need not just repeat conventional social
wisdom. Thirdly, when literary evidence is used in the right way (as a
social referent rather than just as a social reflector) it can sometimes
provide information about particular matters that can be gained
nowhere else. This is true for example of the middle-class psychology of
the Edwardian slum novelists. Finally, the evidence that can be gained
from literature can have a very great 'fullness of account'. Thus
Conrad's investigation of the problems of isolated individuals offers us a
fuller appreciation of the feelings involved than does Durkheim's
account of the same matter.

This discussion of the nature of literature cannot properly be accused
of 'reducing' literary qualities in any way. This charge is often levelled
against the sociology of literature in the belief that social content will be
pulled out at the expense of literary quality; when levelled against the
cruder forms of Marxist interpretation it is perfectly justified. The

position being advanced here, however, is one that insists that form and content go together, or, more specifically, that the literary imagination is pushed to its limits only where its task is to capture social experience. However, it is now the moment to ask whether the matter can be taken further. Can we, in other words, explain the very nature of the literary impulse itself?

The horror of explanation, or the reduction of the literary impulse

Reduction has two relevant meanings in connection with literature: something may be said to be reduced if it is impoverished; or something may be said to be reduced if it can be really shown to be something else. The sociology of literature is not, as we have seen, necessarily reductionist in the first sense, but the fear that it might be reductionist in the second is what in fact explains the extreme hostility the discipline at present attracts. For if the literary impulse could be shown to be something else the self-image of literary departments (as the protectors of the inherently creative powers of the mind) would be dented. Thus the possibility of reduction in its powerful sense is looked upon with horror. This is perfectly proper since the reduction – or, more precisely, the explanation – of any part of human behaviour is morally insulting and, in the case of literature, such as to put literary value in question. This phobia against explanation raises such fundamental issues that it is worth exploring in some detail. Reference to the exemplary work of Chomsky will help us do so.

Chomsky is most famous for his attack on the work of Skinnerian behaviourist psychology. According to this view, children internalise sentences uttered in their presence and then use these sentences in later life; language learning is thus a matter of stimulus and response. Chomsky has two definitive criticisms of this view. First, the range of sentences produced by an adult goes far beyond anything that he himself ever heard in childhood; the complexity of this human 'competence' is such as to make it unamenable to stimulus–response investigation of any sort. Secondly, Chomsky argues that the stimulus–response model, were it true, would still explain nothing; to say that the human mind has responsive qualities is simply empty mentalism unless the manner in which such responsiveness works is specified (Gellner, 1974, *passim*). This second point, which is far too frequently ignored in discussions of Chomsky, is vital in realising his own intellectual programme. His first criticism has caused many to hail him as a defender of human creativity; his second suggests that he is in fact as desirous of cold explanation as Skinner, only he thinks that the full reality of language must be treated if explanations are not to be cheap and ineffective. This means, as Ernest Gellner has brilliantly pointed out, that Chomsky is less a saviour of human powers than their greatest assailant yet:

> Any explanation or human conduct of competence in terms of a genuine structure is morally offensive – for a genuine structure is impersonal, it is an 'it', not an 'I'. Chomskian structures are also known to be, in part, well hidden from consciousness; he himself lays great stress on this. If this be the correct strategy in the study of man, then the *I* is ultimately to be explained by an *it* (alas). The Freudian *id* was beastly but, when all is said and done, it was cosily human in its un-housetrained way; at worst you could say it was all too human; it was human nature seen in the image of conscious man, but with the gloves off. (Like us, but without the advantages we've had, if you know what I mean.) The explanation of our unthinking, quasi-automatic competence into explanatory schemata, outlining structures which are not normally accessible to us at all, is far more sinister. This kind of *id* is not violent, sexy and murderous, it is just totally indifferent to us (Gellner, 1974, p. 99).

Any explanation is thus bound to disenchant us about our human powers since it makes the world less and less an area in which human creative powers are predominant. Something that seemed unique would be, literally and correctly, reduced to something else.

Two points are raised when Chomsky's very powerful theory of explanation is applied to art. Firstly, something can be learnt from Chomsky's argument that, after the rejection of simplistic and brutalising theories such as behaviourism, we should still try to explain language use in all its complexity. A similar tactic needs to be applied in the sociology of literature. It has already been argued that the literary process is not as simple as the metaphor of reflection would have us believe; but it does not follow from this that we should cease to try to explain this literary process once its complexity is recognised. This point could be put another way. The idea of literature as a praxis is useful insofar as it criticises the simplistic reflectionist view; but the idea of a praxis should be treated with caution when used to suggest that no further investigation is necessary. Secondly, explanation, being reductive, will always unfortunately have the disenchanting effect Gellner notes. An explanation of the work of Mozart or Beethoven would turn their uniqueness into something that was, as it were, public property and thus replicable at will. There is then much to be said for the traditional view (often expressed by Auden) that research into contemporary authors should be discouraged since it is capable of drying up their sources of originality. The classic instance of this has been, significantly, that of Genet. Genet was so impressed by Sartre's analysis of his life and work that, rightly or wrongly, he had Sartre's biography printed as the first volume of his collected work; thereafter he was unable to write novels, and instead became a playwright.

The fear of explanation in cultural matters can be more specifically illustrated. A classic instance is provided in an essay by Ernst Gombrich on Johan Huizinga, the greatest of all cultural sociologists. In 1921 Huizinga argued that:

As a result of this luxuration of our intellects the shameful misconception of Marxism could be put about and even believed, that economic forces and material interests determine the course of the world. This grotesque over-estimation of the economic factor was conditioned by our worship of technological progress, which was itself the fruit of rationalism and utilitarianism after they had killed the mysteries and acquitted man of guilt and sin. But they had forgotten to free him of folly and myopia, and he seemed only fit to mould the world after the pattern of his own banality (Huizinga in Gombrich, 1974, p. 1086).

This passage is in fact an attack on something that Huizinga believes to be a false explanation, and thus parallels Chomsky's attack on Skinner. But, in a spirit alien to Chomsky, Huizinga goes on to attack the very idea of explanation. In his celebrated *Homo Ludens* he argued that the play instinct was part of human nature and thus above explanation. In Gombrich's words:

He had found in this somewhat authoritarian approach a defence against those dangers of 'reductionism' which had come to preoccupy him. Play could not be explained. He speaks of 'that irreducible quality of pure playfulness which is not . . . amenable to further analysis', of the 'absolute independence of the play concept'. In other words, play has become for him what Goethe would have called an *Urphänomen*. Goethe had used this strategy to preserve his theory of colour from the analysis of Newtonian optics. Huizinga withdrew into a similar fortress to ward off the onslaught of psychology and the study of animal behaviour (Gombrich, 1974, p. 1088).

Other fortresses have been erected recently. Most strikingly, Saul Bellow, revolted by false rationalisations of artistic creativity, has recently come to suggest that there is much more in a mystic like Rudolf Steiner than we have hitherto allowed (Bellow, 1975). Raymond Williams's insistence on Marxism as creativity, and in particular on language as constitutive and creative, is a similar attempt to preserve human creativity from investigation.

One can have sympathy for this approach as a reaction against meretricious explanation. However, it remains no more than anti-intellectualism. For no self-denying ordinance on explanation is possible; indeed the purpose of Huizinga's own work has to some extent been undermined by animal psychology, notably of Tinbergen and Lorenz, that has shown that play is not innocent but is usually connected with the protection of territory.

The argument that I have been making is that the jump often made in reaction against simplistic and brutalising theories to some sort of ineffable theory of inexplicable creativity is unnecessary and mistaken. But is it the case that we do have properly reductive explanations of the literary impulse readily at hand? The answer to this crucial question seems clearly to be in the negative since serious explanation of the literary impulse has scarcely begun. Chomsky's own work, despite its important philosophical scaffolding, has been content to analyse grammatically simple sentences (i.e. John is easy to please); there remains an enormous gap between such analysis and the understanding of complex poetic diction. For the general structuralist enterprise has told us little about the structure of the human mind; indeed its main contribution has been to make us realise the complexity of the whole literary enterprise. And we may note that a very striking recent book by Barbara Hardy entitled *Tellers and Listeners* (1975) makes us aware that we still have very little idea about why men tell each other narratives in the first place.

This is a depressing conclusion insofar as it reflects on the weakness of our knowledge – although, to that extent, it will be understandably welcomed by those hostile to any understanding of human powers. But if this is the case, it now becomes relevant to describe the third way between the present lack of reductive explanation and the return to anti-intellectual mysticism that sociology can usefully make its own.

The sociological contribution, or 'enabling' and 'expressive'

Sociology's third way consists in two contributions. The first of these has already been outlined, but may be described here in slightly different terms. It has been argued that writers have a degree of freedom with which to investigate and make sense of their social world, and that their works exhibit a social referent comprehensible with the aid of close textual analysis. Put another way, sociology cannot show particular social facts that cause a writer to write in a particular way, but it can reconstruct after the event the 'reasons for action' involved in a particular perspective. This type of approach is close to that of Sartre's search for 'singular universals', and it is, of course, in no way reductive. One could summarise this contribution as one of helping in understanding rather than in explaining a work. The second contribution is the main one which sociology has to offer, and it is the one that will concern us hereafter. The weakness of the first contribution is that it would tend not to lead to higher level generalisations; works may well be found to be unrepresentative of larger patterns of social experience whilst such investigations would often be hampered by lack of information. More secure generalisations about larger social influences and pressures on the form that literary impulse assumes in any particular society can be gained by distinguishing between two concepts of society: one as enabling a literary culture and the other as encouraging particular expressive patterns. But before these concepts are elaborated, we need to say something about the nature of sociology itself.

The archetype of the sociological method should be the structural-functional method derived from social anthropology. The basic principle of this method is not hard to grasp. Societies are to be understood in terms of their functioning elements, the important elements being those based firmly in the structure of society (power, means of subsistence, etc.). It must be stressed that the concern with the structure and functioning of society does not mean that this method is somehow unable to explain social change, as is sometimes argued. The method has often been associated with various consensus views, but this does not prevent its application to the dynamic forces of society; indeed any systematic study of social change must rest upon an awareness of the structural importance of particular factors.

An immediate consequence of this is that sociologists should not be content with explanations of social behaviour in terms of 'ideal' rather than 'material' factors. This is not to say that sociologists are uninterested in belief, merely that they wish to examine not only social forces using belief as rationalisations, but also social forces which are necessary for, as it were, true belief to be supported. A classic example of the sociological method in this matter is Max Weber's thesis about the relations of Protestantism and Capitalism. Weber was obviously deeply interested in the matter of belief, and quite clearly he nowhere goes so far as to say that Protestantism is 'invalid'. Nevertheless, he makes clear that this was a religion that was suited to and was welcomed by the merchants of the European city. A factor of belief, in other words, was made possible by its having a social factor underneath it.

The most basic characteristic of this approach to the social world is its view of the active nature of man. The vision of human nature it embodies is of men choosing and selecting beliefs and values on the basis of their own interests. This is not to say that sociology automatically rules out as impossible belief as basic social force, merely that it will accept belief as an explanation only after all analysis of social structural facts has failed. And, once again, it is essential to note that the realisation that a particular belief is made possible by a conglomeration of social forces is not necessarily to suggest that it is untrue. Social origins and philosophic verity must not be confused.

The stress on the active nature of man is especially important when trying to understand literature. Man is not a passive receptacle into whom society pours its norms and values, but a being concerned to make sense of his experience – one part of which of course includes such norms. This point has been summarised by Duvignaud (1972) in his assertion that art is a 'wager' on man's ability to understand his own society.

These comments on sociology allow us to make four points, some of them explanations of arguments already made.

1. The remarks made about the structural-functional method explain why scepticism has been shown to the claim that literature, simply because it

is known in all societies, is always a significant social force in its own right. Men indeed do create meaning in all societies, but the force their meanings have depends upon social circumstances which vary histori- cally. On certain occasions it does seem as if art is more closely related to the power structure, and can be considered as a significant social force. Towards the end of his life Shaw, for example, was wistfully wont to argue that in primitive societies art had greater impact. Baalbek's monumental art was indeed more 'forceful' since it was designed in part to legitimise the rule of the powerful. Similarly scribes were surely of greater importance to the rulers of society so long as they were the possessors of a scarce skill. Again, it is clear that much of the architecture of seventeenth- and eighteenth-century Europe was designed by European absolutism to serve as a very powerful social force indeed. But, in contrast, it seems likely that a society in which nearly all men are literate is not one which is likely to place such value on art. The function of art is likely to change from the provision of semi- ritualistic legitimations for rulers to, in large part, that of entertainment.

2. The criticism levelled against the structuralist concept of inter- textuality is very close to the above comments and may usefully be reviewed here.

The underlying idea at work on the idea of intertextuality is well known to sociologists since it is a sociological theory in its own right. Kristeva's claim that literature is best seen as a reaction against its own history is paralleled by the argument, used by Popper, and, more recently, by Giddens (1976), that humans in society are constantly reacting to their own history. These authors suggest that sociological laws of any sort are impossible in that men have consciousness, can read and are thus likely to confound them.

These arguments are not altogether happy. They tend to be overly- idealist in presuming that consciousness in itself is the moving force in social affairs. Men do indeed take account of their situation, but the structural-functional approach is more realistic in suggesting that they tend to do so in ways that accord with their circumstances. This is especially true of literature where study of the mere fact of literary influence is not a substitute for examining an author's use of literary sources on the basis of his own experience. The situation then is complex; new social circumstances will in turn lead to a renewed intertextual dialogue that has to be carefully examined. And it is occasionally the case that an intertextual dialogue can precede social experience; but we tend only to be aware of this from the occasions in which society has eventually caught up with something that anticipated its course.

3. Much of the concern of those interested in the sociology of literature has been, to date, the social genesis of literature. The central argument of this whole section is that the specification of a social origin

does not devalue or reduce literature, but merely tells us how the unexplained literary impulse may be guided by a particular society. A corollary of this is that literature must continue to be judged in aesthetic terms. In Gombrich's words:

> Does the fact that the cathedrals were built to proclaim not only the glory of God but also the power of the Bishop make them less beautiful? Are they not in any case astounding structures ... The scientist must indeed frame hypotheses concerning the physical and psychological causation of phenomena, but that need not commit him to denying their autonomy ... (1974, p. 1088–9).

The understanding of the social genesis of literature is the understanding of social forces which allow literature to flourish.

The first important way in which this may be done is by examining those facets of society which enable a literary culture to be born. The specification of social forces is based on the presumption that, albeit it is impossible to explain why great art is produced, it is possible to note the forces that seem to frustrate it; we can discover forces which enable a literary culture to be born but cannot predict exactly what it will produce. These forces are diverse and have not been systematically considered. Peter Burke (1974), for example, has argued that social mobility was a necessary condition of the Italian Renaissance. His case is strengthened when the numbers of artists who were 'new men' is noted; and this theory helps to explain the pre-eminence of Florence in the Renaissance. Furthermore, in a review of enabling theories, he suggests that great cultural periods arise at moments of cultural vacuum when, as it were, a civilisation loses its force and leaves room for another. This might well be a generalisable factor, as is the covering statement that culture tends to be strong when social structure is weak (MacRae, 1970). However, other factors seem to be specific to particular societies. Thus Baron's argument that the Florentine achievement depended on liberty fails to cover other instances. Similarly Lopez's theory that hard times lead to investment in culture is surely not applicable today, whatever its status as an explanation for fifteenth-century behaviour. Finally an argument to be more fully developed later (Ch. 8) concerning an enabling factor for modern European literature may be briefly anticipated. Max Weber suggested that European city merchants were attracted to Puritanism because its emphasis on disciplined conduct as laid down in a book suited their own already regular style of life. Many have since agreed with Weber's claim that discipline was and is a necessary precondition for industrialism. However, it may be argued that the discipline necessary for the workplace had as its unintended consequence the re-creation of rigorous thought; all men have experience worth recording but the discipline provided by 'Bourgeois Literacy' was an enabling factor particularly effective in ensuring that a considerable number of such experiences found their way into print.

These remarks could be summarised by saying that certain factors encourage writing. In contrast, 'Expressive' refers to the way in which society influences the very form of what can be written. Society does so through encouraging conventions, genres and literary movements which accord with its basic character. The convention that has been most exhaustively examined, especially in Auerbach's superb *Mimesis*, is that of realism. Genres are those artistic forms such as tragic drama, epic and the novel whose rise and fall seem to be related to social change. It is worth noting that this area of the sociology of literature is that which has produced (often by authors who would not consider themselves sociologists) particularly sophisticated treatment of the relations of literature and society. Authors whose work fits into this category include W. P. Ker, C. S. Lewis, Lionel Trilling, R. Poggioli and Leslie Fiedler. An analysis of the novel in realist and modernist movements is the subject of Chapter 4.

This approach does not mean, yet again, that literature is being reduced. For example, it is fair to say that Proust was enabled to write his novel in part because he was driven by qualities of determination that seem archetypally those of bourgeois literacy; similarly it is fair to say that his society encouraged him to write a modernist novel. However, these are factors which merely influence the basic literary impulse. That they do not in any sense determine it can easily be seen if the picture is reversed; bourgeois literacy and the modernist novel may have been available, but it is all too conceivable that a Proust might not have arisen to have used them in his own very remarkable way.

4. This is an appropriate moment to summarise the difference between the sociological approach advocated here and that of Marxism. Such a summary is the more necessary in that both approaches recognise that 'material' forces are essential to an understanding of society, and in that both show an interest in the genesis of literature. (The sociology of literature is, as we shall see, also interested in much more.) Three differences between the two approaches concern us.

The first of these concerns the difference between society determining and society enabling and encouraging particular expressive forms. The former of these naturally leads to treating literature as a mere symptom of the social process, the principles of which Marxists believe they possess; an inevitable consequence of this is that the literary qualities of a text come to be ignored or diminished wherever literature fails to fit the Marxist theory of historical development. In contrast, the sociological approach treats literature – in a word – as real, as worth listening to; social forces that push the literary impulse in one direction or another are worth considering, but no theory of determination is possible until more is understood about the literary impulse itself.

This concept of society as enabling explains the second difference, that of the preference here for 'Bourgeois Literacy' over the Marxist notion of 'Bourgeois Literature'. The latter suggests rather crude mechanistic links between a class's economic interests and its literature;

this seems to me implausible in view of the considerable gap between the exigences of literary life and the economic situation of a whole class. 'Bourgeois Literacy' is a more meaningful and modest concept in its suggestion that the bourgeoisie was the carrier of certain qualities that could be translated easily into a powerful literary culture.

A final difference might as well be openly acknowledged. There are very strict limits to the usefulness of the Marxist philosophy of history. Where the Marxist sees the modern world simply in terms of class conflict, the sociologist would wish to insist that the increase in complexity consequent on industrialisation has changed society in ways that are significant even were class conflict to be abandoned. This difference will prove important in developing a view of the novel in Chapter 4 in opposition to that of the Marxists.

The sociology of literature

This chapter may usefully be concluded by giving a brief overview of the whole field of the subject. This overview will also serve as an explanation of the layout of the rest of the book.

The first area of the sociology of literature is that concerned with books-in-themselves. Detailed analysis of texts is bound to form the cornerstone of this area since no generalisations can be built up without such studies. The sociology of the author (Ch. 3) is likely to be of great help in understanding the relations of particular texts and society. However, it has already been suggested that particular texts may not in themselves advance sociological knowledge very far. Sociological appreciation of single texts all too often merely describes their content in different and often appropriate social terms; and, as I have argued, the specifics of a social referent in a text often reveal the atypical idiosyncrasy of its social views. For both these reasons the discussion of the emergence of broader genres and movements is to be preferred since it allows for a greater level of generalisation. A discussion of the novel (Ch. 4) serves as an example of this sort of approach. And the discussion of the sociology of the author is of considerable help in explaining the change in the novel from 'realism' to 'modernism'.

These considerations of books-in-themselves are already familiar from the discussion so far; however, they do not capture the whole of the sociology of literature. The greatest weakness of the reliance on studying the production and content of classics is that it can lead to naive cultural criticism. Far too often in the past critics of one variety or another have felt it proper to read off criticism about the society from a few classics, on the apparent assumption that what is in the text is absorbed in society. There should never be any belief in the automatic correspondence between audience and text. This is true even of popular literature (Ch. 5) although it is likely that the very popularity of a text is evidence of a reasonably close link. It is of great importance to discuss popular literature, however, since its typical themes clearly deny some of the more pessimistic cultural criticism drawn from analysis of the classics; Rockwell's argument about the social control function of literature has some relevance at this level. Moreover, it can be argued that the variety inside popular literature is great and that it is an essential element of literary culture – the true contrast being between literate and non-literate climates rather than between good and bad books.

The discussion of popular literature in large part concerns books-in-themselves, although the element of popularity does lead to some speculations about the audience. Between books and the audience, however, stand the distributors whose social function must be stressed since they have considerable power to influence the publication and reception of books. These distributors (Ch. 6) include publishers, censors, critics and booksellers and their role is sufficiently important to be pointed to, albeit rather little empirical evidence exists about their actual behaviour.

Distributors serve as gatekeepers between books-in-themselves and books-for-others. The argument that there is no necessary connection between these two areas can easily be demonstrated. The truly pioneering work has been done by Leo Lowenthal (1964) on the reception of the works of Dostoyevsky in Germany between 1880 and 1920. This study was based upon virtually all the available critical material on Dostoyevsky in that period, and it was on this basis that Lowenthal was able to show the existence of a distinctive misinterpretation (i.e. a significance for an audience actually removed from the texts' meanings) of Dostoyevsky's work which proved deeply revealing about the state of German society. Lowenthal felt justified in arguing that the critical stress on 'the Russian soul' represented a significant tendency to think in terms of national myths, whilst a similar stress on 'inner demons' in men represented a tendency to passivity on the part of the middle class that was to prove historically disastrous. Lowenthal's conclusion – that the study established the presence of widespread urges on the part of the German middle classes – is rather open to doubt, since it is surely dangerous to deduce the attitudes of a whole class from a critical reception. There is no doubt, however, that such critics represented a significant force in the new irrationalism of the political culture (Stern, 1965); and, most important, his demonstration of a complete gap between the content of the work and the uses to which it was put by at least an influential part of the audience remains valid. Indeed it might be noted that the situation can be even more complicated than this. John Murray the publisher helped make Byron a cult figure with the publication of *Childe Harold*. But Murray felt that Byronism would be killed were he to publish some of Byron's later work. Yet again the divergences in a literary system are striking, and it would be hard to tell whether Murray was right about the audience or merely pushing forward his own view of it.

The audience can be considered at two levels. The historical account

(Ch. 7) provides the basis for a more difficult and intangible discussion of the 'effect' of literary culture. In these areas, once again, far too little is known. It seems likely that the structuralist insistence that readers can actively model themselves on texts accounts for the success of some authors: Kipling's importance may in part be that he provided a model of behaviour for insecure colonialists. However, the dynamics of these processes remain unresearched, and the latter chapters of this study are a report as much on work to be done as on work completed.

Chapter 3

The sociology of the author

Theories of the artist

The most direct approach to the author is by an examination of theories held about the nature of artistic activity. Considerations on this matter will prove to be as contested as those already noted concerning the nature of literature itself. This is, of course, not surprising since judgements as to the proper nature of the artist's work closely reflect evaluations as to what the artist should be doing. Nevertheless, it is possible to find some way through this minefield since the early work of Williams in *The Long Revolution* (1971) and, once again, that of Gombrich have shown themselves resistant to traditional pitfalls.

There are two basic approaches to the artist, namely that stressing his role as imitator and that emphasising his visionary and expressive powers. Both these concepts have an extremely complex history. The emphasis on the artist's imitative, or mimetic, role owes much to ideas of Plato and Aristotle that seemed, as Raymond Williams stresses, on the face of it quite incompatible. The Greek word mimesis stresses the repetitive and secondary nature of artistic activity. This led Plato to believe that the artist might be a danger to society since he would emphasise 'appearance' at the expense of the more important everlasting 'forms'; he considered the poet to be one who 'excites and feeds' the 'worthless part of the soul', and thus destroys the rational part (cited by Williams, 1971, p. 21). Aristotle, on the other hand, suggests that imitation is a function of considerable importance since the poet could describe, not mere appearance, but universals themselves. In the course of the Middle Ages these doctrines became merged in the belief that the poet could pierce appearances when divinely inspired, and thus could give some account of the divine ideal (1971, p. 21). Despite the emphasis on the powers of the poet, it must nevertheless be stressed that such powers were seen to be of use only insofar as they were used to describe and 'imitate' the divine plan.

It must be remembered that great art has arisen from this approach, for current notions tend to assume that art should be 'original'. The Christians of the Middle Ages in comparison held that man in fact fulfilled himself only when he was able to suppress his own wayward individuality and let the design of God find full expression in him. This view stressed that God's design was perfect and that the function of the artist was to try to understand it. In St Thomas's words:

The perfection of art does not consist in the artist but in the work which is accomplished. ... Art concerns things that are made. ... Therefore it is not requested that the artist operate according to the good, but that his work is well made (cited in Josipovici, 1973, p. 53).

This position lay at the basis of Dante's view of his role as an artist, and this view of art can be clearly distinguished at work in *The Divine Comedy*. Dante describes himself as a copyist, not an inventor, and calls on the Muses to help him fathom the wisdom of God. 'Again and again he stresses the difficulty of his task, and we feel the strain and effort of the duty he owes to God and to his reader, the duty to be absolutely accurate' (Josipovici, 1973, p. 54). And this view of art can be seen at work in the structure of the poem which commences on Good Friday and ends on Easter Sunday, so that Dante's descent to Hell and journey to Heaven symbolically parallel the Passion and Resurrection of Jesus. Thus the reader is invited to enter a world of pre-established truth and not one which could be praised on account of any fanciful or playful creative imagination; indeed the exercise of any such imagination would be deemed irresponsible.

It is, of course, the case that many medieval artists were nevertheless aware of their own creative powers and creative problems. However, a new social situation was called for before these perhaps universal feelings could make themselves felt in the nature of views as to the proper function of art. This new social situation was achieved in the Netherlands and the great Italian cities in the fifteenth century, and its importance has been summed up by Blunt:

The artist was no longer a purveyor of goods which everyone needed and which could be ordered like any other material goods, but an individual facing a public. ... In this spirit of competition he began to carry out works other than those directly commissioned. We are here at the beginnings of those modern ideas which make of the artist a creator who works for himself alone (cited in Josipovici, 1973, p. 62).

The full extent of change has been obscured to some extent by the injunction that the artist respect nature. But Josipovici has pointed out how great a change had nevertheless occurred:

... it is no longer, as with Dante ... an *action* that has to be imitated, but a thing. And it is clear that the greater the freedom of the artist to invent, the more he will need to refer himself to external objects. But verisimilitude can never be the sole criterion, for however accurately the artist has imitated the objects of nature the question will still remain as to why he should choose *this* subject to imitate rather than that, or why he should select *this* detail rather than that (since he cannot reproduce all the details) (1973, p. 63).

And the logic of the position stressing the creative powers of the artist has been worked out to its limits in recent cultural history. In Shelley some concept of the imitative responsibility of the artist remains, but the greater emphasis is now clearly on the visionary powers of the creator. Kermode's *Romantic Image* traces the development of the idea of the originality of the creator's imagination, and shows that it is present to a very considerable extent even in the case of those who wish to consider themselves 'anti-romantic' – notably T. E. Hulme (Kermode, 1971, Ch. 7). Kermode points out that this position has become well enough known to be the subject of jokes, as was the case in the *New Yorker* when a cartoon showed an unkempt genius saying 'I paint what I don't see' (ibid, p. 16).

These two general positions have been rigorously schematised, and are only meant to serve as ideal types in a Weberian sense. However, both can clearly be seen at work in different approaches to understanding literature. The Marxist approach already extensively reviewed is the epitome of all those views stressing that the proper role of the artist is to imitate his society. This position can be held in various degrees of complexity. 'Socialist Realism' might be considered as one pole of crudity in this matter; but Lukács's insistence that the great 'realist' artist must penetrate below the appearance of mere surfaces to historical patterns is potentially more subtle and has interesting links with Plato's concern to penetrate behind appearances. Similar degrees of complexity can be seen at work in the stress on creativity. A rather extreme view of the artist in this manner is that of Freud. Freud's theory stresses that the artist is indeed a man of genius; but the price of such genius is neurosis. The artist is thus a man unable to live in normal society; he is, above all, characterised by a failure to accept the 'reality principle'. The view of the artist as a special visionary has grown since Freud – not surprisingly as it has been a view partial to many artists themselves. As Al Alvarez (1974) has argued, we have come to listen with reverence to those artists who, in one way or another, have lived in extreme situations. A masterly chronicling of this view is Lionel Trilling's account of the increasing stress given to social and aesthetic matters in *Sincerity and Authenticity* (1973). This book ends fittingly with a discussion of the 'anti-psychiatry' school associated with Laing whose views, especially in popularised form, represent a complete antithesis to those of Freud. The artist is again seen as visionary and as 'mad'; but this madness is seen as a sign of the artist's distinction since the 'reality principle' of the world is judged to be inherently alienating.

Weaknesses of both these schematised 'ideal-typical' views are all too evident. The greatest weakness of the Freudian view is that it presupposes that imagination is not part of normal psychic functioning; further criticism of this point offered by Rank is noted below. More generally, the 'original' artist is limited in crucial ways if he wishes to be understood; if, for example, he were driven to invent a language or symbolism that was entirely new he would not be understood at all. This is a point frequently made by Gombrich who stresses that artists may be driven by various psychic urges but that they do not succumb to them;

the important thing about them remains their ability to translate these feelings into form of one kind or another. Comparable weaknesses of the 'mimetic' theory have already been noted. The concern with 'social content' leads to an absurd belief that the convention of realism is clearly superior to others in which social experience is contained. And this view, as argued, tends to stress the idea of reflection which has already been ruled out of court on the grounds that it fails to realise the 'active' nature of artistic work.

At this point it is pertinent to point out that both approaches tend to suffer from a similar failing. Both tend to oppose art and reality, although each chooses one or the other as the bearer of all that is worthy and excellent. This division may be seen to be false once we remember Gombrich's argument that perception is only possible through socially given conventions, 'spectacles' or, in Popperian terms, searchlights. Raymond Williams, whose position is close to Gombrich's, has summarised the position thus:

> The new facts about perception make it impossible for us to assume that
> there is any reality experienced by man into which man's own
> observations and interpretations do not enter. Thus the assumptions of
> naive realism – seeing the things as they really are, quite apart from our
> reactions to them – become impossible. Yet equally, the facts of
> perception in no way lead us to a late form of idealism; they do not
> require us to suppose that there is no kind of reality outside the human
> mind; they point rather to the insistence that all human experience is an
> interpretation of the non-human reality (Williams, 1971, p. 36).

It has been argued that the understanding of individual texts is concerned with the reality seen through particular approaches; a most important concern of the sociology of literature is with the social origin of various conventions and genres. The reason for this is simply that we know rather little about 'the literary impulse'. This is not, however, to say that we should not be interested in theories which help direct our investigations in these matters. Three such theories can be specified. These are by no means mutually exclusive, and it is indeed rather easy to see continuities between the various positions. Ultimately they add little to the general view of literature as making sense of the world, but as constituents of that vague covering statement they are worth discussing if only for heuristic purposes.

The first theory under consideration may be best termed, somewhat clumsily, that of art as natural biography, and is most clearly seen in the work of Rank (1968) and, to a lesser extent, in that of Sartre (1963). Rank's unduly neglected *Art and Artist* was designed (as is much of Sartre's work) as an attack on Freud's views that art represented a neurotic obsession with fantasy at the expense of serving as an upright citizen of the reality principle. Rank opposed this view completely by stressing the 'health' of the imagination. His own studies of neurotics had led him to believe that their 'hostility' to the imagination prevented them from coping with their problems which they were unable to 'work through' in their imagination. Rank came to believe that neurotics were thus failed artists, rather than that artists had failed to live up to the reality principle. His own therapy for neurotics consisted in encouraging their imagination so they could become like artists in being able 'in the plan of illusion, in the act of creating ... to conquer creatively the problems they faced' (Rank, 1968, p. 109). This view of art can also be seen at work in a fine essay on *David Copperfield* in which Blount argues that the writing of the novel enabled Dickens to understand and accept his experience (1971). Perhaps the most helpful part of this approach is, however, indirect. The stress on the 'success' of the artist is likely to encourage the necessary interest in detailed investigations of the way in which an artist approaches his society; such detail is likely to undermine studies that move too brutally from the intentions of a text to an accepted vision of the society. It is at this point that Sartre's work is also important. The means by which the individual relations with the larger society are mediated by particular local connections and feelings appear in a very complex manner in Sartre's work. But this complexity need not detract from his signal service in encouraging detailed investigations.

This first approach would be generally psychological in orientation, but for the insistence (of Sartre in particular) that a biography is worked out in relationship with the larger society. It is this emphasis that links the first approach to the second which stresses the need to put social experience into words. This theory has been well argued by Burns and Burns (1973), Duvignaud (1972) and Williams (1971). Amongst the constituents of this theory is the belief that an artist can put into words feelings which will become generally recognised only at a much later date. This naturally leads to considerable respect for the importance of the artist. In Williams's words, 'we depend for growth on new descriptions being offered' (1971, p. 52). This argument has much in common with the Barthesian insistence that literature can provide models for social behaviour. Examples of this phenomenon include Kipling and Balzac; the success of both is partly ascribable to their ability to provide standards of behaviour for those groups facing entirely new experiences in the colonies or in Paris. This can be exaggerated but the general position has much to be said in its favour. Above all this approach allows for a conception of art as activist. Duvignaud considers that the artistic enterprise is thus a permanent 'wager' to establish better understandings of social life. Burns and Burns suggest that this approach is best understood as a 'reconciliation' of Durkheim's stress on social structure with Weber's insistence on the importance of an action approach in sociology.

The final approach is that of 'intertextuality'. This has already been extensively discussed and is only mentioned again for the sake of completeness. Rank noted that an artist could be as concerned to 'free himself' from the constraint of a literary tradition as he could be to 'free himself' from more obvious social pressures (1968, p. 372). It is indeed the case that some interest in formal matters is more immediately important than social concerns. This is perhaps especially the case inside a 'literary culture' which leaves a certain number of formal possibilities open. Consequently, the relations of an author with his own literary tradition must not be ignored. But two particular limitations to this view must be stressed. Firstly, this approach can tend to swallow too easily the cliché that what the avant-garde says is new will be seen to be such in the end. Besides being manifestly untrue, this view tends to overestimate the innovative concern of many of the greatest authors. In Gore Vidal's words (writing of great writers in general):

> ... and though it is true they did not leave the form of the novel as they found it, their art was not the result of calculated experiments with form so much as it was the result of their ability, by virtue of what they were, to transmute the familiar and make it rare (1977, p. 74).

Secondly, this viewpoint is prone to make the opposite error of the Marxist concern with content at the expense of form – namely to consider form without content. As argued, new formal demands are necessitated in large part by the need to capture new experience. One striking example of this concerns the social background of many of the best of twentieth-century British writers. It will be demonstrated below that the literary stratum of late-Victorian and Edwardian England was comprised overwhelmingly of those from middle-class (especially professional) backgrounds. Given the argument that few can 'transcend' their social position, it would seem likely that the novel would have a very strong middle-class base to it. However, an awareness of the achievements of the novel has led to a realisation that sources of renewal inside English literary culture came through the acceptance of outsiders in the literary establishment. 'The importance of new social groups in much of the most original social thinking of the nineteenth century, and of these groups and of women in the major period of the Victorian novel, is a positive correlation' (Williams, 1971, p. 265). The incapability of the literary establishment to produce great writing has been interestingly explored by Eagleton and, more controversially, by Green. Green's argument (1977) centres on the impact of the First World War on British life and is thus rather limited, despite its pungency, in its scope. Eagleton's *Exiles and Emigrés* (1970) is of more general interest. Eagleton notes that the great twentieth-century figures of English literature have either been exiles (Conrad), émigrés (Eliot, Yeats, Pound, Joyce and James) or outsiders (Lawrence and, at a slightly lower level, Wells, Bennett and many 'provincial novelists' including David Storey and Margaret Drabble). Acceptance of such figures by the establishment is to its credit even if the failure to breed its own is disquieting. The three theories outlined here go some way in suggesting why the sources of renewal came from the outside. Socially displaced artists will suffer from exactly those tensions which the biographical approach emphasises. Furthermore, it is clear that these new and forceful social experiences naturally led to the revision of traditional forms precisely in order that the new experiences could be successfully captured in words. Here then is a prime example of form and content marching together.

The social position of the writer

These last remarks have already taken us to the question of the social position of the writer. This social position obviously varies in different cultural climates. However, the mass of available material necessitates some principle of selection; consequently the social position of the author in Britain will be considered. Even here there is a massive amount of biographical material: this has given rise to one excellent general discussion on *The Rise and Fall of the Man of Letters* (Gross, 1973). A broad picture is, however, made possible as a result of the surveys into social position carried out by Williams (1971), Altick (1962), Laurenson (1969), Bradbury (1971), and Bradbury and Wilson (1971); but even here rather rigorous selection is necessary.

Saunders's *The Profession of English Letters* offers an excellent guide to the historical development of the social position of the writer in England; some of the key points of his account may usefully be restated here. It is possible to begin to talk about the profession of English letters only in the fourteenth century since until then a 'national' language was missing. The position of the writer at this time was precarious since creative writing was not held in high esteem – the proper models were judged to be those of the past. Moreover, creative writers were potentially opposed to the interest of the Church which held a virtual monopoly on literacy and education; the Church was largely responsible for providing clerks to government and to individual nobles, many of whom did not feel it important enough to learn to read themselves. Added to all these hostile circumstances was the fact that an author would have no control over his manuscript once it was printed; no royalty system existed, and his work could be taken over by another printer without his permission. Despite these circumstances, some nevertheless became writers. It is important to realise that most of these came from non-aristocratic backgrounds. Their social position was of the middling sort – Chaucer being a civil servant and Gower a merchant. In Saunders's words:

> Until the Renaissance, then, the most dynamic forces behind the
> development of English Literature were middle class in origin, English
> rather than Anglo-French, of the guilds and the yeomanry rather than of
> the Court and the aristocracy. This fact was to have potent influence
> upon the development of a literary profession at the crucial time when
> printing presses came into use (1964, p. 25).

Saunders adds to this picture of the new profession the observation that the spread of literacy amongst the middling orders was responsible for an increasing multiplication of manuscripts, and later of printed books, in the very kinds of literature which middle-class readers preferred (1964, p. 25).

The lack of interest in the literary arts on the part of the powerful changed dramatically as a result of new renaissance humanism. Castiglione's *Courtier* was influential in England as elsewhere. A ready and easy pen could help one flatter one's way into the favour of monarchs – as proved the case with many of Elizabeth's courtiers, especially in the later part of her reign. This in itself, however, does rather little to alter the general picture of literature being the product of 'the middling sort'. The true professionals were of such social origin and the quality of much of the rather sickly courtly love poetry of the 1590s is open to question – and was certainly much criticised by Shakespeare (Cruttwell, 1960). Moreover, Saunders points out that courtly interest in literature tended to militate against the actual act of publishing; once private flattery was in print it could all too easily be attacked: 'For the professional the achievement of print ultimately became an economic necessity: for the aspirant to courtly promotion the avoidance of print was a social desirability' (1964, p. 56).

The most difficult question to resolve concerns the court's link to the Elizabethan theatre. An oft-repeated orthodoxy in this matter is that of Raymond Williams who argues that the achievement of Elizabethan drama was due to its popular nature (1971, p. 193). This is strenuously opposed by Saunders who considers that the court was responsible for keeping the theatres open and for employing dramatists. This was not to say that a popular element was lacking but merely that it was held in check:

> ... the plays of the time were homogeneous, because they were written for homogeneous audiences by writers who could confidently anticipate the public response craved for by all literary professionals, mass popularity strengthened by the support of the intelligentsia. It is rare in literary history for such a happy combination of circumstances (Saunders, 1964, p. 78).

This view gains support from Cruttwell's dated but striking *The Shakespearean Moment*. Cruttwell argues that the tragic vision of Shakespeare and others was made possible by a neo-aristocratic and pessimistic vision that was eventually displaced by the improving outlook of Puritan rationalism.

It is a sad comment on the failure of English sociologists of literature to confront the giants of their literary heritage that it is impossible to point out the truth of the matter in any rigorous manner. Williams's argument as to the popular nature of the theatre is surely exaggerated in that only a very few people could have regularly attended performances at the Globe. Moreover, as Saunders demonstrates, popularity is in itself no guarantee of quality. The degeneration of the English theatre after

1660 meant that plays were produced by hacks to demonstrate the qualities of great actor-managers; this did not prevent such plays being extremely popular. Nevertheless, the image of discriminating courtly patronage is equally suspect. C. Hill has recently argued that the image of the Puritans as destroyers of the theatre has been exaggerated; certainly Milton's own background was far from narrow (Hill, 1977, p. 23). Moreover, the beneficial effects of the court are surely exaggerated; Chesterton pointed out long ago that the image of a 'well-balanced' Elizabethan era simply fails to take account of the treason and plotting in the plays – especially, perhaps, in Jacobean revenge drama. The position then is extremely complex but it seems that neither the populist nor the aristocratic version is satisfactory.

In contrast to this uncertainty is the relative confidence with which the real establishment of the profession of letters can be dated in the century or so after the Restoration. In this period writers, helped in part by the passing of the Copyright Act of 1709, finally became free of patrons. This freedom was often much appreciated since many patrons had only marginal interest in purely literary matters in any case; this was the subject of the famous rebuke Samuel Johnson delivered to his aristocratic patron, Lord Chesterfield.

> Seven years, my Lord, have now past, since I waited in your outward rooms, or was repulsed from your door; during which time I have been pushing on my work through difficulties, of which it is useless to complain, and have brought it, at last, to the verge of publication, without one act of assistance, one word of encouragement, or one smile of favour. Such treatment I did not expect, for I never had a Patron before. . . .
>
> Is not a Patron, my Lord, one who looks with unconcern on a man struggling for life in the water, and, when he reaches ground, encumbers him with help? The notice which you have been pleased to take of my labours, had it been early, had been kind; but it has been delayed till I am indifferent, and cannot enjoy it; till I am solitary, and cannot impart it; till I am known, and do not want it. I hope it is no very cynical asperity not to confess obligations where no benefit has been received, or to be unwilling that the Publick should consider me as owing that to a Patron, which Providence has enabled me to do for myself (Boswell, 1960, p. 185).

This freedom was, of course, not easily gained and the writers of Grub Street came to symbolise those who were unable to make a decent living out of literature. Nevertheless the increase in literacy and the rise of new genres, especially the novel, the essay and the biography, did allow for at least some to succeed in the profession of letters.

Something of the social composition of the profession of letters can be seen by making use of the investigation of Altick on the period 1800–1935. Before examining his figures, it is worthwhile remembering that one of the most striking facts about the nineteenth-century novel

is that it was very largely the product – in terms of quality as well as
quantity – of women writers (Chesterton, 1913). Turning to more
empirical matters, Altick offers interesting information about the
social class of the fathers of authors in his survey:

Table 3.1

	1800–35 (%)	1835–70 (%)	1870–1900 (%)	1900–35 (%)
Upper class	12.7	11.3	7.9	10.0
Middle class	83.9	87.8	90.3	84.2
Lower class	3.4	0.9	1.8	5.8

(Adapted from Altick, 1962.)

The general character of the literary culture of nineteenth- and early
twentieth-century England is thus overwhelmingly indebted to those of
middle-class origin. This picture is reinforced by some of the detailed
figures offered by Altick that have not been included here: two points
are important. First, in the course of the nineteenth century the
'aristocracy of wealth' (bankers, merchants, shipowners and brokers)
provided fewer members of the literary profession; the aristocratic
embrace of English culture presumably turned such figures into
consumers rather than producers of culture. Secondly, Altick demonstrates that the vast proportion of writers in his survey had fathers in the
arts and professions (i.e. civil servants, clergymen, journalists, school-
masters, lawyers and artists).

Altick's survey also includes the following, perhaps predictable,
information about the education of authors:

Table 3.2

	1800–35 (%)	1835–70 (%)	1870–1900 (%)	1900–35 (%)
Little or no schooling	11.3	5.9	4.1	7.2
Education ended at secondary level	36.2	27.9	25.0	20.5
Education continued into university or comparable institution	52.5	66.2	70.9	72.3

(Adapted from Altick, 1962.)

These figures mislead unless several other points – mostly concerned
with questions of quality – are borne in mind. The increasingly
established nature of English literary culture evidenced by the increasing
number of authors going to university does not militate against the
picture that has already emerged of the profession of letters being
predominantly middle class in character. As noted, the sources of
renewal were typically not 'established' in nature. Secondly, it may be
argued that insofar as English literary culture has become more closely

linked to the establishment it has simultaneously declined in its power and range. Thus the powerful bourgeois and dissenting culture that produced George Eliot and the Mills as well as Bennett and Lawrence has been replaced in some degree by a new semi-aristocratic and significantly weaker style. The accommodation of the bourgeois culture to that of the establishment can be seen at work in Larkin's *Jill* and in the fascination of two very considerable recent writers, Evelyn Waugh and Anthony Powell, with a gently declining aristocratic world. Some of the reasons for this decline have been offered by Shils (1972) and Green (1977).

One final point about social position may be noted. Even in the heyday of the Victorian three-volume novel it was hard to make a living from literature. Both Dickens and Disraeli managed to get £10,000 for a novel, but this contrasted unfavourably with the £250 that as good a novelist as Trollope commanded for his *Three Clerks* (Sutherland, 1976). Consequently, many novelists themselves had second jobs:

Table 3.3

	1800–35	1835–70	1870–1900	1900–35
Clergymen	29	38	16	3
Practising solicitor or barrister	5	10	2	4
Government official, civil servant, diplomat	17	27	17	13
Artist, architect, musician, actor	11	21	10	13
Teacher, professor	4	17	25	37
Practising physician	8	10	2	4

(From Altick, 1962.)

Once again the impression is gained of the literary culture being one that was supported by middle-class groups.

Altick correctly notes that the social groups supporting and comprising the literary culture changed rather little in the period from 1800 to 1935. This is the more surprising given that the audience itself was changing so completely. 'Most nineteenth century writers found themselves in the unprecedented position of having to adapt their techniques and messages to the limited capacities and special expectations of a newly formed mass audience' (Altick, 1962, p. 403). This proved to be a fact of very great importance to the literary profession's conception of its own role.

The spread of literacy in the nineteenth century was met in large part with optimism on the part of the literary profession. The 'hero as man of letters' glorified by Carlyle presumed that he would be able to capture the newly literate for the organs of respectable opinion for which he wrote, notably the *Edinburgh Review*, the *Spectator* and the *Nineteenth Century*. The duty to raise the newly literate was taken seriously;

Dickens, for example, took inordinate care (and insisted that authors he published did so as well) to educate his readers (Sutherland, 1976, Ch. 8). This optimism was confounded by discoveries made during the course of the nineteenth century. Most importantly, it became clear that the newly literate preferred the *Daily Mail* introduced by Northcliffe to, say, the improving tones of the *Daily News*.

Authors were confronted with a realisation that their audience had now become fragmented, and some of them, most immediately Meredith, learnt to accept the fact. But the realisation that the mass of newly-literate readers were not likely to be led by liberal intellectuals caused much soul-searching and anxiety. The role of the artist came to be conceived in rather different terms; the role of general educator was dropped for that of preserver of high culture. This latter role naturally linked itself to various types of elitist view; this in itself is scarcely surprising considering that the early works of the modernist writers appeared in 'little magazines' like the *Egoist* and *Blast* which were read by a very small audience indeed.

This change in the conception of the role of the artist will concern us in the next chapter when the social roots of modernism are discussed. This chapter may be concluded with some comments on the social position of the writer at present. The best source of information on the position of the modern author is offered by Richard Findlater in two surveys done for the Society of Authors (1963 and 1966). In 1965 half the writers Findlater considered lived off a second job; and only 44 per cent of those who did live by literature were able to make more than £500 a year. Thus two thirds of all writers earned less than £6 a week from their work, and only one sixth made more than £20 a week.

Per Gedin has recently pointed out that these conditions may well get worse for imaginative writers. At the beginning of the sixties many Western countries devoted about 30 per cent of their book production to imaginative literature, but Escarpit (1966, *passim*) has shown that there is currently a tendency for an increase in the proportion of 'functional' books published – including as a basic staple school books (up to 25 per cent) and as a growth point books in social science. In Sweden, considered by Gedin a forerunner of trends of publishing likely to catch the rest of the industrial world, this situation is becoming worrying. In the early 1940s Sweden too devoted about 30 per cent of its output to fiction; this had fallen to 18.3 per cent by 1969. Further to this Gedin notes that it is much harder for new writers to be published (158 new writers in 1965, 118 in 1971) (Gedin, 1977, Ch. 5). Gedin's prognostications about the difficulties facing *belles-lettres* will concern us again; but their relevance for any consideration of the social position of the author cannot be overestimated. As we shall see below (Ch. 6) the economics of modern publishing make it more and more important to have some best-selling books on a publisher's list since even a well-known author such as Margaret Drabble is likely to gain only moderate profits for her publishers (her hardback sales are, according to Gedin, about 15,000 per novel). The temptations to ignore new fiction and to commission fiction-cum-film script, as was the case with *Jaws*, increases daily.

The writer has two new sources of patronage whose effects cannot as yet be fully assessed. The first of these, the patronage of the media system, has been briefly discussed by Bradbury (1971) and its importance cannot be doubted given that the BBC is the richest and largest patron in history. Virtually nothing is known about the social effect of this form of patronage, but the observation might be hazarded that corporate patronage, perhaps naturally, tends to support already established literary talent at the expense of new writers. But this is only an observation, and as such merely a call for research. The second corporate patron is the university, especially the American university, which has been able to support many authors as 'creative writers' or 'writers in residence'. This new corporate patronage has generated a mass of comment, much of which is uninformed. Those who are opposed to such patronage point to the sterility of the university novel genre, and the narrowing of social experience that inevitably follows. It is in this light that Tom Wolfe observes that the services of fiction in the nineteenth century have been taken over by 'the new journalism'.

> There is no novelist who will be remembered as the novelist who captured the Sixties in America or even in New York, in the sense that Thackeray was the chronicler of London in the 1840s and Balzac was the chronicler of Paris after the fall of the Empire. Balzac prided himself on being 'the secretary of French society' (Wolfe cited in Gedin, 1977, p. 142).

And it is worth stressing that the greatest diatribe against the universities is made by distinguished writers. Saul Bellow has argued that the whole academic teaching of English has been 'an intellectual disaster' in which students are told what to think about particular books at the expense of developing their own critical faculties (Bellow, 1977). Gore Vidal, the most celebrated castigator of 'the hacks of academe', has gone so far as to argue that the obsession with form in the modern American novel is a consequence of the academic status of the authors; such novels he argues with customary brilliance are not written to be read but to be taught (Vidal, 1977, 'Plastic Fiction'). Similar arguments about the limitations of what has been called 'post-modernist' fiction have been made by Lodge (1977).

Arguments on the other side tend to be weaker yet more effective. Writers are pointed to (Jerzy Kosinski, and, ironically, Bellow himself whose *Sammler's Planet* in fact contains a rather considerable discussion of the 1960s) whose powers have not been diminished by intellectual life; but whether this is because of or in spite of the new corporate patronage remains an open question. More cogently, however, supporters of academic patronage can point to the undoubted fact that it is becoming harder, except for the very few, to make a living out of writing and that universities do provide jobs; though a brutal argument, this is undoubtedly a forceful one.

Chapter 4

The novel, realism and modernism

The character of the novel

The discussion of the nature of the novel has recently advanced to very dizzy heights as a result of structuralist interest in the nature of the novel (see Halperin, 1974). However, for our purposes only three striking attempts to relate the novel as a genre to society are of real interest. All these theories are such as to allow for the achievement of realist and modernist novels; they are thus distinct from some of the cruder views of the later Lukács which tend to restrict 'the novel' to the nineteenth-century novel almost without exception.

The first interpretation that concerns us was offered by Hegel. The 'epic' is seen by Hegel as a form which suited and gave witness to the 'total' man of classical Greece; this totality was the result of there being no division between society and state so that no distinction between private and public realms could be distinguished. The novel, in comparison, Hegel views as a 'bourgeois prose epic'. He judges this form to be essentially inferior since it reflected the alienation of modern man consequent on the breakdown of the early harmony of man and society (1920, Vol. 4). This general view was also shared by the early Lukács whose *The Theory of the Novel* provides the second contribution that is of interest here.

Lukács offers a more positive version of Hegel's theory but this is in fact only a development of Hegel's own comments on Diderot's *Rameau's Nephew*. In those comments Hegel argued that the proper response to the newly fragmented world is not a retreat into a false and spurious new 'totality'; rather social contradictions should be embraced in the hope of arriving at new and proper authentic values. Thus Hegel praises Diderot's portrait of Rameau's unstable and romantic nephew on the grounds that the very graspingness of his ambitions shows that he had advanced beyond any sterile acceptance of now empty social conventions. Lukács extends this view by arguing that the novel is the form in which a hero searches for authentic values. Thus characteristic heroes of the novel as a genre are judged to be Julien Sorel and Rastignac who work their way through a number of different social situations in the search for a reasoned creed to live by. It is worth noting that even this early and striking theory of Lukács is excessively dependent on examples drawn from France. When applied mechanistically to different situations it can hide more than it reveals. Thus Swinge-wood, who follows Goldmann in adopting the theory of the novel proposed by the young Lukács, very nearly writes off the English nineteenth-century novel since its heroes are not quite enough like Julien Sorel (Swingewood, 1976, Ch. 2).

For all the brilliance of *The Theory of the Novel* it is both obscure and perhaps overly idealist. However, Lukács's main contributions are capable of clear and less question-begging statements, and they have received it in a superb essay by Lionel Trilling on 'Morals, Manners and the Novel' (Trilling, 1950). Trilling's great merit is that he is not dogmatically married to any philosophy of history and is not in any case keen on the re-creation of the 'totality' of man. Hence his arguments restate the core of the positions of Lukács and Hegel in a manner which is much easier to accept. Trilling argues that the novel is indeed born out of the social differentiation symbolised by the rise of monied economies. Money allows social mobility, and such mobility brings in its train difficulties as to how to understand and behave in newly discovered social situations. Three important points about the novel can be made as a result. Trilling suggests that the novel is well suited to describe the experiences of a single individual who begins to move in unfamiliar social strata. Its very form is thus 'liberal' in being most suited to explore the experiences of the individual; the corollary of this is that the novel, as Malraux's *Days of Hope* demonstrates, is rather poorer than, say, the epic, in describing a collectivity. And the novel is suited to contrast the illusions of the hero with the more sordid realities that he encounters. Trilling gives a very large number of apposite examples on this point, drawn significantly from a very wide range of literature. Amongst these examples is that of the manner in which Don Quixote's dreams are destroyed by reality; and the celebrated scene in which the dying Swann, come for consolation to his friend Mme de Guermantes, is forced to realise her selfishness when she tries to ignore his illness so that she can go out, is also cited as an exemplary instance of the novel's capacity. Secondly, Trilling's theory is of considerable use in emphasising that the novel has its origins in the very rise (and, one might add, continued existence) of complex societies. This position allows for the important criticism of Heiserman (1976), Kristeva (1976) and Spearman (1966), that novels were written before the rise of the bourgeoisie, to be taken into account. Precursors of the novel are, of course, to be expected in earlier moments of social complexity, although this in turn does not diminish the important contribution made by eighteenth-century developments. Thirdly, Trilling emphasises that factors other than the purely economic may be at work. His argument about social complexity leads him to quote with approval Henry James's famous diatribe on the 'thinness' of American life:

> No State, in the European sense of the word, and indeed barely a specific national name. No sovereign, no court, no personal loyalty, no

aristocracy, no church, no clergy, no army, no diplomatic service, no country gentlemen, no palaces, no castles, nor manors, nor old country houses, no parsonages nor thatched cottages, nor ivied ruins; no cathedrals, nor abbeys, nor little Norman churches; no great universities nor public schools – no Oxford, nor Eton, nor Harrow; no literature, no novels ... (James cited by Bergonzi, 1972, p. 97).

Trilling uses this argument to suggest that the stress on equality has prevented the American novel from producing memorable characters:

I think that if American novels of the past, whatever their merits of intensity and beauty, have given us very few substantial or memorable people, this is because one of the things that makes for substantiality of character in the novel is precisely the notation of manners, that is to say, of class traits modified by personality (1950, pp. 261–2).

And this general view stressing the importance of an ideological factor not obviously related to any particular class interest has been stressed with very great insight by both D. H. Lawrence and L. Fiedler; their works provide a most convincing account of American literature in the light of the American ideal of equality and democracy.

The general conception of the novel adopted here can be summarised by quoting Jean Duvignaud who has also sought to escape the more rigid points of the Marxist approach:

We shall not discuss the interpretations put on the novel by Hegel or by Lukács, because it seems to us that the great proliferation of this type of imagined experience in prose form owes its importance, not to the momentary situation of a class, but to the discovery, which remained unresolved, of the existence of a tension between groups in the whole society. *Moll Flanders, Lady Roxana, Le paysan parvenu, Marianne,* Julien Sorel, and Rastignac do not reflect a determination to be 'bourgeois', they are the result of a question posed by the writer concerning the multiplicity of possibilities available in a society whose organisation remains 'mysterious', according to some, and 'anarchic' according to others. ... The experimental attraction of examining the real world by making use of the imaginary is striking when we consider that the novel, far from reflecting the values of a class (which was never really aware of them) increases the surprise of belonging to a society where human relations and social situations are multiple (Duvignaud, 1972, p. 122).

Realism and the novel

The awareness that the novel springs from a larger background does not mean that the achievements of the eighteenth-century novel need be ignored. It will be seen later (Ch. 7) that the rise of the middle-class reading public was important in creating a receptive audience in its own right; it also allowed a degree of financial independence for the author.

These factors were necessary conditions for the emergence of the novel as an important genre. But the concerns of a middle class may be seen at work in the novel in more particular ways. Diana Spearman, generally reluctant to admit the influence of society on the novel, argues that:

> ... the eighteenth century novelist ... differed from writers of prose epics in choosing characters in private life instead of historical figures, from the picaresque tale in placing them in a much higher station and giving them many amiable, if not heroic, qualities (1966, pp. 113–14).

The 'democratic' concern with and interest in the lives of ordinary people is the prime characteristic of 'realism' and it can be seen at work in many facets of the eighteenth-century novel. Ian Watt notes, for example, that the naming of characters in such novels is personal and sensible, and typically no longer heavily overladen with symbolism of one sort or another. He also suggests that the Puritan emphasis on individualism is important, for:

> By weakening communal and traditional relationships, it fostered not only the kind of private and egocentric mental life we find in Defoe's heroes, but also the later stress on the importance of personal relationships which is so characteristic both of modern society and of the novel – such relationships may be seen as offering the individual a more conscious and selective pattern of social life to replace the more diffuse, and as it were voluntary, social cohesions which individualism had undermined (Watt, 1963, p. 183).

Watt further relates the realism of the eighteenth-century novel to more general changes in philosophic climates of opinion. He notes the similarity between individualism and the distrust of abstract universals; following Descartes, the preferred notion became that of the individual himself building up a correct picture of the external world through rigorous use of his own sense organs. In its turn this encouraged the novel to embody new attitudes towards time. Whereas time in tragedy had been restricted to the canonical twenty-four hours prescribed by the Greeks, the novel concentrated on the slower, more realistic unfolding of the pattern of events; the difference, for Watt, symbolises the fact that tragedy is focussing attention on the facts of life and death so that we shall be able to face eternity, whilst the novel is a form of this world, providing information about different social strata (1963, pp. 23–4). Finally, Watt notes that the novel broke with the canons of classic style in favour of a less elevating prose style:

> Reading *Tom Jones* we do not imagine that we are eavesdropping on a new exploration of reality; the prose immediately informs us that exploratory operations have long since been accomplished, that we are to be spared that labour, and presented instead with a sifted and clarified report of the findings (p. 30).

A comment on this point is in order. Watt broadly accepts the claim of the eighteenth-century novel to describe reality more accurately. One modernist critic, Josipovici, has questioned this rather stolid trust on a number of grounds, one of which may be mentioned here. Josipovici suggests that puritan readers are invited to:

> ... close their eyes and allow their imaginations to play on what is presented to them; neither, while engaged on this, would dream of questioning the reality of what their imagination provides. Unlike our ordinary experience of life, there is nothing, we feel, that could happen to [the puritan reader] which would make him alter his views of his way of looking at the world ... there is rarely any questioning of the nature of the implication of these things (1973, pp. 146–7).

The problem here for Josipovici is that the overly assured and determined reality of both realist philosophy and the realist novel is oversimplified, and not, literally, 'real' at all. It is interesting to note that these limitations were marvellously transcended by Sterne's *Tristram Shandy*, and it is no accident that this book, which questions the nature of our views of reality with merciless wit, receives scant treatment in Watt's survey.

There is no doubt that Watt's book is excellent when discussing Defoe and Richardson, but it has been interestingly criticised for its attempt to include Fielding in its survey. Swingewood has pointed out that Fielding shared little of the middle-class world or views of Richardson; unlike Richardson, for example, Fielding had been forced to rely on traditional patronage for his subsistence on a number of occasions. Swingewood's careful reading of *Tom Jones* leads him to argue that:

> It is thus difficult to resist the conclusion that while Fielding was critical of certain aspects of the social structure, especially the aristocracy, the Church of England, and the medical profession, he seems finally to assert the virtues of a traditional rural England over the secular, advancing urban capitalist areas. It is hard to see how Fielding can be situated in the history of the novel as a bourgeois writer; in *Tom Jones* society and the need for social order exercise priority of individual motivation and action ... (Laurenson and Swingewood, 1972, pp. 203–4).

Swingewood buttresses the view of Fielding as a 'conservative' with interesting readings of Fielding's views on cities and on sex, finding them in each case diametrically opposed to those of Richardson. Two points are drawn from this. Firstly, Swingewood draws upon the idea noted above, that the novel as such centres on a hero's search for true experience and values. Using this idea, Swingewood is able to demonstrate that Fielding had very considerable technical problems in the novel since he wished to assert that the social values were broadly just, but was using a form suited for exploration of individualism to do so. Hence, Tom himself becomes a rather curious character, who, unlike, say, Julien Sorel, accepts social conventions that seem to harm him and, in general, has things happen to him as a passive victim. Swingewood notes that 'Fielding's flat portrayal of character, his lack of interest in the subjective aspect of life flows from his acceptance of the neo-classicist emphasis of the priority of the plot over character' (Laurenson and Swingewood, 1972, p. 204). One can see what Swingewood means here, and his comments closely resemble the argument made by Leslie Fiedler (1965) that, despite his support for certain social values, Bellow's novels are in fact at their best when they exhibit a 'fertile paranoia'. Nevertheless, Swingewood's theory is ultimately one-dimensional and contrasts poorly with the charity of Henry James who, unhappy though he was about the character of the hero, could yet excuse Fielding in the Author's Preface to *Princess Casamassima* on these grounds:

> (Tom Jones) has so much 'life' that it amounts . . . almost to his having a mind . . . besides which his author – *he* handsomely possessed of a mind – has such an amplitude of reflection for him and round him that we see him through the mellow air of Fielding's fine old moralism, fine old humour and fine old style, which somehow really enlarge, make everyone and everything important.

Secondly, Swingewood adopts an argument from Gramsci which deserves further examination. He suggests that the early eighteenth century did not see a complete ascendancy of the middle-class puritan; rather their economic ascendancy went hand in hand with political subservience to the traditional aristocratic class. He feels, however, that this does not affect the connection between a class and a convention of the novel, but makes it more complex and perhaps stronger. For 'a social class which strives towards some form of economic and political supremacy in circumstances which inhibit its claims will seek to assert itself through culture; as a rising class it must negate the values of the class it seeks to supplant' (Laurenson and Swingewood, 1972, p. 189). Swingewood adds to this in noting that the relationship between the reading public and the history of the novel may be more complex than usually allowed. He suggests that the burgeoning but politically feeble middle class did provide some readership for the novels of Richardson and Fielding. However, once this class was much more self-confident it seemed to demand entertainment rather than the articulation of alternative social values; 'it may be possible', he notes, 'to link the actual decline of the English novel after 1760 with the growth of a middle class, through its insatiable need for entertainment . . .' (ibid., pp. 184–5). This is an interesting observation but it is one desperately needing empirical investigation.

Swingewood's views on *Tom Jones* are a useful bridge to a consideration of the nineteenth-century novel. Most of the work done by sociologists on the nineteenth-century novel, much of which is extremely valuable, is of Marxist origin and generally follows in the path of Lukács. Hence it is perhaps as well to note immediately that there

exists no obvious relationship between larger questions of economic
change and developments in the novel. For the great and admitted
achievements of the nineteenth-century novel took place in France and
Russia, and both these countries were, of course, economically
backward in comparison to England. This is not, however, to say that
there is no relationship between novel and society. Following Trilling,
we may suggest that cultural factors were of the greatest importance at
this juncture. For France was, as a result of the Revolution, politically
advanced, and this made for great intensity in analysing the relations of
individual to society. George Steiner has put the point thus:

> ... the age of Revolution and Empire bestowed on daily life the stature
> and resplendency of myth. It vindicated with finality the supposition that
> in observing their own times artists would find themes in the grand
> manner. The happenings of the period from 1789 to 1820 gave to men's
> awareness something of contemporaneity, something of the freshness and
> vibrancy which Impressionism subsequently gave to their awareness of
> physical space (1967, p. 28).

And this interest led to one notable theme, and one striking example.
The theme that dominated much of European fiction in the nineteenth
century was that of 'Bonapartism', and it received something of a final
statement in Dostoyevsky's *Crime and Punishment*; and this theme was,
as it were, epitomised by Balzac's Napoleonic creation of complete
fictional society.

The Marxist theory of the nineteenth-century novel dominated by the
views of Lukács has already been described. How good is it? There can
be no doubt but that significant readings have come out of this tradition
(for example, Lucas, 1971). But as a whole the theory has considerable
weaknesses, two of which may be mentioned. First, the belief that
realism somehow tells the truth is simplistic. What are we to make of this
account of the obviously allegorical and non-realistic names Dickens
often gives to his characters? At times Marxist readings have been so
doggedly unimaginative that they have reached the right conclusion
largely by accident. It is, for example, true that Balzac may be seen in
part as an examiner of new capitalist attitudes, but this point is made
much more forcefully by examining the structure of his imagination
than by presuming that the social content of, say, *Lost Illusions* is
correct. This is in fact what Brecht did when noting that:

> Balzac is the poet of monstrosities ... he writes vast genealogies, he
> marries off the creatures of his fantasy as Napoleon did his marshals and
> brothers; he follows possessions (fetishism of objects) through
> generations of families and their transference from one to the other ...
> (1974, pp. 47–8).

This sort of detailed literary awareness, so obviously possessed by both
Brecht and Benjamin, is exactly what Marxist aesthetics has hitherto
generally lacked. Secondly, on a matter of detail, it is almost certainly

not the case that Lukács's adulation of Balzac in reference to Stendhal is at all justified (see Turnell, 1950).

Marxism and modernism

The criticisms of the actual theory of realism are not as damning as that already made against Lukács, namely that his condemnation of modernism is wildly unjustified. This section is concerned in large part to show that, *pace* Lukács, modernist novels represent a considerable artistic achievement from which a social referent may be drawn. After this version of Marxism, here termed Marxism 1, has been criticised in this manner the material assembled may be compared with the view of modernism offered by more radical Marxists, whose position is here termed Marxism 2.

One of the weaknesses of the simple-minded theory of Marxism 1 is that it fails to take into account the changes that occur within industrial society. This is a curious omission given that these societies have lived through more rapid change than any others in history. Some of the changes of the 1890s and early 1900s are responsible for making the world we know, and the world to which modernism reacted. Amongst such changes were the invention of the internal combustion engine, the use of oil and electricity as sources of power, the foundation of modern office organisation, the application of organised science to industry, and the birth of the new press (Bullock, 1976). These forces were sufficient to create a unified world. In John Berger's words:

> There was no longer any essential discontinuity between the individual and the general. The invisible and the multiple no longer intervened between each individual and the world. It was becoming more and more difficult to think in terms of having been *placed* in the world. A man was part of the world and indivisible from it. In an entirely original sense, which remains at the basis of modern consciousness, a man *was* the world which he inherited (1972, pp. 138–9).

Berger is able to write suggestively on 'The Moment of Cubism' on the basis of these remarks and it is possible to specify the manner in which these changes affected writers. This can be done by examining three basic sets of changes that occurred at the end of the nineteenth century.

The first changes that must be noticed are those which affect the position of the artist. Perhaps most important for the development of the modernist movement was the loss of status that humanist intellectuals suffered at the turn of the century. Whereas intellectuals of this type had at first felt filled with some degree of optimism about the possibilities inherent in the new affluent and literate societies, their successors had doubts. An intellectual like Matthew Arnold could feel that in writing for, say, the *Nineteenth Century* or the *Edinburgh Review* he was fulfilling a useful function of general social and cultural education. But the turn of the century in England saw such liberal and enlightened cultural periodicals going out of business (W. Martin, 1967, pp. 192–200); and those who felt that they wished to adopt the same role, such as Hobhouse and Hobson, found that they could not reach as large an audience as could less liberal voices, such as Bottomley and Kipling, writing in the new mass circulation papers. Hence, the periodical of general issues and culture was replaced for the artist by work for little read, small magazines such as *Blast*, the *Egoist*, the *New English Weekly*, and the *Criterion*. This loss of status encouraged artists to see themselves as running ahead of popular tastes. And this concentration of attention on a smaller circle of people of similar taste and ambition led in turn to a much greater emphasis on the problems of creation themselves, on originality and on style. Thus was born the avant-garde, described so well by Poggioli (1968) and Shattuck (1970). And it must be noted that this loss of status helped to contribute to the occasional endorsement of reactionary, anti-enlightenment political views.

Secondly, the larger society itself underwent sweeping changes. The modernist movement was above all an urban movement (Bradbury and McFarlane, 1976, pp. 95–110). Benjamin's work treated Paris in the nineteenth century as a symbol of what society was becoming, and it stressed the importance of Baudelaire in focussing attention on the industrial city (1973). Initially this point might seem over-simplified in that Dickens and Balzac are also, in one sense, urban novelists. But the nature of the city changes during the course of the nineteenth century. As Simmel and Louis Wirth realised, the city was becoming the home of the majority of modern men; thus it was impossible to escape it. More important, the city was seen to be more complex and less structured than had previously been imagined. Balzac's heroes are concerned with how to conquer the city, but later heroes of urban novels are much more concerned to establish an identity in a flux that seems to have no meaning at all for them; the heroes of the former may be defeated by the predatory nature of the city, but the heroes of the latter may end up not knowing exactly who they are.

A part of this greater awareness of complexity came as a result of the realisation that many previous assumptions about the social world were in fact untrue. This was true, for example, of the concept of social class. Sociologists working at the turn of the century realised that Marx's view of stratification was extraordinarily over-simplified, as well they might have done with the advantage of hindsight. Michels suggested that even radical organisations suffered from an 'iron law of oligarchy', whilst Weber suggested that the society of the future, free even of capitalism, might well present an 'iron cage' of bureaucracy. Above all, perhaps, Sorel and Pareto suggested that the working class was less motivated by immediately 'rational' goals than Marx had believed; and for all the criticisms that one might level at their theory, it was felt that they were, given the absence of revolution, discussing new and important social realities. Some of this spirit of scepticism was also felt by modernist writers who realised that a mere deterministic and external portrait of society such as that of Balzac did not really get to the core of social reality. One writer manifestly touched by this scepticism was Proust. In *À la recherche du temps perdu* he suggested that class operated in far more complex ways than his predecessor Balzac had allowed. His analysis of the role of snobbery in social cohesion was typical of modernist concerns in suggesting that society was, as it were, a mental construction as much as a solid reality.

Thirdly, the intellectual climate had changed markedly as was perhaps to be expected in view of the changes in the position of artists and in the larger society already noted. Many of these changes are, of course, well known. In general they represented a reaction to 'positivism'. The argument between those believing that sociology could be considered a science and those who felt it to be a cultural humanism was typical of a general awareness that man was far more complex than enlightenment thinkers and positivists had allowed. This emphasis on human complexity, of course, helps account for the reception given to Freud, whose insistence that there were deeper unconscious forces in the mind than had been realised merely confirmed what many artists had already come to believe. The pieties of the Victorian period – faith in progress, free trade and democracy – seemed shallow in view of the deeper forces that were felt to exist in the mind. This joined with the belief that the artist was somehow an innovator ahead of his times to help create a climate in which artists were often prone to adopt social values of reactionary hue. Whilst such adherence is regrettable it should not, on account of the insistence of Engels and the New Critics on separating intention from performance, itself serve as a reason for condemning modernism. For although we may wish to disagree with Samuel Beckett that life is quite as meaningless as he would have us believe, there can be no doubt that such anti-enlightenment views helped in a pragmatic sense to push modernist artists towards greater self-exploration. It is not necessary to accept the half-baked social theories of D. H. Lawrence to realise that his vitalism encouraged him to penetrate further inside his characters than had typically been the case before. Moreover, as we shall see, there is no reason whatsoever to believe that modernist art is inherently biased in a pessimistic direction. And Lukács's distrust of such art is in one sense irrelevant anyway. For, in David Caute's words, 'modernism is the authentic artistic movement of our century; by and large, it has failed to flourish only where it has been censored out of existence' (1972, p. 121).

It is now possible to go on to establish my main contention, namely that modernism is a movement that extends the area that an artist can describe and his means for so doing, and that consequently it is the story of a considerable success. It was naturally the case that new formal capacities arose as a result of the search for means of describing new social realities, so that form and content cannot be separated here at all.

But, bearing this in mind, one can characterise the spirit of modernism accurately in these words of Trilling:

> No literature has ever been so shockingly personal as that of our time – it asks every question that is forbidden in polite society. It asks us if we are content with our marriages, with our family lives, with our professional lives, with our friends. . . . It asks us if we are content with ourselves, if we are saved or damned – more than anything else, our literature is concerned with salvation (1967, p. 23).

The modernists were, of course, writing with full knowledge of what had been achieved by the realists before them, and their emphasis on the complexities of personal identity and self-consciousness is a result of their seeing weaknesses in their ancestors. First, the world itself had changed in ways that could no longer be captured by traditional realist means. This can be seen in the image of society proposed by realistic and modernist fiction (Zeraffa, 1976, *passim*). Balzac could almost attempt to control a world through his attempt to portray a whole society; the image of society as such was simple, and, although Balzac disliked some social tendencies, there is little generalised scepticism about society as such being a danger to human individuality. But by the time of Chekhov a similar desire was capable of producing not a hundred linked novels, but only of a series of magnificent short stories (Bellow, 1975). And the increasing concern with the nature of human consciousness made the very fact of the social nature of man sometimes appear as the cause of human unhappiness; this view was given further respectability by Freud who argued in *Civilisation and Its Discontents* that social order depended upon some curtailing of the 'pleasure principle'. The logical consequence for some was that social reform could only touch the surface, and would not alleviate more basic problems. Secondly, the new attitudes of modernism to such things as human consciousness and time led to the necessity of employing rather different language in order to capture their experience. David Lodge has argued that modernist writing uses metaphor rather than metonymy (1977). Lodge suggests that this can be seen even in the contrasting title of typical realist and modernist novels: *Kipps* and *Anna of the Five Towns* contrast strikingly with *The Rainbow* and *Heart of Darkness*. Finally, the portrayal of the limits of human powers and consciousness naturally flowed over in a distrust of the powers of the nineteenth-century omniscient narrator. This point has been well put by Bradbury and Fletcher who argue that the self-consciousness of technique of Sterne, despite its subtlety, is not characterised by the anxiety that leads modernists to similar experiments:

> In other words, although there is a certain similarity of intention, most of the earlier devices served to draw attention to the autonomy of the narrator, while the later techniques drew attention to the autonomy of the fictive structure itself. And whereas the former versions of self-

conscious narration functioned usually for humorous effect, the later ones were normally serious and 'literary' in a way that would have been incomprehensible a century or so previously (Fletcher and Bradbury, 1976, pp. 395–6).

These three characteristics of modernist writing can be seen in detail in Proust's *À la recherche du temps perdu*. Proust's novel has as its very theme the problem of self-consciousness, or, more accurately, the problem of ever knowing anything for certain. In Proust's words:

> For even if we have the sensation of being always enveloped in, and surrounded by, our own soul, still it does not seem a fixed and immovable prison; rather we seem to be borne away with it and perpetually struggling to break out of it into the world, with constant discouragement when we hear endlessly, all around us, that unvarying sound which is not an echo from without, but the resonance of a vibration from within (Proust cited in Shattuck, 1974, p. 105).

Marcel, the hero of the novel, becomes aware that his personality interferes with his interpretation and understanding of the world. His own imagination encourages him to romanticise love and art; this leads to disillusion once he realises that the reality of these 'worlds' is quite other than he had hoped. Marcel's position might seem to be one in which man is doomed by his febrile imagination to disappointment consequent on the discovery that previously romanticised objects and people are in fact no better than the ones he already knows and possesses. However, as argued, the novel ends on the triumphant note whereby Marcel does manage to establish an identity of his own. In order to do so, Marcel feels it necessary to abandon the false trails of love, society and of the idolatry of art; salvation can only be found through actually working at writing. At the end of *Time Regained* we realise that the book that Marcel must write is the one that we have just read; we are thus the readers of his successful attempt to make sense of his life. This optimism will concern us in a moment.

David Lodge has himself discussed the use of language in Proust, and we can do no better than to follow his comments on this second point. The very theme of Proust's novel is essentially metaphoric – indeed some have gone so far as to argue that Proust's account of involuntary memory serves well as a theory of poetry. However, the matter is more complicated than this, and it is complicated in a way that allows Lodge to argue that metonymy is necessary to modernist writing albeit the use of metonymy is idiosyncratic. In Proust's case the action of involuntary memory is useless unless the rigorous, puritanical and metonymic exploration of a particular memory is undertaken; Proust stresses the worthlessness of mere involuntary memory without metynomic discipline time and time again. Nevertheless, Lodge follows a brilliant essay of Genette in noting that the purpose of metonymy is less that of exact description than that of capturing authentic experience. Consequently Proust's descriptions of two similar church steeples are vastly different since resemblance matters far less than authenticity. This, of course, is opposed to the spirit of traditional realism but Lodge suggests, surely correctly, that the investigation of metaphor by metonymic writers would perhaps show that metaphor can also be used in idiosyncratic ways (Lodge, 1976, pp. 492–5).

Finally, the differences between realist and modernist writing are themselves one of the major themes of Proust's novel. Proust himself remains unparalleled as an aesthetician of such matters. Near the end of *À la recherche du temps perdu*, Proust tries to show the ways in which the realist novel was limited by its easy presentation of an untroubled world. He offers a brilliant pastiche of the Goncourt brothers' arch-realist journal in which they discuss his own characters. Whereas Marcel does not know them well enough to know whether they are putting on fronts or are presenting themselves 'sincerely', the Goncourts, trusting naively to the veracity of the perception of a moment, offer an amusing, rounded and utterly false picture. Proust in this matter is trying to reverse our traditional expectations of a novel: 'it undoes our trust in the characters, consciously setting itself up against the impulse of the novel form' (Josipovici, 1973, p. 150). This is a point of some moment since it is the view of modernist theorists (including Proust and Josipovici) that the questioning style of narration calls for a new type of active and critical reader; in comparison the realistic novel is scorned by the early Barthes, Caute, Josipovici and others as a novel of mere entertainment. In Proust's classic words about his own novel: 'Every reader is, while he is reading, the reader of his own self' (Proust cited in Josipovici, 1973, p. 44).

This self-assessment amounts to saying that modernism is a replacement for realism. How seriously should this self-assessment be taken? There is one thing that must certainly be said in its favour, namely that the modernist novel has permanently expanded the equipment available to the novelist. This can be seen in a number of ways. David Lodge has interestingly demonstrated (1966) how the refusal to use modernist techniques and perspectives has come to limit as good an artist as Kingsley Amis. Moreover, it is interesting to note that a number of gifted writers (e.g. Naipaul and Mailer) have, despite their great achievements as 'realists', recently been attracted to various modernist practices. However, this said, there remain extremely strong reasons for insisting that the modernist novel is merely extending the possibilities of a genre whose basic characteristics were well laid down in the argument of Trilling noted above. Firstly, one must note that the novel is still 'about' the individual and society, although the complexity of this has been emphasised. Secondly, and in relation to society, what is finally impressive about the modernist novel is how 'realistic' the modernist novel is: how, in other words, it has managed successfully to describe our experience. When Beckett tells us through Molloy that language is a useless tool ('Not to want to say, not to know what to say, not to be able to say what you want to say, and never to stop saying . . .') what impresses us is the fertility, not the impotence, of language (Caute, 1972, p. 161). Similarly, those novels which tell us about their own gestation are more likely to breed a faith in illusion than their advocates might allow. It is tempting to think that Proust was, as a result of his telling the story of the creation of his novel, somehow telling the truth; but the early drafts for his masterpiece, *Jean Santeuil*, show the gap between reality and artifact to be as great as ever. This point can be put in other ways. Modernism has more in common with realism than is usually imagined, and indeed both are but part of the long Western tradition of *Mimesis* analysed by Auerbach. And it must be realised that such pleas for increased realism can never in fact be taken absolutely seriously since the very activity of reading is one that will always involve some suspension of belief. This has been beautifully put by Wayne Booth in his masterly *The Rhetoric of Fiction*. He notes that: '. . . our entire experience in reading fiction is based . . . on a tacit contract with the novelist, a contract granting him the right to know what he is writing about. It is this contract which makes fiction possible' (1966, p. 52). After analysing the contract drawn between Henry James and his reader, Booth notes that the reader accepts James's convention 'provided it serves larger ends that I can also accept. But in no case do I pretend that I am not reading a novel' (ibid., p. 53). This leads to the third point that critical reading is always necessary. This is true of modernist novels which are capable of greater sleight-of-hands than is sometimes allowed. There are modernist novels that do invite critical reading, and this is to be welcomed. But the lack of an invitation should not suggest that critical reading is impossible. Barthes, in his *S/Z*, and Kermode (1974) have both argued that readings of nineteenth-century novels in the light of the difficulties of the modern theory of the novel have shown them to be often just as complicated as their modernist descendants. This is perhaps not surprising. For, whilst new techniques are to be welcomed, communication in literature still occurs very largely through imagery that the author cannot consciously control. Hence despite the formal and substantive developments in the novel between God-like author and modernist who lets you, or pretends to let you, into the secrets of his creation, between fixed self and the search for identity, and between society as promise and as danger, there remains a great deal in common between realist and modernist novels. In fact all the social and intellectual changes mentioned in this section do not obscure the measure of continuity in Western society since the Renaissance and Reformation. If the latter are taken as the origins of modern Western man then the novel need not be seen as undergoing a decline as Marxism 1 would have us believe, nor as becoming utterly new as some modernists would have us believe.

Marxism 2 can be assessed against this position. This more radical Marxist argument makes similar claims for modernism as do Caute and Josipovici. The most interesting exponent of the view has been

R. Barthes, but the general position is neatly summarised for our purposes in a lecture by Adorno on 'The *locus standi* of the narrator in the contemporary novel'.

Adorno's argument is complex but centres on the assertion that the post-1848 world is one in which the condition of man is that of complete alienation. In such circumstances Adorno believes that 'surface realism' must be abandoned since it can only show the false exteriorities of life that are being used to manipulate men in such a way that they become unconscious of their true needs. Adorno further adds that it has now become impossible to tell a straightforward story. The changes in the position of the narrator in the novels of Kafka, Proust, Joyce and the late novels of Thomas Mann show that the theme of the novel is now nothing more than the direction of irony against any narrator who still tries to tell a traditional story. Under these circumstances, writes Adorno, the work of art re-acquires the character of 'higher fun' that it once had, before it presumptuously claimed to be an image of reality (Pascal, 1977).

It has already been admitted here that substantial changes have taken place in the position of the narrator, but the position reached in this chapter is much less strong than that of Adorno. Above all, his cultural pessimism, seen particularly in the belief that man was once whole but is now hopelessly alienated, ends up creating as exaggerated an image of modernism as Lukács created of realism. Whilst it is true that Proust is concerned with the difficulties of knowing reliably both in the world and as novelist, this does not stop his novel being able to tell a very striking story which, moreover, is able to hold out some possibility of escaping alienation. And a very similar argument has been made in a much more considered form by R. Pascal in an excellent essay on Thomas Mann's *The Magic Mountain*. Pascal demonstrates how the theme of the novel is indeed the alienation of which Adorno complains; but Mann exhibits his theme by telling a story which significantly offers some hope of overcoming the sorry condition. Pascal notes correctly that 'if, as Adorno says, story is no longer possible, it would mean that man's self-understanding is grievously maimed' (1977, p. 20); there is no reason to believe this is already the case, and certainly no reason to believe that the changed position of the narrator in modernist novels prevents narrative art. And insofar as Adorno's justification of almost cabbalistic complexity can be seen at work in post-modernism, an hostile accusation may be levelled at Adorno. Such art is necessarily elitist, and consequently destroys all unity in literary culture. We shall see that there is good reason to be unhappy about such a rupture, perhaps especially if it is not strictly necessary.

The great profanation

No discussion of modernism is now complete without considering the recent work by Daniel Bell on the matter (1976, 1977a, 1977b). Bell's account of the social origins of modernism is rather similar to that offered above; in particular, Bell stresses the importance of the new technologies that suddenly made the world much smaller:

> What was true of the physical world was equally true of the social. With the growth of numbers and density in the cities, there was greater interaction among persons, a syncretism of experience that provided a sudden openness to new types of life. . . . In modernism the intention is to 'overwhelm' the spectator so that the art produces itself . . . imposes itself on the viewer in its terms. . . . In all this there is an 'eclipse of distance', so that the spectator loses control and becomes subject to the intentions of the artist. The very structural forms are organised to provide immediacy, simultaneity, envelopment of experience (1977b, p. 216).

Nevertheless, Bell's work on modernism departs strikingly and interestingly from the interpretation that I have offered. One of his arguments, that the effect of the diffusion of modernism is so great that it is now 'the cultural contradiction of capitalism', will be considered in Chapter 8, but his general portrait of modernism as an anti-rational movement in the service of instinctual gratification needs to be assessed immediately.

Bell's portrait of modernism stresses that many modernists were attracted by anti-enlightenment views, and in this it of course resembles the diatribes of Lukács against modernism. But Bell's reasons for disliking modernism are much more idiosyncratic and interesting than those of Lukács. A vision of human nature which was implicit in his early work has come to the fore in his work on modernism. Bell seems to think that the mind of man is some sort of pool filled with instincts and desires, prominent amongst these being those concerned with domination and with sexual gratification. Historically these impulses were held in check by religion, whose power, according to Bell, lay in its ability to provide some sort of explanation for the finitude of man. With the decline of religion man began to be haunted by the fear of nothingness. Those impulses hitherto held in check by religion came to be examined and celebrated by modernism, which replaced religious moral law with a philosophy of the aesthetic. Bell's dislike of this approach, although he admits that it explains the force of modernism, can be seen when he discusses Nietzsche:

> In this proclamation of the autonomy of the aesthetic – indeed, in the argument that only as an aesthetic product can life be justified – Nietzsche declared war on the most profound tradition of Western culture. The writers of the Old Testament, as any religious Jew knows, had a horror of the aesthetic because of the implications of its claims. For if the aesthetic was autonomous, it was not bound by moral law, and anything was possible in its search for experience lived to the highest peak as art (1977b, pp. 229–30).

Bell's theory is in effect a slightly exaggerated version of Trilling's argument that the classics of modernism represent an 'adversary culture' opposed not just to our societies but to the social as such (Trilling, 1967). However, Bell's argument goes slightly further in adding that the very artistic discipline of modernism that kept their play with previously hidden instincts in bound has now fallen before the meretricious popularisation of its most questionable ideas.

Bell's analysis may be criticised at this point in two ways. The first of these is the most important and concerns the actual character of the modernist imagination. Bell in fact far too easily accepts Trilling's view that the classics of modernism all have an adversary intent. Some do indeed consider the social as alienating; a clear example of this is provided by Sartre's *Huis Clos* and *Nausea*. However, this is certainly not the case with all the modernist classics, and indeed perhaps not the case with the best of them. Thus Proust ends *À la recherche du temps perdu* on a note of affirmation as Marcel discovers his true vocation as an artist after having been misled on the false trails of love and worship of high society. The same is true of *Ulysses* in that Molly Bloom's soliloquy is popularly and justly celebrated as one of the most striking 'affirmations of life itself' in all of Western literature. And for someone who claims to appreciate modernism his taste is curiously conservative. He considers, for example, that modernism is an attack on 'the rational cosmos'. This is wildly exaggerated and seriously misrepresents the very strong moral sense in, again, Proust whose work is representative of modernism in desiring to rationally investigate matters that had hitherto been overlooked.

Secondly, Bell's account may be criticised in a way that introduces the topic of the following chapter. His belief that the adversary values of modernism have been popularised is surely open to doubt. As we shall see, romantic novels and popular drama tend to be rather conservative in their moral values – as a glance at any of Barbara Cartland's novels would show. In this matter, moreover, Bell is amusingly at odds with another theory that is suspicious of popular art, namely that of the Frankfurt School which chose to stress the conservative and 'ascetic' character of the 'culture industry' (Jay, 1973, Ch. 6). Bell has in this matter little sense of where his allies might lie, and would perhaps do better to join with those such as Kingsley Amis who has often used the common sense and morality of popular art as a tool with which to berate the pretensions and anti-enlightenment views of modernist authors.

Chapter 5

Popular literature

At the beginning of their book on *The Popular Arts* Hall and Whannel place Kingsley Amis's comment that 'I have only reached the stage of firmly opting for any straight hour's worth of mass culture in preference to again being told about it' (Hall and Whannel, 1964, p. 19). The warning sounded by Amis has not lost its worth since it first appeared in 1960; indeed its note of common sense may become even more relevant since there are signs that the theoretical exuberance characteristic of the sociology of literature as a whole is about to turn its talents loose on popular literature. Already recent discussions of popular literature have been influenced by the structural-hermeneutic position (Bigsby, 1976). But these discussions have not yet been sufficiently profound to shift the centre of gravity away from the questions posed earlier by mass society theory. The first such question has already been noted, but may usefully be recalled here as a point of focus for this chapter. The question is that of the relations existing between 'high' and 'low' literature. Some mass society theorists have complained that popular literature borrows from high culture and in the process depletes it. Such a statement implicitly raises the question of the components for a healthy literary culture. More particularly, does such a culture in fact depend, as Raymond Williams believes (1958, conclusion), on a free interchange between high and low culture, or is it the case that masterpieces can be produced entirely independently, and that it is their production alone that counts?

If the first question concerns the relations of 'high' and 'low', the second is that of the exact character of popular literature. It may be as well to state immediately which supposed characteristics of popular literature or mass culture are not, since they are so obviously wrong-headed, going to be discussed here. Herbert Gans's *Popular Culture and High Culture* (1974) enables us to recognise two such highly questionable theories. The first of these is that mass culture is aesthetically poor since it is produced for profit. This vague anti-capitalist theory combines uneasily with a love of high art in general, for it is obviously the case that, say, art galleries are as devoted to profit as perhaps is Harold Robbins. Moreover, as Mrs Leavis (1938) discovered and as any pronouncement on the subject by Barbara Cartland makes clear, the creators of popular culture are very often motivated less by money than by a conviction of the importance of their moral vision and task. And, of course, this position is debilitated by its failure to notice the very great diversity of popular art; as we shall see when briefly looking at three genres of popular art, such diversity belies nearly all simplistic conclusions. Secondly, it is often asserted that popular or mass art is emotionally harmful and that, in particular, it can even lead to totalitarianism – a fear already seen in Bell's hostile reaction to the supposed popularisation of modernism. Very little empirical evidence is available with which to establish the actual effect of popular literature. But the work that has been done in mass communications in general is sufficiently relevant to discredit the general approach. This evidence may be summarised by saying that whilst the debate over effects is not conclusively terminated, it is nevertheless clear that a massive amount of information has been accumulated that makes it most unlikely that mass culture has such deleterious effects. To some extent this is obvious. If there had been very massive effects of, say, television programmes featuring violence then one would have expected crime rates to have risen far faster than is in fact the case. More importantly, Katz and Lazarsfeld began that school of investigation (currently represented by the 'uses and gratifications' approach) which has produced evidence of the audience being more than a passive receptacle for whatever any manipulator wishes to put in it. And a moral may be drawn from this: there is more to be said for asking what the readers of popular literature want from their books than in simply asking what these books are doing to the readers. Such an approach has already been put to sensible use in Jarvie's discussion of the cinema (Jarvie, 1970).

Despite these negative comments, two alleged characteristics of popular art and literature may serve us heuristically as further foci of discussion. Both of these are in a sense watered down versions of the previous arguments, but this process of dilution makes them less question-begging. In general the two characteristics fit together, but this is not strictly necessary and in some authors they are actually opposed to each other. The first of them concerns the function of popular literature. Adorno and Horkheimer's essay on 'The Culture Industry' is quite representative of the many mass society theorists who argue that popular literature serves as 'escapist' fare (1977). This theory has different versions which can be distinguished by the stand they take on the issue of manipulation: the strongest insist that such manipulation is consciously designed to fit the masses to their place, whilst the weakest argue that the choice of popular literature is made freely whatever the objective result may be. The second alleged characteristic is that popular literature is judged to be politically innocuous or conservative. The reasoning behind this frequently heard charge is interesting. It is argued that smaller and more specialised audiences allowed for an author to speak in very direct ways: thus literary allusions were understood within an elite audience whilst politically radical opinions could be addressed to similarly discrete audiences. The argument then suggests that this happy situation has been changed by the constraints imposed once production is geared to a mass audience. An author must rely only on symbols which are generally known if he is to be understood: special allusions and reference to the politically discomfiting are thus ruled out. Again this theory is held in different strengths according to the degree of manipulation imputed to rulers of various hues.

These questions about the relations of 'high' and 'low' and about the character of popular literature can guide our discussion. Unfortunately, it must be admitted immediately that hard and fast answers will elude us simply because there is insufficient evidence to hand. But a very great deal may be gained by a realisation that matters are far more complex than the theories noted allow. And it is perhaps worth warning the reader that the position taken here is in general rather positive in its appreciation of popular literature.

Understanding content

The manner in which the content of popular culture is to be understood has recently become a subject of controversy, and this methodological question needs to be considered at once. Broadly speaking, the argument is whether content can be analysed by counting procedures or whether structuralist-hermeneutic procedures discussing the meaning of particular social codes are alone adequate to the task. This is an issue already considered in rather different form in Chapter 2, and the conclusions reached there can help us here. Counting procedures perhaps come naturally to sociologists, and the sheer quantity of popular literature makes their use understandable. There are very good arguments to be made for counting procedures when applied in a sophisticated manner. A glance at some of the research work actually done along these lines shows its value but also exhibits the curious paradox whereby the result of such work is often misunderstood.

Berelson and Salter's (1946) 'Majority and Minority Americans' illustrates this situation well. The authors of this celebrated piece of research discovered that counting procedures applied to popular American short stories revealed that 'heroes' tended to be dispropor- tionately White, Anglo-Saxon and Protestant. Minorities, in contrast, tended to be under-represented in sheer numbers whilst their individual appearances tended to be either in subservient or anti-social roles. This state of affairs created a considerable amount of anger in the breasts of the researchers who seemed to feel that literature was not living up to its duty of 'reflecting' social reality. But, in fact, this excellent piece of research really tells us, as the idea of a social referent would lead us to expect, about the self-image of an age in which minorities were given low status. Surely this is what we would expect to find, and in this sense the social referent of the short stories seems extremely accurate: social reality is falsified but the state of social values beautifully described.

The paradox whereby impressive empirical research is misunderstood by its own authors is sufficiently common to justify another example.

Weitzmann (1971/2) produced a short study of the 'sex-roles' implicit in children's books. Her results stress that the sex roles portrayed favour boys rather than girls: boys, in contrast to girls, tend to be seen as active, independent and, in general, seem to have interesting things to do. Again it is rather curious to find a sociologist angrily accusing these books of distorting reality; the authors concerned have simply not realised that the real social referent of the book is precisely that prejudice they abhor. Such prejudice is indeed responsible for distorting some sort of natural equality, and one could only expect significant changes in children's books if feminists were free to have their own commendable values written in at the expense of widely accepted values. It is doubtful if this is completely possible, and it is not in any case desirable. But it is very curious to see books blamed for distortion when they in fact describe all too accurately a very sorry social condition.

These comments suggest that counting exercises can yield results (in fact we do not have nearly enough of them), but that such results must be carefully interpreted. This is as much as to say that the more extreme criticism of the structuralist-hermeneutic position, that counting can have no significance, is incorrect. It is, of course, the case that counting alone is no good since, for example, the death of a hero has a different weighting to that of the death of some minor character, but this has in fact been realised all along by those who have used quantitative methods. The studies of sex roles in children's books gain their merit from asking questions only about an issue that has obvious social meaning. If a day comes when quantitative methods are used to count anything and everything then structuralist-hermeneutic criticism will gain in force. But this is not the case in the present situation which seems to offer a helpful blend of quantitative investigation with an understanding of social codes. That such a mixture is a good one becomes all the more obvious once we examine the licence to which the unfettered structuralist-hermeneutic position is prone.

There can be no doubt that the structuralist-hermeneutic position is fortunate in having tremendous talents at work on its behalf. The most formidable of these is surely Roland Barthes whose ability to discover hidden meanings at work is quite unrivalled. In his *Sade, Fourier and Loyola* (1977b), for example, Barthes deliberately ignores the differences in actual content to argue that a resemblance does exist between the three writers in terms of their passionate desire to organise their texts. Whilst Barthes' book is in this case convincing, the general approach raises the issue of whether, in Frank Kermode's words 'Can We Say Anything We Like' (1977). Much recent work has drawn elaborate theories on the basis of very limited material indeed. And theoretically a certain licence has been introduced by the Tel Quel Group (with which Barthes is associated) which has recently, under the influence of Derrida, tried to encourage a proliferation of readings of particular texts. Whilst imaginative readings of texts are to be welcomed, Derrida's argument that standards of judgement should be freed from Western standards of rationality conjures up the picture of absolute and probably uninteresting relativistic licence (Culler, 1975, Ch. 12).

It is the possibility of such licence that makes counting procedures, where appropriate, a useful check on the structuralist-hermeneutic approach. Such a combination has always been present in the very striking work of Lowenthal. In his study of the heroes of American popular biographies, for example, Lowenthal began by establishing that it was in fact the case that heroes of production had been replaced by heroes of consumption. On this basis he was able to establish something about the changed social statuses consequent on the development of industrial society (1961).

The structuralist-hermeneutic position thus makes its greatest contribution when its understanding of the nature of social codes is combined with an interest in empirical work. And it must be stressed that such work analyses only the actual content of popular literature. On occasions it has seemed as if the structuralist-hermeneutic position presumes that understanding a social code is equivalent to understanding both content and audience who share that code. This is quite as unjustified an assumption as has been every presumption that the audience accepts or understands the content of a text. Two different processes must be distinguished: the encoding of the message in the text itself and the decoding performed by the audience.

Three popular genres

Another way in which the hasty generalisations of the structuralist-hermeneutic position can be curtailed is by studying the character of whole popular genres. Many such genres could be chosen, but three have been selected here on the grounds of the quality of the secondary literature to hand. In the course of the discussion it will prove possible to note some of the typical social codes at work, and, above all, to describe the diversity that exists inside these genres both synchronically and diachronically.

1. Detective stories into crime novels

We are particularly well served in discussing detective and crime stories by Julian Symons' exemplary *Bloody Murder* (1974) since this contains a myriad of interesting suggestions about the social relevance of such stories. Symons opens his account by examining some proposed explanations for the appeal of detective stories. Charles Rycroft has proposed a psychoanalytic explanation. The detective appeals to us, in this account, since he allows us a feeling of power with which to investigate an equivalent to those matters, archetypally the 'primal scene' of childhood, which were hidden from us as children. The criminal, on the contrary, represents the repressed hostility to the parents. Symons suggests that this interesting view gains some support from those examples of the genre whose heroes are criminals or behave like them (1974, p. 13). A second theory may be seen as following Durkheim's description of the necessity of redressing any threat to the social order; thus the hounding of the criminal represents the removal of a threat to social solidarity. Both these theories, however, offer constant features of human nature or of the nature of the social, and to that extent are not very good at explaining the development in the genre that is Symons' main theme, and which is rather convincingly explained by a sociological explanation for the appeal of such stories. Broadly speaking, Symons' book is a gloss on a famous essay by George Orwell on 'Raffles and Miss Blandish'. In this essay Orwell compared the moral tone of *Raffles* with the violence and sadism he felt were present in a typical and more recent American crime novel, *No Orchids for Miss Blandish*. Symons recognises this change but refuses to deprecate it as Orwell had done. Instead Symons suggests that the earlier, closed world of detective writers such as Agatha Christie corresponded to a different social reality than that of the later, American-influenced, crime novels. The appeal of the former can be seen broadly as that of preserving the middle-class values of law and order against subversives of various sorts:

> The aloof, super-intellectual and slightly inhuman detective like Holmes, who occasionally acts outside the law, was particularly attractive when posed against such terrifying figures because he was a kind of saviour of society, somebody who did illegal things for the right reasons, who was really *one of us*. An intelligent French critic, Pierre Nordon, has pointed out that the whole Sherlock Holmes cycle is 'addressed to the privileged majority, it plays on their fears of social disturbance and at the same time makes use of Sherlock Holmes and what he stands for to reassure them'. These comments apply primarily to British society, which was powerful, prosperous, and marked by clear divisions between classes ... (Symons, 1974, p. 17).

The appeal of the more recent crime novels for Symons lies in the realism with which they depict the world of crime and the inherent interest of their attempt to understand the workings of character. And it may also be noted that the American crime novel is one of the few literary genres that centres itself in the urban world where most Americans actually live.

Symons stresses that the earliest criminal stories are strikingly different from those offered by later writers such as Agatha Christie. 'Villains' were admired in a romantic manner as social rebels, and some of their activities were seen with a sympathetic eye. This sympathy can be seen in the heroic proportions in which Balzac cast his arch-villain Vautrin. But the most striking case is that of Godwin's *Caleb Williams*. The hero of this book is pictured as innocent and pure until corrupted by society which is consequently blamed for the development of his criminal activities.

However, this early romanticising of criminals was soon submerged by a glorification of detectives and a detestation of crime, only too natural a consequence of the dangerous life of the early industrial cities. Undoubtedly the greatest detective-saviour produced by this social climate was Sherlock Holmes, and it is all the more to be pitied that no sociologist has carefully analysed the growth of the Holmes mythology. But despite his great social appeal, it is only fair to point out, as Symons does, that the myth often served at the expense of the quality of the genre. G. K. Chesterton pointed out on many occasions that the readers are offered a demonstration of dazzling powers which the humble reader could not hope to emulate. His own reaction to this was to create in Father Brown a character whose reasoning, at its best, was based on such ordinary observations that the average reader had a chance of reaching similar conclusions. And Chesterton's ins...tence on considering certain rules of the genre which the average reader could follow proved of importance in the early 1920s when quite general agreement was reached about such rules, or, more exactly, social codes. Amongst these codes were the insistence that clues be provided that the reader could follow, the preference for a murder as the crime to be solved and the demand that the criminal commit the crime for personal and rational reasons but that he must not be a servant since 'the culprit must be a decidedly worthwhile person' (W. H. Wright cited in Symons, 1974, p. 107). This last point gives its own clue to the development of the genre in its 'Golden Age' in a conservative direction that would have been anathema to Chesterton.

> It is safe to say that almost all of the British writers in the twenties and thirties, and most of the Americans, were unquestionably Right-wing. This is not to say that they were openly anti-Semitic or anti-Radical, but that they were overwhelmingly conservative in feeling. It would have been unthinkable for them to create a Jewish detective, or a working-class one aggressively conscious of his origins, for such figures would have seemed to them quite incongruous. It would have been equally impossible for them to have created a policeman who beat up suspects ... (ibid., p. 109).

But these rules produced thousands upon thousands of puzzles to be solved, sometimes easily, but often only with difficulty when produced by, say, Agatha Christie at her best. And such puzzle-solving has been loved by many – from Stanley Baldwin to Sartre and Bertrand Russell.

The formalism and limited social context of such novels was bound to be attacked in the long run, and it is perhaps no surprise to find that it was challenged most effectively at the end of the 1930s when the settled world of the detective story was being destroyed by the brute facts of history. Dashiell Hammett, a former private detective with radical views, lamented that in the detective story the real world of crime was ignored:

> That the law-breaker is invariably soon or late apprehended is probably the least challenged of extant myths. And yet the files of every detective bureau bulge with the records of unsolved mysteries and uncaught criminals (Hammett cited in Symons, 1974, p. 142).

Chandler added to this a commendation of the world that Hammett actually created in which murder was committed by people who do it 'for reasons, not just to provide a corpse; and with the means at hand, not with hand-wrought duelling pistols, curare, and tropical fish' (Chandler cited in Symons, p. 142). The novels that these two writers produced remain amongst the most distinguished of all crime stories and they played a large part in formalising new rules or social codes that may, following Symons, be seen to differ from the detective story most strikingly thus:

(a) The detective is the key figure in the detective story since the discovery of clues often depends on the brilliance of his reasoning powers. This contrasts with the crime story which may in fact have no detective, but merely a central character suffering at the hands of sinister forces he does not understand.

(b) The method of the murder differs as a result. The detective story's appetite for clues and for puzzle-solving is satisfied by bizarre means of death. The crime novel, on the other hand, is perhaps more realistic in placing much less emphasis on sophisticated methods of killing.

(c) Clues are of the essence of the detective story, but may play no significant part in the crime novel.

(d) Characterisation is very weak in the detective story, not surprisingly as too great an interest in the characters might detract from the logic of the puzzle presented. The crime story, however, is based on the analysis of character, and indeed the main claim to importance of the crime story lies in its interest in psychology. This was well put by Symons himself when explaining something of his own justification for writing crime stories:

> The thing that most absorbs me in our age is the violence behind respectable faces, the civil servant planning how to kill Jews more efficiently, the Judge speaking with passion about the need for capital punishment, the quiet obedient boy who kills for fun. ... If you want to show the violence that lives behind the bland faces most of us present to the world, what better vehicle can you have than the crime novel? (Symons, 1974, p. 198).

(e) The setting of the crime novel tends to be of great importance since an interest is often shown in social and psychological forces explaining the origin of crime. The classic detective story tended, in contrast, to have a much more limited social setting – at its most stylised, especially in country houses.

(f) The social attitude of the detective story has been conservative. The changed historical and social circumstances perhaps encouraged something of a reversal of attitudes, for the crime novel is often politically critical and radical.

On the basis of such a set of social codes novels of varying importance have been written. The best include those of Hammett and Chandler, but the genre is sufficiently wide to allow for the very considerable and slightly idiosyncratic achievements of Georges Simenon. Not surprisingly, however, some authors have followed the example of Mickey Spillane in revelling in various unpleasant combinations of sex and violence.

Symons finishes his survey with some speculations on the possible future of the genre, and these are worth considering as they once again exhibit a diversity that is customarily overlooked. Symons suggests that the detective story is likely, despite individual talents, to lose its popularity at an even faster rate than is already the case. The gentility of its settings has already been to some extent overtaken by the far rougher world of a new but distinct sub-species, the police novel. The popularity of the police novel is perhaps especially evident in America where the danger in the large cities resembles that of the earlier Victorian city, and produces a similar admiration for the guardians of law and order. But this is not to say that the genre is now openly conservative. Crime novels retain their critical capacity and are 'capable of any sort of development, according to the talents they attract' (Symons, 1974, p. 254). At the moment Patricia Highsmith is undoubtedly the most notable writer of crime novels and she has made clear that she has no interest in any straightforward adulation of the forces of law and order:

> Criminals are dramatically interesting, because for a time at least they are active, free in spirit, and they do not knuckle down to anyone. . . . I find the public passion for justice quite boring and artificial, for neither life nor nature cares if justice is ever done or not (Highsmith, cited in Symons, 1974, p. 188).

This philosophy can be seen at work in a series of extremely striking novels, not least those dealing with the celebrated Mr Ripley. Finally, it may be noted that Symons' own bet for the future is on the adventure story which he considers to be currently attracting the greatest talents.

2. Westerns

No discussion of popular literature would be complete without mention of the extraordinarily stimulating work of Leslie Fiedler. His characteristic interest is in the social myths of the collective unconscious of society. This concern with 'literary anthropology' derives in part from

Fiedler's familiarity with Lawrence, Freud and Marx and can clearly be seen at work in his *The Return of the Vanishing American* (1972). Fiedler argues that the European novel naturally centred itself on questions of class since the feudal past of such countries made the class system particularly real. In America the absence of any such past meant that the American novel's myths tended to be those concerned with race and sex. To some extent the idea of the 'savage' has European origins that Fiedler describes with his usual Freudian relish:

> The Savage Man is associated with sexual assault rather than cannibalism. He can be read, indeed, as a projection out of the darkness of the European mind, of all in man's passionate nature which resisted not only the bonds of Christian marriage, but the conventions of Courtly Love as well (1972, p. 42).

But the American experience alone turned this into a central myth. This seems to be a consequence of the refusal to acknowledge that the treatment accorded women and racial minorities went against the ideals of the American dream; such repression, in Fiedler's eyes, is the breeding ground for social myths. And in America only the Western was able to deal effectively with the memory of the Indian for the 'Northern', 'Southern' and 'Eastern' already had their own characteristic themes.

Fiedler distinguishes four basic myths at work in the Western. Each of these has been treated by several authors, and the charm and merit of Fiedler's account lie in the manner in which he demonstrates the slight variations in treatment. This makes his argument particularly rich and consequently hard to summarise, so that the following sketch is really scarcely more than a brutalisation. The first myth is the least developed and satisfactory, and Fiedler dubs it 'the myth of the Runaway Male'. The archetypal figure in the myth is Rip Van Winkle whose story received its classic treatment at the hands of Washington Irving as early as 1819. Fiedler considers the genius of Irving's account to lie in its ability to capture the misogyny of the American male:

> ... it is Irving alone who fully realises the importance to the Rip myth of drinking, the archetypal significance of gin ritually consumed with the boys as a protest against home and wife. So, also, it is Irving who creates the first drunk to come reeling through the pages of a native American work ... (1972., p. 56).

This desire to escape the female presence is considered at greater length in Fiedler's celebrated *Love and Death in the American Novel* (1969). Certainly this 'myth' can be seen at work in as fine a novel as Bellow's *Henderson the Rain King*. Interestingly enough in this novel Henderson spends a great deal of time with a companion who is both black and male. In contrast, Rip Van Winkle only has a dog as a companion – although Fiedler slyly points out that he is called Nig. It is this failure to confront repressed desires that makes this first myth unsatisfactory for Fiedler. He insists that it is '*real* coloured men that we want by the side of our Runaway Whites, not beasts with metaphorical names – Indians, if possible . . .' (1972, p. 59).

The second myth, that of 'love in the woods', is based on the legendary encounter of Captain John Smith with the Indian Princess Pocahontas. This encounter might seem to allow for those simple and uncomplicated feelings about sex that Fiedler has already denied the male. But in fact the legend is much less about 'love in the woods' than about Pocahontas's saving of John Smith from an attack of her own tribe. Fiedler bitterly notes that 'our first celebrated traitor to her own race is . . . a model long in advance for Uncle Tom' (1972, p. 70). The myth then is one produced by the White Anglo-Saxon Protestant mind dreaming of forgiveness for its terrible treatment of Indians by some sort of reconciliation through love and marriage. Fiedler demonstrates that the details of the myth change with different social circumstances. Thus in Catholic Canada, the legend of Catherine Tekakwitha, a pious Mohawk maiden who died in the love of Christ, may be seen as an analogous figure of reconciliation. Fiedler offers these sardonic comments on her death:

> . . . speech had failed her as she mumbled the names of Jesus and Mary. A little later she was dead, and a few moments afterwards the French priest praying beside her cried out in astonishment because her face had turned white. White – the complete conversion. No wonder she is proposed year after year for sainthood . . . (1972, p. 79).

The third myth of 'the White Woman with a Tomahawk' has received notable literary treatment from Cotton Mather, Hawthorne and Thoreau. These authors give varying accents to the story of Hannah Duston, who was captured by Indians and forced to escape by murdering her captors. Fiedler sees two great attractions to this myth. The first attraction lies in the thought of Hannah captured and dragged away naked.

> And, indeed, this primordial image has continued to haunt pulp fiction ever since (often adorning the covers of magazines devoted to it); for it panders to that basic White male desire at once to relish and deplore, vicariously share and publicly condemn, the rape of White female innocence (1972, p. 93).

More importantly, however, the myth is that of American feminism since:

> What makes the story American is not merely that the Ogre has become an Indian, or a 'Savage' as the old chronicles prefer to say, but that the Maiden has to deliver herself. Any nearby male is either ineffectual . . . or inappropriately reasonable (1972, p. 97).

Cotton Mather's early treatment is in a sense orthodox in turning Hannah into a heroine along the Old Testament lines. Hawthorne clearly turns the tale into another version of the myth of the Runaway

Male by arguing that Hannah Duston was quite capable of looking after herself and that her husband in fact had hidden courage of his own. Thoreau's version is, however, the most significant, and nicely illustrates the important point that a myth of this popular type can provide material for reworking by a major writer. Thoreau's version of the story takes the opportunity of considering the role of the American as a whole. The story is seen from the Indian side, and turned into a fable of lost innocence.

The fourth myth is that of 'Good Companions in the Wilderness' and seems to be the one that Fiedler considers to penetrate most deeply into American hidden desires. The story of a meeting in the wilderness between the white fur-trapper, Henry, and the Indian Warrior, Wamatam, was first told in Henry's *Adventures*, but the theme has been dealt with by Thoreau, Faulkner and Cooper. This choice of a companion is seen as a working out of an observation of Crèvecoeur that:

> There must be something in their [the Indians] social bond singularly
> captivating, and far superior to anything to be boasted of among us; for
> thousands of Europeans are Indians, and we have no examples of even
> one of the aborigines having from choice become European . . .
> (Crèvecoeur cited in Fiedler, 1972, p. 112).

The power of his myth to which so many writers have turned lies in its ability at once to contain the misogyny of the American male, hopes of reconciliation with the Indian, and a retreat from the pressures of civilisation itself.

If these are then the four basic myths, Fiedler demonstrates that their potency has varied in different historical periods. In their origin they represented an attempt to treat the problems of collective life. However, Fiedler insists that their power was nearly destroyed at the end of the nineteenth century with the rise of the 'southernised Westerner':

> The desexing of the West . . . is of critical importance in the deposition
> of the Western from the centre to the periphery of our literature. . . .
> Only when this myth goes is the Western deprived of its essential power:
> when chivalry *à la* Sir Walter Scott replaces the dream of Wamatam, and
> the Westerner comes to be portrayed as an Ivanhoe in chaps: i.e. one
> who does not flee the good White woman at home, but rather risks his
> life to defend her against the forces of savagery (1972, pp. 138–9).

The first of such 'southernised Westerners' was Owen Wister's *The Virginian*. And Fiedler further suggests that such novels (and the films taken from them) represent the type of wildly falsified image of the West that became popular at about the time the urbanisation of America was completed. He himself shows a definite dislike for such novels on the ground that they so clearly favour the indiscriminate use of violence – provided violence is used for the right cause.

Fiedler's discussion, however, finishes on a note of optimism as he feels that the potential of the genre is against being mined by authors as diverse as Leonard Cohen and John Barth. His own preference is for Ken Kesey's *One Flew Over the Cuckoo's Nest*, and it is a merit of his general argument that his previous discussion makes his reading of the book so convincing. For Fiedler suggests that the core of the book lies in the attempt of Big Nurse to castrate her male rivals, and that the response to this lies in the 'companionship' of McMurphy and Chief Bromden. However, the novelty of the book lies in its not being set in the geographical West. A step has been taken from 'thinking of the West as madness to regarding madness as the true West'. The reason for this is simple:

> We have come to accept the notion that there is still a territory
> unconquered and uninhabited by palefaces, the bearers of 'civilisation',
> the cadres of imperialist reason; and we have been learning that into this
> 'schizophrenics' have moved on ahead of all the rest of us ... (Fiedler,
> 1972, p. 185).

Such beliefs are probably wildly misguided, but it is Fiedler's achievement to show the extent to which they have become part of the American self-image.

3. Romance

Romantic novels sell something over thirty million copies every year. These sales can be measured in part by realising that whereas only 5,000 copies of a novel make it a best-seller, a new Victoria Holt sells between 30,000 and 40,000 copies, a new Mary Stewart no less than 95,000 copies, and a new Barbara Cartland about 7,500 copies – but she, of course, has over a hundred and fifty novels to her name. Given these figures, and the fact that such reading is the only reading done by a considerable number of women, it is particularly sad to discover that very little research has been done into romantic literature. A part of the reason for this, as Rachel Anderson has pointed out in *The Purple Heart Throbs* (1974), is that our attitudes remain, like those of Flaubert, highly puritanical and thus resistant to novels supposedly offering some sort of sensual gratification. Perhaps more important, however, is the difficulty of defining the genre tightly. Mann (1971) has studied the Mills and Boon novel readers, but it is clearly the case that 'high' literature can be dependent on romantic themes, *Wuthering Heights* being, presumably, the most striking and extraordinary of all studies of romantic passion. That romantic themes should hold such a central place is not surprising given the importance of the idea of love in western culture, and this has given rise to one famous study, (Denis de Rougemont's *Passion and Society*, 1940) that considers this idea at a suitably generalised level. Nonetheless, Anderson's study of the best-selling romantic authors offers us the best limitation of the genre for the purposes of this section.

De Rougemont's study is essentially of European literature which glorifies stories of passion that take place outside the bonds of marriage. Very possibly as the result of the moralising influence of the Puritan family (cf. L. L. Schucking, *The Puritan Family*, 1970), this element of 'immorality', albeit an immorality with great costs attached in the cases of *Madame Bovary* and *Anna Karenin*, has been missing from the romantic novel in England. Indeed, Hall and Whannel are correct in saying that the basic theme of defending virtue has not changed since Richardson's *Pamela* first popularised the romantic story (1964, p. 170). Thus the most important characteristic of the romantic popular novel is its stress on upholding conventional morality. Anderson considers that the popular genre can be seen emerging most clearly with the publication in 1853 of Charlotte Yonge's *The Heir of Redclyffe*. This book is typical of the genre as a whole in its attempt to manipulate emotions, to link passion with the playing of music and to insist that tragedy hovers closely behind a love affair. But this highly successful author was also a friend of the religious reformer, Keble, and was much vexed by questions of moral improvement. And so was Mrs Stannard whose *Soul of a Bishop* apparently contained all of the 39 Articles. The book was, according to Anderson, typical in that the central relationship was never consummated. This element of the social code has scarcely changed today. The object of the exercise, to put it bluntly, is for the woman to catch a man, and no interest is shown in later events. This characteristic of the genre has been recognised with great forthrightness by one current writer of romantic novels:

> It is not, and never has been, the function of a romantic novelist to
> continue further than the first dawning and final declaration of true love.
> To take the next step would be to enter into an entirely different field. I
> am glad this is so. It would take the gilt off the gingerbread to follow the
> idyllic dream with realism. How sad to watch the heroine, now married
> and pregnant, trying to do up her shoes. Her expression of mystery
> would be replaced with a look of grim determination to eat mustard
> pickles at all costs. And how on earth can she give light lilting laughs
> while speeding to the loo for a bout of morning sickness? (Irene Roberts
> cited in Anderson, 1974, p. 244).

Thus in general the basic morality underlying so many of the codes at work in the romantic best-seller, most notably in the mythology surrounding 'the kiss', should be seen not so much as connected with fulfilment but as representing a desire for goodness. Real passion is almost never shown, and, on those occasions when it is, it is always seen in a very cursory manner.

This basic moral dimension can be seen at work in the history of the romantic best-seller. Ouida at the end of the nineteenth and Marie Corelli at the beginning of the twentieth century were, in effect, mass producing morality tales for modern women warning them of the disasters that follow any lapse on the road to marriage. Some changes have, of course, occurred but these are largely of secondary importance. Thus villains have ceased either to be simply evil or to be foreign and Jewish and have quite often become 'psychopaths' instead. In such matters romantic literature is a particularly good recorder of changes in social attitudes. But the basic desire to preach remains very prevalent: just as Marie Corelli had insisted that electricity was somehow linked to the divine so Barbara Cartland offers advice on numerous topics, including the importance of natural foods.

It might have been expected that the romantic novel would become more relaxed in its views towards sex. Elinor Glyn's *Three Weeks* suggested that such a change was coming in the Edwardian era, as did E. M. Hull's *The Sheik* after the First World War with its revelation that rape was to be enjoyed. But in retrospect perhaps the most important characteristic of the latter was that the Sheik proved to be an English nobleman in disguise who married his victim in the end along very traditional lines. Anderson even argues that we are, on the evidence of reading habits, becoming quietly more puritanical, since a reissue of R. M. Ayres's *Weekend Woman* (1939) in 1969 necessitated making several cuts on moral grounds (Anderson, 1974, p. 200). And Victor Anant (1976) has argued that domesticity still triumphs in women's magazine stories as it has always done.

The romantic novel then has as its referent social values rather than social reality. We know far too little as yet about these novels: this argument would, for example, be supported if it were shown (as I think it could be) that the heroines of women's magazine stories always have slightly higher incomes than their supposed jobs would in fact give them. But it is quite clear that these moral tales have nothing to do with gratification or the release of instinctual demands as Bell believes. And some critics have sought to criticise romantic literature precisely on these grounds. The most brilliant attack in this manner has been made by Germaine Greer (1971), but a more typical one is that of Hall and Whannel whose analysis exhibits the same curious distaste for popular literature that seems to mark their whole book (1964, Ch. 7). Indeed in some senses Hall and Whannel appear to be, as it were, 'new Puritans' on the basis of their analysis of the mass arts. Their views provide a convenient point for trying to reach some conclusions about the two questions concerning popular art raised at the start of this chapter.

Popular literature – an assessment

Hall and Whannel argue that there was once indeed a worthy and meritorious literature of the people that has now been overtaken by the much less meritorious mass literature they analyse. Their dislike of the new popular literature is the result of their considering it politically suspect and aesthetically poor: these two charges are in effect but the questions as to escapist/conservative character and effect on high art raised at the start of this chapter, and each may be considered in turn.

The question of the character of popular literature may be considered in stages. Firstly, is it the case that the function of popular literature is to provide escapist fare for the masses? In its extreme form this theory conjures up the image of a passive audience, and this has already been rejected on the grounds that mass communications sociology has provided sufficient evidence of the active choices made by the audience. This question properly belongs to our discussion of readers in Chapter 7, rather than in this chapter which has been much more concerned with the content of popular literature in its own right. However, this hard and fast distinction may be dropped as something may be learnt about the functions of reading by looking at the work of Albrecht, Rockwell and Goodlad on the content of popular literature.

Albrecht's famous article asked the question 'Does Literature Reflect Common Values' (1956). Albrecht undertook a content analysis of popular literature in order to discover the values that it contained, and then compared these with the state of societal values established through sociological surveys. His interesting finding was that only social values that were under strain and thus difficult to uphold became the subject of popular literature. Something that everyone was in agreement about presumably failed to create sufficient tension for artistic treatment. The theory that underlies this is in effect that of Joan Rockwell applied to popular literature:

> ... the pleasure of participation in fiction, which gives the unreal lives
> presented there the fascination they hold for us, has its origin in the
> functional necessity of small-scale societies. The excitement of sharing in
> the enforcement of taboo, and in the repetition of the 'history' of the
> clan and of its godhead, were an essential part of the social bond,
> cementing ties of identity with the group and reinforcing self-identity
> (Rockwell, 1974, p. 57).

This theory in turn could be described as Durkheimian in its insistence that social solidarity is something that society seeks to preserve at all costs. Sinclair Goodlad, in one of the most striking recent contributions to the sociology of literature, has argued that whereas social solidarity used to be maintained by religious ritual, it is now maintained in part by popular literature and drama. The great merit of Goodlad's *A Sociology of Popular Drama* (1971) is that it provides very suggestive empirical work to back up this argument. Goodlad created a typology of possible themes that could concern popular drama including an interest in the outcast, in money, power, love, and in themes drawn from various idealist and moral questions. Through a very sophisticated content analysis Goodlad discovered that the themes centring on questions of morality or love dominated popular drama: his first three conclusions were that:

1. Plays containing either morality themes or love themes or both
   account for 79 per cent of all plays. Morality themes are the most

frequent, occurring in 52.6 per cent of all plays. Love themes occur in 43.9 per cent of all plays ...

2. The morality plays deal with transgressions against society. Most commonly the transgressors are motivated by a desire for more than reasonable power (social control), a desire for money, the wish for revenge for some (supposed) wrong, and illicit sex ...

3. The love plays deal with problems raised by monogamy. Nearly a third of the love plays are concerned with misunderstandings that arise within marriage ... (1971, p. 167).

The conclusions to be drawn from this fine piece of empirical research are broadly in line with those of Albrecht, that the audience likes to see those areas of life examined in which it finds it hard to uphold particular values or institutions such as monogamy. One slight weakness must, however, at this point be noted in Goodlad's study. He presumes that the audience's feelings can be read from the content of the plays. His reason for adopting this position is that empirical evidence on the mass media audience has shown that standards of appreciation do not notably vary by social class. Whilst this is an accurate report of McQuail's findings, it ignores the fact that McQuail's research (for example, 1970) suggests that other social indicators such as social mobility can be used to demonstrate that the content has a different impact in different social circumstances; and it fails to consider that the case might anyway be different in the case of literature. Goodlad should really have followed up his excellent and highly plausible study with a uses and gratifications study to give his theory about the functions of popular drama complete conviction. However, this criticism does not apply to the finding that critical plays such as those of Beckett and Pinter always received low ratings. If the audience wishes to see its problem area examined, it does not, apparently, wish to have the meaning of social existence in general questioned.

These studies could be summarised by saying that the audience is aware of what is presented to it and makes conscious choices of preference that deny the escapist theory. The evidence assembled also suggests that it would be a mistake, secondly, to presume that the content of popular literature is all conservative in tone. That this is not uniformly the case has already been seen in the crime novel which is so often critical of the manner in which social justice is meted out. However, it does seem to be the case that popular literature endorses, although it does so more self-consciously than is usually allowed, established values relating to private life. In a sense, it is difficult to imagine how things could be otherwise, and thus says really little more than that popular literature is a social institution. And, lest popular literature alone be tarred with this 'conservative' taint, let it be remembered that such classics as *Madame Bovary* and *Anna Karenin* are even more remorselessly puritanical.

The general case against the character of popular literature is far from proven. The same is true of the argument that popular literature depletes classic literature. The most vigorous champion of popular literature in this matter is Leslie Fiedler who has, moreover, little time for its 'conservative content' theory. Fiedler insists that the novel in its earliest days was a popular form and approves this popularity wholeheartedly:

> But the authors and audience of Popular Art, and the marketplace mechanism which is their nexus . . . operate on levels beneath the perception and control of anyone, even of the authors themselves. The novel is subversive because it speaks from and for the most deeply buried, the most profoundly ambivalent levels of the psyche of the ruling classes . . . (1974, p. 193).

He goes on to suggest that:

> It seems, in fact, a psycho-social law that the social and economic oppression of certain groups in any society entails always the psychological repression of certain parts of the individual in the oppressing group (ibid.).

Fiedler's study of the Western is, of course, one of his main attempts to justify this argument as to the ability of popular literature to make a contribution to the understanding of the repressions at work in the collective unconscious. And a corollary to his argument is that the more the novel becomes formalised in 'post-modernist' directions the more it will lose its vital role.

It is equally important to stress that the line between 'high' and 'low' literature is far more fluid than mass society theories allow. Are Dickens and Balzac to be considered as 'high' or 'low'? When Kingsley Amis decides to write a criminal story does this make him suddenly an inferior being? It can be argued, on the contrary, that the presence of genres of various types is something of a blessing in allowing authors to begin their writing career somewhere. When the Brontë sisters began to write the fact that they had a model in romantic literature must have helped them considerably. And just as the borderline between high and low is fluid for authors, so surely is it for readers. This is to argue against the insistence of Mrs Leavis that:

> . . . a habit of reading poor novels not only destroys the ability to distinguish between literature and trash, it creates a positive taste for a certain kind of writing, if only because it does not demand the effort of fresh response . . . (1938, pp. 136–7).

This is wildly exaggerated and far too puritanical in disallowing any catholicity of taste. In contrast, Goodlad has declared:

> It is common experience that an individual may enjoy different types of drama at different times. Personally, I thoroughly enjoy mind-stretching experimental drama such as is provided by the Royal Court Theatre. However, at other times and in other places I also enjoy a good detective

play or a Western. This is not evidence of schizophrenia. It is important to draw this distinction between the different types of satisfaction, because much confusion arises from the confounding of the two separate activities. Once the distinction between the different types of need is clearly understood, much fruitlessly polemical literary criticism may become unnecessary (1971, p. 197).

This is to argue, as Gans (1974) does, that different taste cultures exist, all of which have a claim to be satisfied on the democratic ground that literature is ultimately a way of providing information, advice and consolation and thus of making life bearable for all of us.

Perhaps the most effective rebuttal of those seeking to attack popular literature has been that of Chandler:

It is no easy trick to keep your characters and your story operating on a level which is understandable to the semi-literate public and at the same time give them some intellectual and artistic overtones which that public does not seem to demand or, in effect, recognise, but which somehow subconsciously it accepts and likes (Chandler cited in Symons, 1974, p. 257).

This is to repeat the argument from democracy, that attempting to provide literature for all is something to be endorsed. But in conclusion three more definite points may be made which argue that there is something to be said for the insistence that 'high' literature depends on support from a popular base. First, one needs ordinary literature as a background against which to recognise masterpieces when we are lucky enough to have them. A diet of nothing but the classics would be intolerable, although it is only by supposing some such standard that the case against popular literature is even made to look plausible. Secondly, it may be argued that a literature that consciously scorned its readership would become introverted and eventually trivial. Denis Potter has defended this 'philistine' view thus:

The modernists and their heirs, in a series of dazzling innovations, have succeeded in turning literature back into itself, with the result that even literary criticism has precious little truck with anything so arcane as (chuckle) human values. It is this sad inheritance which so enrages Solzhenitsyn after his flight to the west leaving a tyranny where words are bent and twisted to fit the convenience of a spiritually dead bureaucracy, he found not the opposite pole, not an engagement with the central dignity and vulnerability of humankind and human freedom, but a sterile, in-turned trivial and trivialising abdication by the writer from the concern with the strivings which characterise all of our lives at some points (1977, p. 7).

Finally, we shall see in the next chapter that the economics of publishing are such that 'high' literature (and especially poetry) depend on the money produced by best-sellers for its very existence: thus the end of popular literature would entail the destruction of the whole literary culture. This is not, of course, the utopia dreamed of by the critics of mass society: to the contrary, they dreamed of a society in which the classics themselves would be best-sellers. But the arguments advanced in Chapter 8 suggest that it is conceivable that modern society is moving in a direction which may make the worry over 'high' vs. 'low' literature comical in that the true discovery of the future may be that reading as such will be at a discount. It is this pessimistic but realistic vision that has made the evaluation of popular literature offered here so favourable.

Chapter 6

Gatekeepers

The concept of the 'gatekeeper' has been developed by mass communications sociology to refer to those whose role is that of selecting the type of communication that the audience is to receive. This concept can usefully be applied to the sociology of literature; indeed, that this concept needs to be applied can be seen from the general tentativeness of the discussion and from the complete absence of any discussion of literary agents and literary prizes. Gatekeepers in the sociology of literature can exercise their function in two different places. Publishers can prevent manuscripts reaching the market, as can censorship of the type which demands pre-publication licensing. On the other hand, gatekeepers may have some influence on the book once it has been published; the fate of the book depends in part upon critics, libraries, distributors and, again, censors – though this time of the post-publication variety.

A few general comments about the character of the inquiry are in order. The purpose of the general approach is to isolate factors which come between books-in-themselves and books-for-others. A serious difficulty arises from the attempt to discover whether such forces do have a powerful distorting effect. This difficulty can be put bluntly: how is it possible to identify and measure an absence? In other words, where most of the sociology of literature is a form of the sociology of knowledge relating social factors to literature, the study of gatekeepers, insofar as they are successful in their tasks, is best seen as an eminent branch of the sociology of ignorance. This is less true of censorship (court battles may produce evidence of a sort) than it is of publishing (no knowledge is available by definition of masterpieces unrecognised). This lack of detailed evidence cannot be remedied, and our task instead must be that of trying to locate more general factors at work. The one that will repeatedly concern us is that of the economic dilemmas of publishing, but one other should be mentioned immediately. No study of gatekeepers can be complete without reference to intangible factors of public opinion, since such factors may be more powerful than the gatekeepers themselves. An example of this is Hardy's famous decision to turn away from novel-writing as a result of the hostile criticism that *Jude the Obscure* received in 1896. This is a classic example of the difficulty noted about the sociology of ignorance for it is possible to conceive of more Hardy novels had the general climate been more propitious. These intangible factors are hard to discover but must be borne in mind.

Publishers

The origins of publishing as a profession lie in the Middle Ages. Printers began by producing on demand but quickly began to produce material that they could manage themselves. They found that the time-gap between printing and selling often placed them in financial difficulties and were consequently naturally drawn both to find themselves better properties and to seek their own bookshop outlets. This expansion of interest neatly illustrates the general character of publishing, namely that it is inherently speculative. Publishers have to guess whether a book is going to appeal at all, and have to take even more agonising decisions as to whether to keep it on their lists when it is only doing moderately well. In Lane's words:

> ... picking the 'classics' of the future is somewhat akin to picking Derby winners with a pin, the difference being that picking a Derby winner is hardly likely to be a matter of individual survival, whilst picking future classics may well affect the ultimate survival of a publishing house.
> Hence, there tends to develop an endless balancing act between current losers that may make good, and the back-list profits. When the balancing act fails, the house has two options: to be taken over by someone who has capital ... or to cease publishing ... (1970a, p. 248).

Publishers could be approached by telling anecdotes about famous works that found great difficulty in gaining a publisher. But a more general approach towards novel publishing offers some incisive examples of the gatekeeping role. We may begin by considering Victorian publishers, such as Smith and Elder or Chapman and Hall, whose work has painstakingly been described by Sutherland (1976). These publishers were able to promote the spacious three-volume novel until it became the dominant genre of the time. The reading public had expanded considerably in the 1850s and the puritanical reformation of manners in English society encouraged by Prince Albert also gave a boost to novel reading. The 'three-decker' novel usually sold at thirty-one shillings and sixpence; this was a considerable sum of money and thus not truly in the interest of the reader – as some publishers realised (Sutherland, 1976, p. 20). But the corollary to high prices was the ability to provide a considerable number of novelists with a decent livelihood. A Disraeli or Dickens could occasionally command £10,000 for a single novel, but Trollope in his early days managed only to get £250, and less than this was the rule. This was, nevertheless, a living, and it was increased by pre-book publication in parts and magazines. These economic conditions allowed for the spaciousness of the classic Victorian novels; but they also proved a constant worry for novelists as diverse as Ainsworth and Trollope who felt themselves driven to unnatural wordiness.

It should not be imagined that the Victorian publisher was all-powerful. As we shall see, they did not always want to charge so much for novels, but were forced to do so by the power of the great circulating libraries who could be relied upon, providing they considered the novel suitable for family reading, to take most of their stock. Nor were they free to ignore public opinion, especially if the feelings of that opinion were interpreted for them by Mudie, the head of the most important circulating library. Thus in 1851 Chapman rejected Eliza Lynn's novel *Realities* since she would not revise passages which 'excited the sensual nature and were therefore injurious' (cited in Thomas, 1969, p. 251). But within the limits laid down by public opinion and Mr Mudie, the publisher could exert considerable influence. Sutherland has shown this influence at work in a series of detailed studies. Kingsley was persuaded to drop a first person narrator in his *Westward Ho!*, whilst Dickens (as a publisher in his own right) insisted that books were written clearly enough for his very large but rather unsophisticated audience. And influence could extend to more substantial matters. Three early works of Hardy were refused whilst *Far From the Madding Crowd* was given an uncharacteristically 'happy' ending to accede to the demands of Leslie Stephen. Raymond Williams has argued that it is possible to detect the moments in Hardy's work when he leaves his central interests to produce a picture of rural life calculated to appeal to London readers (1973, Ch. 4). Sutherland argues much the same point when he suggests, on the basis of his knowledge of Hardy's relations with publishers, that his 'creaking plots' were indebted to advice given to him by Meredith (a famous publisher's reader), that his appliqué morality owed something to the advice given by Macmillan and that the light badinage of his occasional dialogue might owe something to his having been told to emulate Thackeray (Sutherland, 1976, Ch. 10).

The Victorian world was favourable to both publisher and novelist: it was correspondingly characterised by a massive self-confidence. The position today lacks such confidence and is riven by considerable conflict. There seem to be two general factors that are relevant here that help explain the changed state of affairs. First, the increase in literacy did not lead to increasing the size of a 'single' reading public but rather to the creation of separate taste-publics. As argued, this fragmentation was accompanied by fears of loss of quality that led many modernists to conceive of their role as protectors of elitist culture rather than as having the duty to bring 'sweetness and light' to a wider readership. Secondly, publishing has become more dependent on non-literary books. Escarpit (1966) has shown that publishing is increasingly dependent on 'functional' books, about a quarter of current book production being for the school audience. Such captive audiences are important here insofar as their predictability contrasts poorly with the much more independent novel reading public; it is not hard to see that strong arguments encourage publishers to specialise in these newer and safer areas.

Conflict in the publishing world today can be seen to occur between an ideal-typical 'traditional' publisher and an equally ideal-typical 'modern' publisher. Traditional publishers very willingly embrace the role of gatekeeper since they tend to see their duty as that of maintaining cultural standards. The cultural standards they accept are elitist ones (Lane, 1970b, *passim*). Thus the publication of masterpieces is seen as a duty that transcends business logic. In this spirit many publishers have gone out of business and have been honoured for it; and this spirit was clearly at the back of the minds of Leonard and Virginia Woolf when they founded the Hogarth Press (which survived thanks to the considerable organisational ability of Leonard Woolf). The traditional publisher consequently sees it as his duty to serve authors, and to 'catch' them for his house by himself taking some part in the literary world. All this is superficially attractive, but Lane stresses that there are less favourable aspects. Books tend not to be commissioned, and the gentlemanly nature of the whole enterprise is often such as to lessen the amount the author receives – certainly less emphasis is given to selling a book once it is published. The organisation itself is often marked by internal conflict. The relatively small size of the concern allows for a non-hierarchical division of work and great stress is laid on the common serving of a cultural mission. However, these attitudes may be only skin deep since they depend upon employees accepting the definition of culture of the owners: if this is contested, decisions tend very quickly to revert to the top.

Traditional publishing is currently under attack. This can most obviously be seen in the increasing size of many publishing concerns. Longmans, for example, was forced to go public in 1947. In 1968 the firm became a part of a large finance group which later absorbed Penguin and currently has a turnover of over £20m. Greater size seems to be related to attitudes the reverse of those so far considered. Books are commissioned, and much greater emphasis is laid on the necessity of financial viability. Moreover, culture itself is seen in less overtly elitist terms and books tend to be seen as just another product that has to be sold. These attitudes encourage the firm to be more active, and may, in one sense, be considered more democratic. Books are commissioned to make money but there is also an awareness that this depends upon the filling of unrecognised public needs. Moreover, modern publishing organisations tend to have less internal conflict since a greater formality means that different individuals are responsible for different stages of a book's life.

Both traditional and modern publishers will select books to suit their different conceptions of their role and of culture itself. However, Dan Lacy (1970) has argued that this in itself matters little since there is no actual evidence of quality being overlooked and a massive amount of evidence of much that is poor that does reach the public. In the last six months of 1972, 16,394 books were published by 1,673 publishers (*Bookseller*, 6.1.73), and this would seem to bear out Lacy's argument. However, reservations are in order. Lacy himself notes that publishers operate at consistently low profit margins; this is especially true in the case of the novel. Novels are only likely to make money if they appeal to the middle class. The disturbing implication of this is seen by one New York writer:

> The price of hardcover books has been so inflated that only the middle class and up can afford them. Publishers are therefore careful to publish only books about subjects, and written in styles, attractive to such people. It greatly limits the freedom of a writer who has to live off his books. I wouldn't embark upon a novel about factory life or street people for example, because I probably could not sell it, whereas anything about Power or Money, Suburban Anxieties, or other middle class obsessions are surefire. Real social criticism is permanently out to lunch (Weatherby, 1977).

And Per Gedin's account of the Swedish publishing crisis (1977) holds out little hope for improvement. Indeed costs are now so high in Sweden that profits can only be made on a novel after 90 per cent of a 10,000-copy printing has been sold: this is a very high figure indeed, and certain not to be met by the average novel.

It is easy to imagine a frightening scenario with these facts in mind. The activist publisher commissions vigorously to catch the latest public fad. The cost of back lists becomes virtually prohibitive so that fewer and fewer risks are taken on books that might prove themselves over time, whilst the number of first novels published plummets. In a nutshell, books would become the playthings of immediate circum-stance and would not have any chance to prove themselves. It is encouraging to note, more optimistically, that small audiences and publishing at a loss have not seemed to hinder the achievements of contemporary poetry. But the novel, in comparison, is so much more a social form that this analogy may mean little.

Censors

Societies are keen to be known through the self-image they diligently propagate. Such self-images need to be considered by the sociologist, but should be handled with care. The bias often inherent in self-images can occasionally be remedied by examining the skeletons hidden in societal cupboards; this can make for an awareness that a society is not all that it pretends to be. The richness of this sort of approach in literature has been amply demonstrated by S. Marcus's *The Other Victorians*, and it is surprising that this approach has not been adopted more often. This section, however, is concerned with more obviously institutional matters. An excellent guide, Thomas's *A Long Time*

Burning (1969), allows us to locate three particular skeletons in the cupboard (political radicalism, sex and religion) whose changing inter-reaction make up the history of censorship in England.

Attempts to censor began with the spread of printing. Such censorship throughout Europe was directed particularly at religio-political material – the two being inseparable since political struggles were argued in religious terms. The most celebrated attempt to censor was, of course, the Index of the Catholic Church, but the temporal powers were as keen to control the new source of ideas, especially once it started turning out material in the vernacular. Febvre and Martin (1976) have no doubt but that the early attempts to censor failed. The protestant printers were driven out of France but this did not stop the dissemination of their ideas; instead a minor industry of smuggling across the border from Geneva arose. They are in no doubt about the importance of the printing press's ability to spread ideas and suggest that, had the Hussites had the new presses, the course of European history might well have been different.

In England censorship was initially of the pre-publication variety. The Tudor State was notably active in giving itself an armoury of controls over literature. In 1538 it declared that any manuscript needed a licence from a privy councillor in order to be published; in 1586 it added to this by allowing printing only in Oxford, Cambridge and London. These controls were enforced by the Star Chamber and lasted through the reigns of the first two Stuarts. It seemed briefly that the defeat of the royal cause might increase liberty of opinion and it was to promote this that Milton wrote Areopagitica (1664) – although it should be noted that the freedom of opinion he advocated was not to be extended to papists. But these hopes were premature for the 1662 Licensing Act restored the pre-publication licensing system. This system became less and less workable in the face of the burgeoning volume of publication. Hence in 1695 it was allowed to lapse. It must be understood that this represented no general advocacy of freedom of opinion; on the contrary, the most powerful argument for the lapse of the licensing system was the harsh one that there was a mass of law already enacted that could be used against anyone who ventured beyond discretion. But perhaps equally important was the awareness that the old system had never had much success. Those drawn to radical or heretical views were not fools enough to expose themselves by asking for permission to publish; instead they took advantage of the relative simplicity of early printing technology to publish and be damned. Thomas doubts that any idea was suppressed by the licensing system (1969, p. 319). This is not, of course, to say that penalties for those who were caught were light. Their harshness can be seen in the fate of Prynne; the publication of his *Histrio-mastix* cost him, on different occasions, his ears, the stumps of his ears and a branding with the initials S.L. (for Schismatical Libeller).

After 1695 it proves increasingly possible to consider censorship of religious, sexual and political work separately. The fact that the end of the licensing system was not a libertarian measure can be seen in the passing of the 1698 Blasphemy Act – which (as existing laws covered possible eventualities very thoroughly) is to be understood as a warning to both nonconformist and catholic not to undermine the state. That this political fear underlay most political censorship can be seen from a curious double standard that developed. The resolutely sceptical works of Hume and Gibbon were not prosecuted since their high-minded intellectual tone presented no clear and present danger. But Thomas Woolston's *A Discourse on the Miracles of Our Saviour* (1727) was not so lucky since it was judged to have potential popular appeal (Thomas, 1969, Ch. 4). This belief in the necessity of protecting the establishment was neatly exhibited by the reply of one Lord Chancellor when refusing in 1793 to repeal laws that prevented Presbyterians from holding certain public offices:

> Gentlemen, I'll be perfectly frank with you. Gentlemen, I am against you, and for the Established Church, by God. Not that I like the Established Church a bit better than any other church, but because it *is* established. And whenever you get your damned religion established, I'll be for that too (Lord Thurlow cited in Thomas, 1969, p. 180).

These attitudes on the part of the state changed completely in the course of the nineteenth century. The importance (or at least the imagined importance) of religion as an agent of social control was emphasised in the uproar that followed the discovery in the religious census of 1851 that most of the population did not in fact go to church on Sundays. But much more open and fundamental doubts about religious truth were allowed; no attempt was, for example, made to suppress the publicised loss of faith of George Eliot, Leslie Stephen and Froude. The reason for this tolerance was simple; these thinkers were eminently respectable and clearly did not degenerate into lascivious revolutionaries as a result of their agnosticism. Very great freedom of religious opinion is thus recorded by Thomas who observed in 1969 that 'it is a symptom of something approaching absolute tolerance that it was never even thought necessary to abolish the Blasphemy Act of 1698, since it was impossible to imagine that an attempt would ever be made to enforce its provisions' (1969, pp. 299–300). With the successful prosecution of the magazine *Gay News* for publishing a blasphemous poem this confidence seems now less well founded, and shows that the study of censorship is by no means yet an irrelevance.

If religion occupied the establishment rather little after 1695, the battle in political matters increased in tempo. The initial establishment fears were of Jacobite invasion and revolution from below. This led to the passing of the first of the Stamp Acts in 1712; these stamp duties on periodicals were designed to prevent the circulation of ideas amongst the 'dangerous classes' and were, not surprisingly, increased significantly at the time of the French Revolution. However, three factors at work

prevented censorship becoming fully effective. The two-party system
served to bring in some restraint on the part of governments towards
their enemies since it was realised that harshness was suicidal when one
might be voted out of office. Secondly, printing technology was still
cheap enough to allow the founding of new papers; thus Bolingbroke at
the very height of Walpole's near-Venetian oligarchy was able to found
The Craftsman. Finally, it was not long before ways around censorship
were discovered. Anonymity provided protection for some, but the
greatest safeguard lay in allegory. A persecution of *Gulliver's Travels*
would have been tantamount to admitting the very case that Swift had
presented.

However, very considerable government attempts to censor in the
years between the Wilkes affair and the Reform Act of 1832 were made.
The fear of revolution led to continual persecution of certain offenders.
Works such as Godwin's *An Enquiry Concerning Political Justice* were
not prosecuted since they were judged too expensive to be dangerous;
but continued attention was paid to the works of Paine which were both
cheap and clear. In 1797 a new Stamp Act was passed and in 1799 an Act
controlling reading rooms (which had grown as a response to the
increased expense) received the royal assent. None of this, however,
stopped men of the character of Cobbett and Richard Carlile. The
victory they eventually gained was not in the end without some
unfortunate side-effects. One of the reasons why the government lost its
battle to control the press was that papers were getting too expensive to
be bought out; and the cost and size of papers naturally continued to
increase throughout the nineteenth century. Thomas argues that a
notable concentration allowed nineteenth-century governments to
negotiate with a smaller number of people whose composition changed
less frequently. This in turn enabled governments to grant very
considerable extensions to press freedom since they were secure in the
knowledge that such freedom would be 'responsibly' used. And there
remained, of course, very considerable reserve legal powers. In 1889
these were enhanced by the Official Secrets Act which (especially when
extended in the Edwardian period) was loosely enough defined to
strangle many an investigation. Further to this the contempt and libel
laws remained; and it is well known that these laws, currently under
review, create a situation in which the power of the press is curtailed in
ways that are, for example, unheard of in America.

The final area of importance is the one that has affected literature
most directly. Pornography came to seem of public importance as the
result of the 'puritan' attempt to reform manners. That this was a
novelty could be seen when the attempt of The Society for the
Reformation of Manners at the end of the seventeenth century to bring
cases against literature on the grounds of obscenity initially foundered
when it was argued that only Church Courts could concern themselves
with the issue. However, the society had some impact in the long run as
can be seen from two facts. First, Thomas shows how closely

Richardson's attempt in *Pamela* to underwrite higher moral standards followed the puritanical ethos. An equally important example of the newly respectable morality was Bowdler's famous version of Shakespeare suitably neutered for 'family' use. Secondly, the society gained a considerable success in making governments think that it was their duty to prosecute obscene literature. Neither of these successes prevented other societies being formed. The Proclamation Society was given impetus by Wilberforce and was followed by the Society for the Suppression of Vice; its modern descendant is, of course, the Festival of Light masterminded by Mary Whitehouse.

Thomas has very interesting words on the Victorian societies:

> In an age so conscious of education and the educative effect of all that was considered best in literature, it was inevitable that critics should have issued stern warnings of the likely result, in terms of moral conduct, of all that was worst in literature as well. This preoccupation with the power of erotic literature to corrupt its readers was much less evident in the earlier eighteenth century but, as the pre-Victorians and Victorians themselves recognised, to believe in the educative power of literature is to believe in its ability to deprave and corrupt. In this they showed themselves more logical at least than those who would deny that books can corrupt while maintaining that 'good' books exert an influence for moral improvement (1969, p. 122).

The greatest triumph of these groups came with the passing of the 1857 Obscene Publications Act. When this act was passed it was insisted that it would not be used against literature of any value. But the judicial insistence that the act referred to anything that could deprave or corrupt came to be used against Zola. And Walter Pater declined initially to publish the full version of *The Renaissance* for fears of the possible consequences. Nevertheless, the act merely drove pornography below the counter. There in Thomas' view it developed into a curious form of social criticism. In the pages of *The Pearl*, for example, stories tended to direct themselves against the aristocracy and the virtues of marriage (largely by developing incest themes).

The great difficulty with the attack on pornography was that the 'deprave and corrupt' requirement was used so often against literature of obvious quality. Both *Lady Chatterley's Lover* and *Ulysses* were banned; in both cases injury was added to insult by the authors losing money as the books, without copyright protection, appeared in various pirated editions. The 1959 Obscene Publications Act tried to remedy the state of affairs by allowing expert witnesses to be called who would be allowed to testify about the literary quality of the book. The crucial test of the law came in 1960 when the courts considered the fate of *Lady Chatterley's Lover*. The prosecution asked revealingly whether it was 'a book you would even wish your wife or your servants to read?' (Thomas, 1969, p. 4), but could not stop publication. But this should not be allowed to disguise an ambiguity in Lawrence's own view of the matter.

Though he naturally favoured his own book's publication, he did so only on the grounds that it was not pornography:

> But even I could censor genuine pornography, rigorously. It would not be very difficult. In the first place, genuine pornography is almost always underworld, it doesn't come out into the open ... you can recognise it by the insult it offers, invariably, to sex, and to the human spirit (Lawrence, cited in Thomas, 1969, p. 313).

We may conclude with some general comments about the position of censorship today. The Blasphemy Act has been used again and the Race Relations legislation is in logic such as to allow prosecutions. This has not happened but one could imagine a latter-day Céline under legal attack. By and large, censorship of sexual literature has waned. Some social theorists feel very strongly about this. Herbert Marcuse, for example, has developed the observations of Aldous Huxley's *Brave New World* in arguing that instant gratification is creating *One-Dimensional Man*. David Caute (1972) too notes regretfully that the absence of control does not mean a recognition of the importance of literature but rather its diminution into 'mere' entertainment. Finally, it is probably the case that political censorship is the strongest of the three varieties remaining since contempt, libel and secrecy laws have a considerable range. Greater tolerance can be seen in some areas: theatrical censorship was effectively abolished in 1968. However, one eminent theatre critic has noted that of all the new liberties the one least used is the political (Billington, 1976). He suggests that the reason for this may well be fear of hidden censorship; theatres or companies that question too much fear that they may face 'rationalising' economic stringencies and the tailing out of government subsidies before some of their colleagues do.

Critics

The first two of our sections have concerned themselves primarily with how books come before the public; the last two sections discuss ways in which selection of the material once available is undertaken. A discussion of critics is, as it were, between these two approaches. Certainly the critic as reviewer occupies a role which tries to influence selection. The same is true of more academic critical approaches: Leavis's discussion of the English novel has probably done something to get his favoured authors into Penguins. But some critics are much more than this. Henry James, for example, probably had no immediate impact on the public but had a significant one on certain authors (especially, perhaps, the Bloomsbury Group). James, in other words, produced a new 'aesthetic ideology' that influenced, not selection, but creation. It is immensely difficult to judge whether the vast legion of modern critics is capable of having a comparable influence on creators. James's criticism had so much authority in large part as the result of his own achievement; only T. S. Eliot has been able to exert authority in a similar way more recently. It is then at least a possibility that the sheer number of modern academic critics does not denote much of real importance for the literary system. Comments on this matter must be extremely tentative, but some will be offered after examining some landmarks in the development of English critics. The analysis examines social background, manner of earning an income, publication outlet, role and characteristic ideas of selected English critics.

Three general comments are necessary before the analysis is undertaken. First, it is useful to adopt the distinction made in Watson's excellent *The Literary Critics* (1973) between legislative, theoretical and descriptive criticism. The first of these wishes to tell people how to write and, though the staple of past ages, is currently in abeyance. Theoretical criticism is by no means absent in contemporary Europe and has a very distinguished English antecedent in Thomas Hobbes whose distinction between court, country and city literature has, in Watson's eyes, by no means been fully explored. However, more recent English intellectual life has discouraged theoretical criticism so that as important a theoretical critic as Coleridge has scarcely received his due. Descriptive criticism has, then, been dominant since the time of Dryden. Such criticism is best characterised in Watson's words:

> ... whereas the legislative critic had said 'This is how a play should be written', and the theoretical critic, like Aristotle in the *Poetics*, 'This is the nature of tragedy in general', Dryden simply says: 'This is how I have tried to write my play, and why'. Descriptive criticism, uniquely, is particular and, to a unique degree, falsifiable. It is about one thing, a given text to which critic and reader may appeal equally for confirmation (1973, p. 7).

The description of recent criticism is not altogether happy in that it is usually impossible to describe without some theory of significance as a guide. Modern critics are certainly more rigorous in the manner in which they approach the text, but this does not mean that they are, despite their disclaimers, without critical standards. Frequent use of loaded terms such as 'life-enhancing', 'ambiguity' and 'community' represent a covert smuggling in of critical standards that would have been better explicitly endorsed. Secondly, the developments within descriptive criticism that will be described do not comprise a history in the sense of being a slow accretion of the wisdom of the ages. In Watson's words attacking this evolutionary view:

> Where they see a tidy evolution of doctrine, I see a record of chaos marked by sudden revolution. Where they see a continuing debate down the centuries around the same questions, I see a pattern of refusal, on the part of the major critics, to accept the assumption of existing debate. The great critics do not contribute: they interrupt (1973, p. 3).

Frank Kermode has made the same point when refuting the idea that 'we can say anything that we like'; he suggests that critics can only say what their critical 'paradigms' allow (1977). Finally and most importantly, criticism does not create great literature. Elizabethan England had very little criticism and virtually none that would be granted the title today. But, of course, the age produced Shakespeare and his colleagues.

Following Watson, three periods of descriptive criticism may be distinguished. The first of these covers the period from Dryden to Johnson. The social background of the critics in this, as in most of the later periods (with significant individual exceptions), has been described by Kramer:

> ... after Dryden, the critic was from the urban upper-middle and middle-middle classes ... and tended to be Protestant (Pope was the only one who was not Protestant by birth). His father was either a professional man (usually clergyman) or a relatively prosperous tradesman, and the critic himself usually had a university education. This means that the eighteenth-century critic was from a class whose members possessed reading and writing skills anchored in business and were religiously and socially motivated to improve themselves (1970, p. 438).

At the start of this period, critics were still dependent on patronage; Dryden, Dennis and Addison all benefited from court or government appointments, but by the end of the period this was changing and both Pope and Johnson were able to become independent literary professionals. This change was made possible by new outlets for their writing. Dryden had often published his critical work as prefaces to his plays and his single independent critical work, *Of Dramatic Poesy*, was circumspect in its judgements since Dryden probably had no desire to flaunt independent opinions which his patron might require him to change (Watson, 1973, p. 33). The rise of periodicals at the turn of the seventeenth century allowed for greater independence and proved both cause and consequence of the critic seeing his task in new terms. Dryden's prefaces were written largely for fellow professionals, but the criticism of Johnson and Addison was written for the new middle-class reading public. In Watson's words:

> The Man of Taste is king: the consumer, at last, has won his right of choice. In theoretical criticism ... the issue is now joined not on conformity to precept ... but on the reader's response. By which of the five senses is the human imagination most gratified? How is true taste to be defined? And if a democracy of taste, a mere counting of heads, is not sufficient, what *does* constitute true taste in reading? These are issues which Dryden never once raises; and Pope raises them for professional critics only. Addison, in the *Spectator* essays, raises them for all polite society (1973, p. 59).

On this social basis the characteristic eighteenth-century criticism grew. The great revolution of Dryden was to make descriptive criticism respectable. His analysis of Ben Jonson's *A Silent Woman* was a piece of cross-cultural criticism that allowed English readers to consider their tragedians the equal of Corneille and Racine. This great achievement cannot disguise Dryden's rather slipshod handling of actual texts. Johnson's great *Lives of the Poets* unfortunately followed his example in this respect. In these lives Johnson combined biographical introduction with critical comment. The great weakness of the work lay in the relative failure to integrate the two halves of the study into a coherent whole. However, Johnson's open endorsement of historical perspective did point forwards:

> Every man's performances, to be rightly estimated, must be compared with the state of the age in which he lived, and with his own particular opportunities ... Curiosity is always busy to discover the instruments, as well as to survey the workmanship, to know how much is ascribed to original powers, and how much to casual and adventitious help (Johnson cited in Watson, 1973, p. 83).

The second and more historically minded moment of English descriptive criticism runs from Lamb and Hazlitt to Matthew Arnold. The critics of this period were able to make their living through continuing to provide for the now greatly expanded middle class, both in periodicals and in public lectures. These critics saw their task less as that of improving taste than that of educating the members of the new industrial society:

> The criticism of this century, although interested in defending the functions of literature, was not so much concerned with the improvement of taste. What disturbed the later nineteenth-century critics was that the middle class had become the dominant social class so rapidly that it never had had time to acquire the more fundamental things that are the foundations of good taste ... (Kramer, 1970, p. 444).

The periodicals in which they wrote were evidence of the importance they assigned to their work. These periodicals:

> ... presupposed widespread public interest in many topics which have since been handed over almost exclusively to students and specialists; they offered serious writers an enviable amount of space, to say nothing of handsome rates of pay; they set a precedent for the solid journals of opinion – what the Russians call the 'thick journals' – which were to play such a central role in the intellectual life of nineteenth-century Europe and America (Gross, 1973, p. 17).

This school had very high hopes of their historical approach. This had first been mooted by Coleridge whose work was, however, curiously ignored. But it gained immense status from the historical criticism of the Bible, especially as undertaken in Germany. This criticism led some to believe that this approach might prove definitive and scientific. This ideal was perhaps by its nature illusory and was certainly made so by the lack of a clearly worked out theory of the relations of an author to his society (Watson, 1973, Ch. 7). Nevertheless, the historical sense did benefit some criticism: Leslie Stephen's criticism of the novel, for example, remains of permanent value.

The historical approach was not directly discredited but was overtaken by new concerns. The newly literate masses did not swell the general reading public which was to listen to the august seriousness of the great periodicals. Critics, like modernist artists, began to see themselves as defenders of a beleaguered elite culture. This meant that the critical outlets tended to become the little magazine rather than the general periodical. There were exceptions to this such as Arnold Bennett who, at the *New Age* and the *Evening Standard*, was able to introduce Dostoyevsky and others to a wide audience. However, the general move was towards greater specialisation. Many critics now have PhDs and their typical publication is now usually too complex to be understood by a general audience. Along with this specialisation often went a view, memorably expressed in Leavis's *Education and the University*, that academically institutionalised criticism should consider its duty that of passing down the values, usually considered to be endangered, of civilised life.

No single school of criticism dominates the present scene. The break up of the historical approach led naturally to one group emphasising the importance of more strictly formal concerns. This group may be seen to stem from Eliot's *The Sacred Wood*, and includes the work of I. A. Richards, William Empson, and 'new critics' in America such as Wimsatt, Beardsley and John Crowe Ransom. This group often had strong views about society but these were not closely related to the practice of formalistic criticism. This criticism pioneered close textual analysis. However, it has already been attacked above (Ch. 1) as excessively 'internal'. This, too, is the conclusion that Watson came to when suggesting that Richards's discovery that students analysed poetry badly out of context proves little:

> It seems more natural to suppose that all but the simplest poems exist in traditions which dictate in some sense the significance of the poem, and that poems torn from their historical context tend to mean some other thing, or to descend into the merely meaningless. If this is so, then *Practical Criticism* and its record of failures in response is not an indictment of English education ... but an impressive body of evidence to suggest that unhistorical reading is bad reading (Watson, 1973, p. 191).

It is a measure of the complexity of the situation that a second group also includes Eliot as a founding father. This group advocates the 'English Dream' of a 'collective, unalienated folk society, where honest men work together and create together' (Wollheim cited in Filmer, 1969, p. 271). The Leavises tend to place this organic community in the past and to see all as a slow decline from eighteenth-century communal solidarity; Williams, on the other hand, is not so romantic about the past but perhaps even more so about a future in which socialism will establish a society at once equal, democratic, fraternal and cultured. But these differences do not detract from the common position which is open to criticism on two points. The first of these is that understanding texts is by definition understanding society and thus doing sociology. This view has been attacked above (Ch. 2) and can be neatly summarised in the words of Filmer:

> Because there are certain to be discontinuities between the experience of the writer and that of his public, none of their interpretations of his work will necessarily correspond with the experience that it has been his intention to convey . . . far from embodying the fundamental general values of a popular or common British culture, the literary cultural tradition of the English dream . . . is a coherent restatement of the similar ideals of a number of writers, artists, literary and social critics since the mid-eighteenth century . . . (1969, pp. 290–1).

Whatever the value of literature as social evidence it is always important to ask about the exact social referent involved. Secondly, the generalised scorn shown for industrial society is surely not justified. Industrial society has provided greater freedom for more people than any society in previous human history. More sophisticated observers such as Keynes realised this. Scientists are thus just as much creators of 'civilisation', as Snow realised in his famous lecture on the 'two cultures' (1959), as are departments of English.

The responsibilities of critics are still the subject of lively debate. Recently, many have tried to import new European ideas. The long-term influence of such ideas is as yet hard to discern, but two strands seem to be important. First, increased attention is being paid to European Marxism of various kinds. This has already led to Raymond Williams (1977) declaring that his critical allegiances now lie in this tradition. The difficulty with these Marxisms, however, is that the most theoretical (especially Lukács and Althusser) are not sensitive in literary terms, whilst the more sensitive Marxist critics (especially Benjamin) suffer from weak or question-begging theoretical stances. Secondly, structuralism's originality has been questioned by Thody (1977) who feels that its contribution, once its theoretical debris has been understood, goes little beyond that of Empson. It is, as yet, too early to tell, but both approaches may be welcomed as combatting a certain recent provincial quality to English intellectual life: criticism, for example, has concerned itself far too exclusively with, say, the English novel at the expense of forgetting that the novel can only properly be understood in its European context.

Two general points may be made in conclusion. Firstly, the gap between critics and practitioner is greater than perhaps ever before. Saul Bellow has gone so far as to talk of the institutionalising of English literature teaching as being 'an intellectual disaster' (1977). Gore Vidal has buttressed the general point in a series of arguments in his scathing *Matters of Fact and Fiction* (1977). In particular he argues that the formalism of American university criticism means that the literary culture is now completely stratified and considers this augurs ill for the future given that the novel at least has depended on being able to bridge the gap between high and low culture. Secondly, the increasing specialisation has in one important sense led to what may be termed a neglect of duty. An Arnold Bennett was able to provide guidance about all types of literature. The current system of reviewing is very elitist indeed; only certain types of literature get reviewed regularly and a dismissive tone is used on the rare occasions that more popular genres do receive treatment. The next section points out that mass paperback publication is likely to incr?ase. This makes Weatherby's argument in favour of critical reviewers changing their role all the more important:

> At present the critical coverage of paperbacks is very spotty and
> generally deals with reprints of bestselling hardcovers. A writer who
> published a novel, much praised in Europe, as a paperback original in
> New York, received one review, and that very condescending. To the
> critics publishing in paperbacks first is still like slumming (1977).

Distributors

Distribution of books is far too often overlooked. Even now it remains possible to set up in publishing with rather small amounts of capital since little more than an office is required. This accounts for there being over a thousand publishers in the United Kingdom: Escarpit has estimated that probably 65 per cent of books published do not bring in any profit (1971, Part 3). In other words, our literary system is very good at publishing books but much less efficient at distributing them. However, historically distribution was taken seriously and it seems as if this will again become the case; and this is very important indeed for patterns of distribution may be such as to constitute one of the more powerful forms of gatekeeping.

The first occasion on which distributors exercised power has already been noted. The great circulating libraries of Victorian England exerted considerable power over both publishers and authors since there were few decent public libraries for the reading public. The circulating libraries exerted their power over the publishers in the following manner. Books could have been produced much more cheaply than they were, but publishers did not generally do so since they could rely on Mudie, Smith and others to take the bulk of their stock; in order to gain this security they sacrificed some editorial freedom. Both Mudie (whose library was established in 1842) and Smith were of nonconformist background and insisted on works of an improving temper that could be read to the whole family. Mudie described his role rather late in his career when involved in controversy with George Moore who felt that this system amounted to censorship: 'They (the public) are evidently willing to have a barrier of some kind between themselves and the lower floods of literature' (Mudie cited in Griest, 1970, p. 145). Perhaps even more spectacular than this was the evidence of Mudie's influence seen in the hegemony of the three-volume novel. Mudie preferred this format since it kept prices sufficiently high to make the public dependent for their reading matter on his library; membership cost only a guinea for most of the nineteenth century whereas the purchase of a three-decker novel cost a guinea and a half. By the end of the century Mudie was forced, in large part by publishers like Vizetelly who were managing to find a market for six-shilling single-volume novels, to abandon his insistence on the three-decker. But the extent of the power that he had wielded can be seen in the fall from 184 such novels being published in 1894 (the year Mudie moved against the three-decker) to only 3 being published in 1897. This is, of course, a spectacular demonstration of the importance of some knowledge of external social matters for the literary critic.

With the ending of the power of the great circulating libraries and the provision of public libraries it might seem as if distribution would become unproblematic; books are made available throughout book-shops and libraries. The achievements and limitations of libraries will concern us in the next section, but something further may be said here about bookshop distribution. Escarpit had made a useful distinction between cultured and popular circuits of distribution (1971). Bookshops tend to serve only the former of these and are in that sense a 'cultural preserve' of a rather narrow group of society. Thus Lacy estimates that an American town of 50,000 or less cannot support a bookshop; and bookshops outside metropolitan areas frequently run on very low profit margins (1970, *passim*). And most bookshops can only afford to stock between 3,000 and 4,000 items; a number which compares badly with the number of new issues.

Dan Lacy has shown how book clubs and paperbacks have changed the manner of distribution in America:

> Both these methods have been overwhelmingly successful in enlarging the audience for books and increasing the number distributed. Last year about 39 million hardbound adult 'trade' (that is, general) books were sold outside book-club channels, together with 26 million higher-priced 'trade' paperbounds sold through bookstores. This contrasts with about 280 million paperbounds sold primarily through mass market channels, and nearly 80 million books distributed through book clubs. This means that of approximately 425 million general adult books sold in the United States last year, about 360 million went through book clubs or mass-market channels. And only 39 of the 65 million moving through traditional channels were hardbound. When it is considered that a very considerable proportion of these 39 million copies were brought by libraries, it becomes evident that four general books out of five bought by or for individual American adults came to them through book-club or mass-market channels (1970, pp. 420–1).

Distribution in Europe is already beginning to follow this threefold pattern. Bookshops, of course, survive, but their health seems to depend on a choice between 'dilution' (i.e. quicker stock turnover, smaller range, stationery carried as well) and that of becoming self-conscious cultural foci (the choice that Escarpit, 1971, recommends). The book clubs have already, according to Gedin (1977) captured very large parts of the Scandinavian and German markets. Their success is in a sense logical. The weakness of book publishing has always been its speculative element; book clubs reduce this element by discovering a particular public taste to which it can cater. As yet the selection made by such clubs has not been systematically studied, but it is likely that they exert increasing power over authors who are presumably encouraged to write in a style that gains 'book-of-the-month' status. It is likely, too, that mass-marketing techniques necessitate a similar attitude on the part of the authors. The great benefit of mass marketing is that it cuts out most of the quite considerable costs of distribution by marketing paperbacks in supermarkets and department stores. But only certain books are likely to be able to sell as large a printing as is required to make a profit. If the rise of book clubs and mass marketing means the end of the bookshop then it is possible that the increased availability of books may be at the expense of the literary culture generally:

> As one veteran hardcover editor put it in New York ... 'It's like asking a salesman to play literary critic. The salesmen run the show in paperbacks and, if they are to say what we publish, too, then they will run the show throughout the book business. Sales potential in both hard and soft covers will be the only standard. A Conrad or a Faulkner, who had low sales even when hardcovers were supreme, wouldn't get published' (Weatherby, 1977).

Public libraries

No study of the role of gatekeepers is complete without some comment on public libraries since these, especially since the important act of 1919, are designed to provide access to books for all the population. One of the ways in which this promise might not be redeemed is as a result of the very books bought; but we are in general ignorant about possible biases. Other factors, however, are important. Bryan Luckham has sensibly suggested that:

> Factors such as accessibility, conformity with social conventions, the degree to which staff can make a bureaucratic impersonal service attractive, the extent of positive discrimination can all have a significant effect upon use (1971, p. 7).

Peter Mann has suggested that libraries would attract more people if they were better laid out so that the choice of book would be made easier for those uninitiated in book culture generally (1971). This might be the case, and interestingly brings to attention the area in which hard knowledge is available, namely that concerned not with the process of selection but with the end result measured in terms of the kind of people who use libraries.

Bryan Luckham's *Library in Society* (1971) provides us with the necessary information about library use. The typical age of users tends to be between 33 and 54. More importantly, users are drawn disproportionately from higher social classes. The following are the percentages of the library users in each social class:

Higher professional	44 per cent
Intermediate managerial	42 per cent
Skilled manual	16 per cent
Manual	10 per cent
Unskilled	8 per cent

(after Luckham, 1971, p. 26.)

The variable which in fact seems most clearly to control library use is in fact education (which itself is related in obvious ways to class). In percentage terms of the social groups concerned, Luckham discovered that library users had these educational backgrounds:

University	74 per cent
Technical College	32 per cent
Grammar/Public School	45 per cent
Secondary Modern	14 per cent

(after Luckham, 1971, p. 26.)

Two final factual findings may be stressed. First, any image of the library user as a relentless bookworm would be mistaken. Luckham shows that those who use the library are frequently also particularly active in community life. Secondly, it is not the case that the use of libraries militates against the purchase of books in any simple way since frequent users also tend to buy books.

This section may be concluded in a manner which points forward to some of the more general questions about literary culture that will concern us in Chapter 8. Usage is clearly limited to certain sections of the population; thus 44 per cent of non-members compared with 27 per cent of members feel that libraries are gloomy.

> Many non-members seem to be saying that the library is not for us and, in a sense, they have a more accurate perception of the situation for, although the doors are open to all, as has been previously demonstrated, the profiles of public library members and users have a marked middle-class bias (Luckham, 1971, p. 82).

Luckham and Mann suggest in a liberal spirit ways in which more people can be attracted into the library. Libraries should perhaps be located closer to shopping areas and should perhaps have coffee facilities; Luckham particularly favours their becoming local centres for Open University courses. But Luckham also suggests that there is perhaps a limit to the numbers who will ever wish to use the library: 'It looks, however, as if for four-fifths of the non-members it is not lack of availability that is a problem. Perhaps they are not deeply interested in reading books at all' (1971, p. 77). If this is indeed the case two possibilities seem open. On the one hand, it can be said that this is 'inevitable' and that the interest of the bourgeoisie as compared to other historically important groups in cultural matters is something to be thankful for. On the other hand, it is possible to argue that cultural matters must be defined on new terms so that all people can participate fully. This is the burden of Raymond Williams's argument that, in a properly constituted society, culture will be 'ordinary'. All depends on the constitution and reconstitution of the society. But the argument of Chapter 8 will be more sceptical in suggesting that the mere destruction of bourgeois literary culture does not mean that something better will automatically replace it. There are reasons to think that the opposite may in fact prove to be the case. But before these reasons are examined it is necessary to find out a little more about the original constitution of the European reading public.

Chapter 7

The reading public

The rise of the reading public

The term 'reading public' can be confusing since it suggests both the ability to read and the habit of reading literature; to avoid confusion here a distinction will be observed between 'reading ability' and the 'reading habit'. But perhaps any discussion of the reading public should begin with a warning against cultural provincialism. This warning consists in the realisation that most societies in history have not depended upon the written word for their functioning. Moreover, some of these societies have been able, as was the case with the Incas, to progress to considerable levels of complexity. In general, of course, we know rather little about such societies historically, although we do know a great deal about those societies of this type that have been visited by social anthropologists. An example of a contemporary non-literate community is provided by the Berbers of North Africa whose language is spoken but not written. For our purposes, however, societies may be divided into those in which there are few readers and those in which there are many. This section is concerned both with explaining the move from the former to the latter, and with noting the relationship between reading ability and the reading habit in the latter.

Societies with few readers tend to justify Lévi-Strauss's view that 'the primary function of written communication, is to facilitate slavery' (1976, p. 393). This view goes against the often embraced idea that 'intellectuals always serve as social critics'. In fact, Max Weber demonstrated in his books *The Religion of China* and *The Religion of India* that literate intellectuals were often perfectly happy, provided their social position was assured, to justify the social order, and, in this sense, to 'facilitate slavery'.

If Max Weber's work is useful in describing societies in which the educated few were able to help in averting social change, its central concern was nevertheless with the forces of social change responsible for the rise of what he termed 'bourgeois rational capitalism in the West'. Weber's argument that the origins of rational behaviour lay in Judaism (1952) is of considerable interest to an understanding of the growth and importance of reading. Weber suggested that the historical novelty of Judaism lay in the insistence that a single God be served whose commands could be seen from the basis of a set of written precepts. The importance of this can be seen at work by reference to defeat in war. Other tribes in Palestine were polytheistic, and tended to adopt the Gods of their enemies when they were defeated – on the grounds that the worth of the various divinities had been shown in battle. Weber argued that the non-integrated, upper-class intellectuals of Israel insisted on different behaviour. These intellectuals became prophets who argued that defeat in war was a judgement of God on the failure of the people to obey his law; they thus called for closer observance of the strict decrees of the single God, rather than the adoption of others' Gods. The importance of Weber's work is that it suggests that there is thus some link between written records (especially when diffused) and rational behaviour. One later analyst has sought to explain this connection by arguing that written tradition alone allows appeal to be made to a single source, and that consequently the presence of such an historical record is likely to be of help to those demanding consistent behaviour (Gellner, 1964, Ch. 8). This case has received further support from Jack Goody in a recent essay concerned with the development of critical science. Goody suggests that it is no accident that:

> major steps in the development of what we now call 'science' followed the introduction of major changes in the channels of communication in Babylonia (writing), in Ancient Greece (the alphabet), and in Western Europe (printing) (1977, p. 98).

Goody offers an explanation of why this should be so. He notes that one critic of a famous recent philosophy of science produced by Thomas Kuhn was able to 'assess' his work as a result of discovering that Kuhn's key term 'paradigm' is in fact used in many, not always compatible, senses. Goody suggests that the ability to discover such ambiguity is necessarily limited to book cultures; oral culture allows ambiguity to escape, whilst textual scrutiny in comparison has almost an inbuilt drive to rationalised consistency.

Weber believed that this rationality could only bear fruit in particular social circumstances. In particular, a social group was needed to act as a 'carrier' of such rationalised and disciplined standards; as is well known, Weber felt that European city merchants naturally formed such a group since their work anyway depended on disciplined work routines. There is some backing for this opinion in the exemplary work of Febvre and Martin dealing with *The Coming of the Book* (1976). These authors also offer support for Weber's contention that the disciplined and rationalised behaviour necessitated by city life encouraged merchants to look favourably upon Protestantism, a religion of the book stressing, precisely, discipline and orderliness. The printers whose career is described by Febvre and Martin were in the vanguard of the struggle for intellectual freedom and gave considerable help, even in the face of persecution, to the new humanist learning. Persecution, however, was unable to limit the spread of new and heretical literature; in France, the expulsion of printers simply meant that smuggling over the border from

Geneva increased dramatically. It is doubtful that any such policy could have worked once the printing press allowed for a massive increase in the number of books available. Febvre and Martin tell us that as many as twenty million books were produced by 1500 by scribes, the scriptoria of monasteries and the earliest of presses; however. this figure is as nothing compared with the one hundred and fifty to two hundred million books produced in the sixteenth century alone. On the basis of this tremendous increase they suggest that had the printing press been available for Jan Hus as it was for Luther, the reformation might well have occurred earlier (1976, p. 288).

The protestant middle-class bearers of rationality considered reading ability important. In the Middle Ages reading ability was not in itself a mark of social status, nor even a necessary achievement for all members of the nobility. Catholicism placed the priest between the believer and God, so that the believer himself had no need to read. Protestantism clashed sharply with this position in emphasising that the believer stood alone before God, and that salvation could only be found through one's conscience – the best guide to which was close study of the Bible. The impact of the religious demand to read the Bible cannot be exaggerated, and can be seen in the manner in which Luther's translation of the Bible and the English Authorised Version of 1611 helped mould their respective tongues. And countries which did have a strong Protestant element were celebrated for the great number who could read; this was certainly true of Scotland and it is one of the crucial facts explaining its intellectual pre-eminence in the eighteenth century. But more mundane factors were also involved. Those who could read were able to plead 'benefit of clergy' when sent to trial, and were consequently able to have their cases heard before the rather more lenient Church Courts (Stone, 1964, pp. 43–4). And more important still was the fight for minds that developed as a consequence of the religious pluralism that the Reformation created. In Stone's words describing the Anglican Church's belated attempt to encourage reading ability for its own purposes:

> It was fear of competition for the minds and loyalties of the poor which prompted some detailed enquiries set on foot by the Anglican hierarchy, and the replies make clear that this was uppermost in the minds of the rectors, vicars, and curates. It was also the explicit purpose of the organisation set up by the Church soon after the first enquiry, as is indicated by its very name: 'The National Society for the Education of the Poor in the Principles of the Established Church'. In 1814, the bishop of London summed up the situation in characteristically military terms: 'every populous village unprovided with a National School must be regarded as a stronghold abandoned to the occupation of the enemy' (1969, p. 82).

The conflict over who should control education continued throughout the nineteenth century and was seen in notably virulent form in the nonconformist attempt to break the Education Act of 1902.

The spread of reading ability may be traced in more detail by looking briefly at some of the milestones in the process as it occurred in England. Undoubtedly the Puritan emphasis on learning helped create the remarkably high level of literacy of early Stuart England. At this period:

> ... it seems likely that in the Tudor and Stuart eras the ability to read was more democratically distributed among the English people than it would again be until at least the end of the eighteenth century. But, since there is a vital distinction between the simple possession of literacy and its active, continual exercise, it does not follow that the reading public in the late sixteenth and early seventeenth centuries was either as large or as socially diversified as the apparent extent of literacy in the nation might suggest. Books were not easy to acquire ... (Altick, 1963, pp. 18–19).

Nevertheless, a privileged few who lived in London were able to undergo a very striking literary education based in large part on the theatre. And even the possession of one book, the Authorised Version of the Bible, allowed for very striking literary achievements. Steiner, indeed, has argued that the possession of the Authorised Version enabled its readers to use a significantly larger vocabulary than do later readers of more varied books:

> The language of Shakespeare and Milton belongs to a stage of history in which words were in natural control of experienced life. The writer of today tends to use far fewer and simpler words, both because mass culture has watered down the concept of literacy and because the sum of realities of which words can give a necessary and sufficient account has sharply diminished (1969, p. 45).

Lest the remarks about 'mass culture' lead to this comment being shrugged off as conservative, it is well to remember that this vitality of language has also been noticed by Raymond Williams from a more radical viewpoint. Williams's explanation is, however, rather different in that he suggests that the vitality sprang from the squeezing of many local dialects into a single national language (1971, p. 242).

Two points may be made about the growth of reading ability at this early period. Typically, the ability to read in the modern world follows from the insistence of a centralised power that all must be skilled in a common language so that the higher levels of communication needed for industrial society become possible. A clear example of such forced mass education in literacy is that of Algeria, which seeks to extirpate French and Berber and to make all its citizens at ease in Arabic. Insofar as the populace willingly choose to participate in such processes it is, as Chinua Achebe has pointed out in many of his novels, because they hope to gain material advantages from, say, having a member of the family at ease in the new official language. In the sixteenth and seventeenth centuries the relatively static nature of the society meant that such material advantages were not typically to be expected, and it is this that makes the seventeenth-century phenomenon all the more striking (cf. Stone, 1969, p. 75). Secondly, this initial point is not such as to suggest that the link between reading and 'rationalised' behaviour already noted did not occur. For it is surely no accident that the political upheavals of the seventeenth century took place at a period when so many could read. Some of the precise reasons for this have been investigated. It has been suggested that unemployed intellectuals themselves formed a significant body of discontent (Curtis, 1963). More important, however, seems to be some sort of general link between growth of reading ability and the growth of independent and critical thought. Tawney remarked upon this spiritual independence of the Puritans, and it was a view widely shared by contemporaries. Indeed, contemporaries were so certain that some connection existed between reading and questioning of the social order that they cut back on the donations to schools in the century following the Restoration. The result was predictable: ability to read was curtailed.

This attack on education was compounded by a rise in the price of books. The plays of Shakespeare had cost but twopence or threepence a copy, but a novel cost three shillings a volume. In Ian Watt's words:

> All but the destitute had been able to afford a penny occasionally to stand in the pit of the Globe: it was no more than the price of a quart of ale. The price of a novel, on the other hand, would feed a family for a week or two (1963, p. 43).

But despite the setback to the numbers able to read it remains the case that many of the characteristics of bourgeois literary culture were first established in the century after the Restoration. Ian Watt has established that the new reading public was predominantly middle class (1963, Ch. 2). The most immediate reason for the rise of this new reading public was probably material: the solitary nature of the very act of reading probably depends on a degree of privacy, and this was achieved by some sections of the middle class in the eighteenth century. This privacy was perhaps especially important for women who, freed to some extent from the early Puritan insistence that only 'improving' works were fit to be read, turned their attention to the reading of novels. As such women had more leisure time, it is not surprising to find one of them, Lady Mary Wortley Montagu, writing to her daughter that 'I doubt not that at least the greater part of these [novels] are trash, lumber, etc. However, they will serve to pass away the idle time . . .' (Watt, 1963, p. 45). The effect of such female readership (and of their servants who were also voracious novel readers) can surely be seen in the development of what Fiedler has often called the 'Sentimental Love Religion' so notably embodied in Richardson's *Pamela*. And it has already been shown that the novel, with its investigations of new social worlds and unfamiliar socialisations, proved eminently suited to a social group whose very life depended on the breakdown of traditional standards and the concomitant increase in social complexity.

The spread of the reading habit among the middle class allowed it to support a periodical literature. Its concern for information and its interest in matters of culture can be seen in such magazines as *The Tatler* founded in 1709. These magazines, archetypally read by barristers, merchants and politicians in coffee houses, proved successful because their editors' 'plain' style combined enlightenment with entertainment. Ian Watt has suggested that the copiousness of eighteenth-century novels, as well as their 'plain' style, can be explained by the reading public's still limited skills. Two factors encouraged the novelist to be long-winded:

> . . . first, to write very explicitly and even tautologically might help his less educated readers to understand him easily; and secondly, since it was the bookseller, not the patron, who rewarded him, speed and copiousness tended to become the supreme economic virtues (Watt, 1963, p. 58).

Such consideration for the audience played its part in a marked increase in the reading habit. This growth can be charted in a number of ways. During the course of the century the reading public grew sufficiently to support nearly eight hundred journals and periodicals. This growth continued in the next century, and was helped significantly by the serialising of novels. Per Gedin has described the impact of this practice in France:

> Successful writers were in a great demand and highly paid, and the constant need for new material from competing journals often resulted in great profligacy. When *La Presse* began publication, its first serial was one of Balzac's novels. At the time, Balzac also agreed to deliver one novel a year to the paper over a period of ten years, from 1837 to 1847. During this period *La Presse* also published the work of Eugène Sue. A rival paper, *La Siècle*, engaged Alexander Dumas, who wrote *The Three Musketeers*, which proved to be an enormous success both for Dumas and the newspaper. Writers could earn tremendous sums. Dumas made 200,000 francs a year and Sue was paid 100,000 francs per novel, while Lamartine amassed 5 million francs between 1838 and 1851. The serial novel was also in fact of decisive financial importance to many newspapers. A serial by Dumas, for instance, increased one paper's circulation by 3,600 to 20,000 (Gedin, 1977, p. 19).

In England the growth of the reading public can be seen from increased book production: 100 books appeared in 1600; 600 in 1820; and 2,600 in 1850.

This is a good moment at which to pause and emphasise that the reading habit was, however many were able simply to read, basically limited to the middle class. This was realised by the *Edinburgh Review*, which also pointed to the lack of interest in reading amongst the aristocracy: 'In this country there probably are not less than 200,000 persons who read for amusement and instruction, among the middling classes of society. In the higher classes there are not as many as 20,000' (cited in Gedin, p. 14). And what was first true in England proved, with the spread of industrialisation, to be true later for other European countries. Gedin has strikingly shown that the successes of such English publishers as Constable and Longman were repeated in Europe by Hachette, Gyldendal and Fischer. He also demonstrates that this bourgeois reading public exhibited a striking degree of homogeneity throughout Europe, both in taste and style of life. And two particular ways in which this bourgeois audience supported a literary culture may be recalled from previous chapters. Firstly, its love of novel reading allowed for a reasonable living for a considerable number of writers. Such a living could be spectacular, but much lesser talents were also able to make some sort of living. Secondly, these habits helped produce a publishing industry that devoted a considerable portion of its output to fiction. In Gedin's words:

> ... stability was the pre-condition for the thriving success of the publishing houses that were founded during the nineteenth century – generation after generation could expand their businesses with ever increasing lists of books that could be reprinted time and time again. For S. Fischer an edition consisted of 1,000 copies, but the number of editions could well run to two figures. The profits earned could be reinvested in the firm – there was little tax to speak of and inflation was an unknown word – and the devaluation of the currency amounted to no more than 1 or 2 per cent per year. The public was loyal and unchanging; the ownership of books carried a certain social status, while reading them was a self evident habit of the whole bourgeois class ... (1977, p. 39).

This bourgeois background of the readers of imaginative works has been emphasised here since it is often overlooked in those works chronicling the spread of reading ability. A typical account is offered by Williams (1971), but undoubtedly the most brilliant is that of Altick in *The English Common Reader* (1963). Altick demonstrates that the common man could have various motivations for wanting to read. Obviously, that complexity of the industrial world that encouraged bourgeois reading also applied to working-class readers. But equally important for some was the desire for political knowledge and discussion. This desire can be seen in the fantastic sales that Tom Paine's *Rights of Man* and Cobbett's twopenny *Political Register* achieved at the end of the eighteenth and the beginning of the nineteenth centuries. Such sales were not perhaps surprising given that the population doubled from 7 to 14 million in the years from 1780 to 1830; the same years also probably saw an increase in readers from 1.5 to 7.8 million. But the desire for information and political discussion probably only touched a few. More important for many in the new miserable industrial towns was a simple desire for the amusement, diversion and comfort to be found in light literature.

Three sets of factors stood in the way of any easy extension of the ability to read in the nineteenth century. The first of these was the clear desire on the part of much of the ruling class to prevent any such extension. This desire represented the most obvious form of censorship, and the reasons accounting for the attitude are well known. On the one hand, and as we have already seen, from the earliest times many have feared that the masses would lower intellectual standards. Lowenthal (1961) has described the eighteenth-century debate with insight. A typical early voice of that period was Steele's, who in 1713 inveighed against the new 'unsettled way of reading . . . which naturally seduces us into as undetermined a manner of thinking' (Steele cited in Watt, 1963, p. 50). On the other hand, the establishment feared that increased reading ability would lead to upheavals comparable to the French Revolution. But despite ferocious attempts to prevent the working class reading what they wanted, the 'March of Intellect' went on; the best that the establishment could hope for was to take control of the development itself. The second general factor that hindered any development only began to change in the second half of the nineteenth century and was simply the terrible material conditions of the Victorian working class. Only with some improvement in housing conditions did reading become a realistic possibility.

The third set of factors involved were at once the most important and the most curious. Middle-class reformers, especially those of Nonconformist descent, were keen to see the ability to read democratised so that the advantages of 'individual self-improvement' could be extended to the masses. However, Altick demonstrates that the very importance attached to reading sometimes prevented its spreading. Where the working classes wanted entertainment, the Nonconformist and utilitarian reformer only offered them the driest of tracts.

> The great majority of the missionaries of reading, who came bearing social soporifics put up by the Church or by Brougham's Society for the Diffusion of Useful Knowledge, simply could not countenance this motive [of simple entertainment]. The result was that their zeal to spread the taste for reading was seriously, almost fatally, misapplied. They preached true doctrine – the rewards that lie in the printed page – but for the wrong reasons. Had they recognised the deep-seated desire for imaginative and emotional release which disposes ordinary people to read, and not insisted upon their own well-meant but unrealistic program, their efforts would have borne far healthier fruit. Any man, observed Wilkie Collins, 'can preach to them [the common people], lecture to them, and form them into classes; but where is the man who can get them to amuse themselves? Anybody may cram their poor heads; but who will lighten their grave faces?' (Altick, 1963, p. 97).

The terrible irony whereby the belief in the importance of reading conspired to prevent its growth can be seen at work in a number of ways. In elementary schools a narrow utilitarian spirit was capable of destroying the first prerequisite for the growth of the ability to read (and certainly of the reading habit), namely, pleasure taken in a book of some sort. Dickens was always aware of the need for pleasure, and satirised the insistence on the provision of mere 'facts' harshly in *Hard Times*. The fate of the Mechanics' Institutes and some of the early Public Libraries was rather similar. These institutions eventually failed in their attempt to draw in working-class readers since they refused to provide the lighter literature that such readers wanted: instead both institutions were left for the middle classes. Finally, it must be noted that the lack of ready availability of books proved a considerable barrier for many years. The cost of the triple-decker Victorian novel was, of course, far too high for normal families. But an equally important obstacle was that the publishers of cheaper editions were, until approximately the middle of the century, unable to get contemporary authors in their series.

All these obstacles were diminished if not overcome by the end of the nineteenth century. Webb (1950) has argued convincingly that approximately 75 per cent of the population could read by the 1880s. Much of this increase was achieved by voluntary effort, and some have in fact seen the Education Act of 1870 as merely an attempt to control a process that had become inevitable. But some of the credit can go to those middle-class reformers who were more tolerant than their brethren. Dickens, outstandingly, took every care to consider his readers' capabilities, and his *Household Words* serialised novels (including *Hard Times*) for as cheaply as twopence an issue. However, probably the crucial breakthrough was made by those publishers who eventually managed to bring out cheap editions. This process had its first successes as early as the late 1820s, but was perhaps symbolised by the appearance of W. H. Smith's cheap yellowbacks on the railway stalls in 1851. Both Altick and L. James have established that the actual taste of those newly able to read was for Gothic and criminal stories. And a particularly profitable popular genre was imitations of Dickens such as *Nicholas Nickleberry* and *Oliver Twiss*. Curiously enough these imitations of Dickens – which made Dickens himself furious – were not noted for their provision of a radical working-class tone. Indeed, somewhat to the contrary, one penny periodical attacked Dickens for views which have since been considered only mildly reformist:

> ... what satisfaction can it give the mechanic, to hear the upper classes attacked in language however eloquent? Does it make their labour lighter or the earth happier? And to what end ought the labours of the philanthropist to tend? (cited in James, 1963, p. 73).

Such readers presumably graduated easily to the type of journalism that Northcliffe finally made general with the establishment of the *Daily Mail* in 1896.

This section can be concluded by offering a final assessment of the relations between reading ability and the reading habit. The achievement of the nineteenth century was in spreading the ability to read, but this did not mean that the reading habit was equally democratised. Certainly some sections of the working class found diversion in popular novels of one sort or another. These stories were often crude, but 'the melodramatic heightening was a natural way to focus the emotional content of the story' (D. W. Harding cited in James, 1976, p. 48). But such readership was only occasional and remained overshadowed by the very large percentage of the population who read no imaginative literature at all. Altick himself admits, when discussing the Mechanics' Institutes, that only a few members of the common people became regular readers:

> Despite their sweeping generalisations, Lovett and his followers actually
> were expressing the feelings not of the rank and file of laborers but of
> the workers' intellectual aristocracy and of their middle-class
> sympathisers. The awakening they did so much to advertise and advance
> – the growing desire for knowledge of all sorts, political, economic,
> scientific, literary – was not a true proletarian phenomenon (1963,
> p. 208).

This ought, in a sense, to have been expected, for, as James has pointed out (1963, p. 25), mere access to culture was not enough in itself – whole conditions of life and work would need to be changed before a real democracy of culture would be conceivable. But the general conclusion must be that the core of the literary reading public was still middle class in composition.

This generalisation may be made with some confidence since this remains the case today even after further improvements in general social conditions. In 1965 European Research Consultants Ltd found that 31 per cent of their sample did not read books at all, whilst a further 32 per cent never used public libraries: only 31 per cent read more than twenty books a year. These figures support the earliest suggestion of Waples, Berelson and Bradshaw that, in rough terms, a third read no books, another third read very few, whilst literary culture, as we know it, is supported by the final third (1940). Other evidence demonstrates the class composition of these percentage groups. It has already been seen that the use of libraries is virtually entirely dominated by the middle class, and Peter Mann has shown that the same is true for a local repertory theatre company (1966 and 1967). Mann has also found that even the readers of the 'popular' Mills and Boon romantic novels tend to be middle class (1971, Ch. 5). Research on the reading public itself is at present rather scarce, but the general picture of middle-class domination is borne out by a piece of research by Michel Zeraffa. His conclusions were that:

> ... there was a great difference between knowing the name of an author
> and reading his work, and also that social class had a definite bearing on

'knowledge' of a writer. Thus, the name of Saint-Exupéry was known to all, while only the 'students' named Maurois, Bazin and Montherlant. Camus, Hemingway and Sartre 'start' from the level of secondary education upwards, while Dumas was 'abandoned' by those who had gone beyond the baccalaureate ... (1976, pp. 141–2).

The implications of this state of affairs will occupy us in the next chapter, but one final admission must be made here. This is simply that we know far too little about the reading public. Mann found that women outweighed men by about two to one in the repertory theatre he studied: is it still the case that women constitute the majority of the reading public? Perhaps more important than such basic social information would be knowledge about cycles of reading (does it reach a peak in the teenage years, fall off in early adulthood and revive in middle age?) and, above all, of literary taste.

The uses of literacy

If some knowledge of the social character of the reading public is vital, it needs to be supplemented by an understanding of what readers bring to and get out of their reading. In other words, the 'uses and gratifications' approach successfully applied in the sociology of mass communications needs to be imported into the sociology of literature. This could well become one of the most important areas of the sociology of literature, but it has so far been rather neglected; consequently the evidence for the following remarks tends to be suggestive rather than conclusive.

The most obvious approach to the question is that of examining the changing reputation that an author undergoes in changed historical circumstances. Lowenthal's study of the reception of Dostoyevsky has already been referred to as a model in this line, but historians of ideas have provided us with others. One of the most impressive is J. R. MacDonald's *Rousseau and the French Revolution, 1762–1791*. Mac-Donald confirms that the simple study of texts is insufficient since men:

> ... may act according to theory, or, having acted, they may explain and justify their actions in terms of those political and social theories which are familiar to them, and to whose authority they can with advantage appeal. ... The generic association between theory and practice is to be found in the conditions of society which give rise to both, rather than in the genesis of the events from theory (1965, pp. 9–10).

This sensible position allows MacDonald to show how creative the eighteenth-century audience was in the uses it made of Rousseau's work. Before 1789 he was little read, but this position changed somewhat when his ideas seemed to become useful for the revolutionaries. Still MacDonald insists that this use of Rousseau was purely pragmatic, and usually such as to distort the objective meaning of his work. He was influential only insofar as he was generally presumed to be in favour of liberty and equality. And the revolutionaries were, interestingly, not alone in attempting to appropriate his work. The counter-revolution-aries pointed out that Rousseau was something of a pessimist who had made a distinction between ideal laws suited for perfect men, and laws appropriate for men in their present debased condition: on this basis they accused the revolutionaries of inconsistent use of their own theories. Further details do not concern us, but the very great merit of this approach is clear. Raab (1964) has produced a somewhat similar study of the reception of Machiavelli in England, whilst G. H. Ford's *Dickens and His Readers* (1965) remains a classic. Many more such studies are needed, especially when it is realised that no detailed work is available on the reception of, for example, Freud and Nietzsche in England.

When we turn away from this historical approach, it becomes apparent that the most immediately interesting ideas about the 'use' of fiction are those of authors themselves. Pre-eminent amongst prac-tioners who have reflected about the 'use' of their work is surely Proust. Roger Shattuck has explained that Marcel in *À la recherche du temps perdu* discovers that, in addition to high society and love, a false idolatry of art itself can prove an obstacle to his search for identity. This idolatry is clearly seen in Baron Charlus, but it also dogs Marcel himself who, from his earliest days of losing himself in romantic novels at Combray, suffers from the debilitating tendency to compare life itself un-favourably with the books he has read. It is this pessimistic experience that leads Proust to openly ask what use novels can serve for those who read them. His answer is summarised by Shattuck thus:

> ... true literature does not divert but directs. The great books affect the economy of life for many individuals by allowing them to achieve personal experience sooner, more directly, and with less groping. This sense, this secret, is what allows certain people to live life at all times as an adventure. Others simply do not recognise that what they are doing, what is going on around them, has any significance as *life* at all. Literature is one of the keys.... Thus Proust could speak of a reader as reading into his own self (Shattuck, 1964, pp. 134–5).

If Proust was aware that a reader of a novel could become the reader of his own self, he was prepared to make another different defence of the value of reading on almost contradictory grounds. One of the central themes of his novel is that of the difficulty of escaping one's own shell of consciousness so that 'things may be experienced as they really are'. At the end of his book Proust realises that art is a privileged way in which such escape is possible:

> By art alone can we get out of ourselves, find out what another person sees of this universe which is not the same as ours.... Thanks to art, instead of seeing only one world, we see it multiplied, and we have as

many different worlds at our disposition as there are original artists
(Proust cited in Shattuck, 1974, p. 160).

These rather abstract suggestions as to the power of reading to both
direct life and to escape the confines of one's own consciousness have
been put in different form by others. Escarpit has argued that the reader
of a fictional book surrenders conscious control and puts his ego at the
mercy of chance; in comparison, the reader of a functional book remains
in control at all times (1966, p. 42). Barbara Hardy's important *Tellers
and Listeners* presents a detailed examination of authors (including
Proust) who openly consider the uses of literature. One point can be
mentioned from Hardy's subtle interpretation. Many of the greatest
authors, among them Cervantes, Flaubert, Homer and Proust, have all
warned that the benefits to be gained from reading depend on avoiding
the Scylla of total absorption and the Charybdis of taking literature only
as entertainment. Hardy suggests on the basis of her reading of authors
concerned with the nature of narration, that a good listener is one who
will accept some distancing from his self but who does so in a controlled
manner (Hardy, 1975, *passim*).

These arguments are rather similar to some typically made about the
importance of the novel. Saul Bellow has argued recently that 'an attack
on the novel is also an attack on liberal principles' (1977, p. 182). This
relation between liberalism and the novel has been put succinctly by
W. J. Harvey:

> We may fairly say that the novel is the distinct art form of liberalism, by
> which I mean not a political view or even a mode of social and economic
> organisation but rather a state of mind. This state of mind has as its
> controlling centre an acknowledgement of the plenitude, diversity and
> individuality of human beings in society.... Tolerance, scepticism,
> respect for the autonomy of others are its watchwords; fanaticism and
> the monolithic creed its abhorrence (Harvey cited in Bergonzi, 1972,
> p. 60).

Bellow's own explanation of the link between liberalism and the novel is
slightly more specific. He argues, firstly, that the very creation of
character in a fictional setting vitiates against certain types of
programmatic pronouncements. Much the same point has been made by
David Caute when noting the lack of creative works produced by Sartre
in his later years (1972, p. 83). Bellow's second point is but a
continuation of the first. Just as the novel will enable us to appreciate
individuality, so the privacy of reading will encourage us to think in
terms other than those officially prescribed:

> At a time when we are wildly distracted and asking ourselves what will
> happen, when the end will come, how long we can bear it, why we should
> bear it, these notions of culture and significant space may seem
> hopelessly naive. But for art and literature there is no choice. If there is

no significant space, there is no judgement, no freedom, and we
determine nothing for ourselves individually (1977, pp. 193–4).

The theory of the novel put forward here goes well with the discussion of
the novel in Chapter 4. Trilling's argument received some support from
studies of 'uses and gratifications' in other media. McQuail, Blumler
and Brown (1972), for example, have been able to show that the socially
and geographically mobile tend to rely heavily on the mass media for
purposes of information about the new social settings that confront
them. Noble has suggested that the same is probably true for the act of
reading:

> If the *faite littéraire* involves a problematic but creative semi-escapist
> response within the role sets of some but not all individuals then novel
> reading (or writing) begins to look rather like a form of vicarious
> exploratory behaviour (1976, p. 222).

Although evidence to confirm this point is not available, it seems likely,
given, for example, the success of such 'provincial' writers as Bennett
and Wells in the Edwardian years when social mobility was rather
strikingly high.

Very few attempts have been made to apply the 'uses and
gratifications' approach systematically to literature. A pioneering
attempt in this direction was made as early as 1940 by Waples, Berelson
and Bradshaw who suggested that five types of gratification (instru-
mental, prestige, reinforcement, aesthetic and respite) were to be found
in the reading of literature. Peter Mann has recently tried to create an
ideal typical model of the uses of reading. He proposes a continuum
from books used for work, via utilitarian reading to social reading of an
'improving' kind (high culture, novel biographies) and eventually to
leisure reading of best-selling genres; he further argues that this
continuum also represents a scale of usage, work books being referred to
frequently, social books being occasionally re-read, whilst leisure books
tended to be dealt with more summarily (1971, p. 7). This is all plausible,
although sadly not as sophisticated as the earlier American model.
Mann has, to his credit, however, a piece of empirical research into
actual gratifications of a particular set of readers. He was allowed to
send questionnaires to the readers of Mills and Boon romantic novels,
and was able to find evidence that clearly contradicted the idea of the
audience being passive fodder ready for manipulation by the establishment. He insisted that the opinionated readers who replied 'are not the
frustrated spinsters of the conventional stereotype of romantic readers'
(Mann, p. 169). The readers were apparently married women of middle-
class social background, who usually had children. Mann concluded
that they 'want a form of fantasy in their reading . . . they have the reality
of a woman's role every day and they look to romances for unreality'
(p. 171). A final piece of empirical research deserving mention is that of
Diana Spearman. Although this was based on a small sample, Spearman

concluded that readers seemed to seek information, models and reinforcement; and she found clear evidence of selective perception on the part of readers (1972).

The discussion so far has been designed to show the benefits that can be gained from an application of the 'uses and gratifications' approach to literature. However, it is only fair to note that this approach has recently suffered criticism inside the sociology of mass communications. These critics have accused the approach of failing to see that 'effects' of mass media are to be found at the level of 'agenda-setting' of issues rather than at the level of changes in individual behaviour. Moreover, they add, the evidence gained about gratifications does not in fact show, as it were, unsullied human nature and certainly does not obviate class analysis – on the contrary, such gratifications as are recorded are held to be the gratifications that people are allowed to feel as their own in present-day society. It is too early to say how much of the 'uses and gratifications' approach will survive these attacks, some of which, it may be noted, are based on circular and unfalsifiable arguments. Whatever the case, two points are worth making in connection with the application of this approach to literature.

Firstly, it is clearly the case that the methods applied by this school are at times far too simple. Spearman admits this in complaining that a brief questionnaire is quite inadequate to capture the possible 'effect' of literature:

> The discovery of such changes, if any, would require continuous contact with each individual over a considerable period of time. Answers which gave details as to how respondents had been affected attributed only good influence to books: none said any piece of fiction had caused a subsequently regretted action, or produced trouble of any kind.
> Moreover, people who answered 'no' may have been influenced without realising it (1972, p. 6).

Something of the same point has been made by a romantic novelist who has complained that the surface of romantic novels hides deeper gratifications:

> I don't really think that romantic novels should be called 'romantic' really. Between you and me, I think they're basically twisted sex stories. I mean it is a bit sadistic, isn't it, to be reading about a man blowing his top because he can't get it (Violet Winspear, cited in Anderson, 1974, p. 243).

What these comments suggest is that 'uses and gratifications' must delve somewhat deeper than it can do by use of the one-off questionnaire. In other words, questions need to be far more carefully thought out so that any gratifications that would not be readily admitted, if there are any, could have a chance to be recorded. This greater sophistication can be imagined without too much difficulty. Certainly the attempt to gain high quality empirical knowledge should be made in preference to retreating once more to the sterile realms of cultural critical observations.

The question of 'agenda-setting', secondly, provides a useful link to the final chapter. What is the impact of the very existence of 'literary culture'? In what ways does such a culture 'prejudge' issues, and what systematic biases may it hide? Such questions are given added point by the fact that the literary audience does exhibit some striking differences from that of the mass media. Whereas the very 'mass' nature of television programmes probably entails a similar response from all viewers, it seems that the reading of literature is sufficiently private to allow class variables to play an important part. Michel Zeraffa has discovered that readers of different social class actually look for entirely different things in the novels that they read. Those of high occupational standing tended, in a survey he conducted, not to identify with particular characters and were much more interested in the fate of the hero than in the story itself; these responses were reversed as the occupational standing of the reader fell (1976, p. 143). Further, the question of value seems central to literary culture, in a way that is not at present the case with the mass media. Few intellectuals feel it incumbent upon themselves to have opinions about television plays, but many would not admit to not having some opinion about certain highly respected novels. Literature is, in a word, more highly regarded than the mass media. Peter Mann found that this high regard could be seen even in the pattern of book purchases. Many buyers of books bought them from a category of seriousness greater than they themselves would wish to read: the giving of books thus seems able to give some sort of vicarious prestige (1971, p. 63). A finding that is close to this is that of Spearman who had no respondent in her survey prepared to admit that books had had a harmful effect on his life (1972). All these points could be summarised by saying that the reading of books seems to be able to attach a cultural prestige that is not given to the viewing of mass media. The question to be addressed in our final chapter follows from relating this fact to the predominantly middle-class character of the reading public: what are the 'effects' of the bourgeois domination of our literary culture?

Chapter 8

The 'effect' of literary culture

The 'effect' of bourgeois literary culture on society can best be discovered by considering the question from two angles. On the one hand, an attempt can be made to assess the impact that culture in a modern society can have as a political force. To consider this question is to take seriously Max Weber's belief that the societies of the West are best described as 'bourgeois', 'rational' and 'capitalist'. Is it then the case that bourgeois culture has helped the stability of this sort of society, and that its demise would seriously affect the larger society? A second dimension of analysis concerns the quality of bourgeois culture. Unless this dimension of analysis is taken into account it becomes impossible to separate some arguments that have a superficial similarity. Any consideration of the 'effect' of a whole culture is necessarily very generalised, and it is quite usual to preface such inquiries with careful methodological warnings and delimitations. But as sociology itself is so full of this rather boring methodological caution, a different tack to the question is taken here by examining, comparing and assessing three actual theories of the state of our culture.

Idealist Marxism, or literature as social control

The first theory that concerns us is that developed in recent years in large part by Marxists. This theory has little affinity to the sort of cultural criticism previously associated with Marxist writings on literature, and this gives it an aura of freshness and originality that is in turn much helped by quite striking empirical work. The origin of the theory may be said to lie in renewed interest in factors in the 'superstructure' that might help to explain the failure of Marx's prediction that capitalist societies would undergo revolution. This line of investigation has spiritual ancestry in the work of the Frankfurt School (perhaps especially Marcuse). However, attention is worth giving to those writers of the French left who have recently given an added sophistication to this general approach; but passing references to the work of Raymond Williams are also designed to show that the theory is more than just another esoteric left-bank product. The argument is, of course, that the element in the superstructure that is crucial and needs to be understood is that of culture. And typically by culture is meant not just the

supposedly 'trashy' debris of 'the culture industry' but supposedly
meritorious 'high' art.

The general theory is elegant and simple. The bourgeoisie is deemed
to pose as protectors of culture, and this pose is held to be of very great
importance in justifying its selfish rule. If this selfishness were seen for
what it is, then perhaps revolution would indeed follow; the bourgeois
ability to give itself the air of defender of something valuable, however,
is judged to have a powerful mystifying effect. Put thus simply, the
theory sounds implausible, but it is one that is often heard. Tawney, for
example, was wont to complain of the mysteries of culture that led to
men 'staring upwards, eyes goggling and mouths agape, at the antics of a
third rate Elysium, and tormenting their unhappy souls, or what in such
conditions is left of them, with the hope of wriggling into it' (1964,
p. 113). This general complaint has, however, led to striking empirical
work by Bourdieu (marxisant rather than Marxist) and Balibar (a
Marxist of Althusserian persuasion). The general theory as to the
function (and thus the political force) of art may be described best by
looking at Bourdieu's work; the question of quality becomes more
clearly focused when turning to Balibar.

Bourdieu's work on the sociology of art is in fact only part of a much
larger project concerned to argue that bourgeois society exerts 'symbolic
violence' in establishing a 'cultural arbitrary' that is not justified by
philosophic reasoning. (See Bourdieu and Passeron, 1977.) However, all
that we need to realise here is that Bourdieu considers that art is a key
means by which the bourgeoisie makes its own rule seem natural. He
argues that this can be seen in the very process of art perception. He
notes sensibly that it is in fact difficult to 'read', say, the pictures of
fifteenth-century Florence without some knowledge of Renaissance
iconography. Bourdieu goes on:

> Since the work of art exists only to the extent that it is perceived, or in
> other words deciphered, it goes without saying that the satisfactions
> attached to this perception . . . are only accessible to those who are
> disposed to appropriate them because they *attribute a value to them*, it
> being understood that they can do this if they have the means to
> appropriate them (1968, p. 601).

The training and educational standards necessary to decipher works of
art would lead one to expect that the difficulty of understanding would
be generally acknowledged. Bourdieu feels that the opposite is the case,
and this horrifies and angers him. He considers that the most
connoisseured are keenest to stress that art is the product of inexplicable
genius, and that it should be capable of moving everyone with any
sensitivity. He acidly comments that:

> . . . silence concerning the social prerequisites for the appropriation of
> culture or, to be more exact, for the acquisition of art competence, in the
> sense of the mastery of all the means for the specific appropriation of

works of art, is a self-seeking silence because it is what m kes it possible to legitimatise a social privilege by pretending it is a gift of nature (ibid., p. 608).

This same point has been made even more bluntly by Williams:

Loutishness is always easy, and there can be few things more loutish than to turn, at the end of a long training, and sneer at those who are just entering on it, and who, harassed and insecure, are making the inevitable mistakes (1958, p. 298).

The bourgeoisie is thus judged to pose as the agent of civilisation while simultaneously making it difficult for the common man to understand culture in order so to preserve its special position. Bourdieu feels that he has found further evidence for this view in an empirical study of the image of museums in various European countries. He is able to show without difficulty that museums are used only by the highly educated higher social classes; in contrast, the mass of the population are afraid of museums and tend to associate them with churches (Bourdieu and Darbel, 1969). This information parallels Bryan Luckham's findings in connection with the image of public libraries (see Ch. 6). But Bourdieu goes further than Luckham in showing no surprise that no attempt is made (at least in Europe) to help the ignorant viewer once he is actually inside a museum.

Bourdieu's position is one that is best seen as moderate in that it seems to suggest that great art should be made available to more than the few. This stance naturally leads to calls for reform and may be contrasted with the more radical versions of the social control theory of art. These extreme versions are the result of accepting what might be called 'the argument for the abolition of bourgeois art on the basis of the sociological premise'; the perfectly accurate premise in question that art is the 'preserve' of the bourgeoisie leads into the very questionable argument that it cannot therefore be of high quality and should be abolished. These extreme versions have as a starting-point the observation that turning art into a barrier of social distinction militates against real artistic appreciation. This argument has been made with force by Goblot (1973), Veblen in his classic *The Theory of the Leisure Class*, Barthes in his *Système de la Mode*, and Toffler in more popular guise in his *The Culture Consumers*. Their general case as to the inevitable lack of appreciation consequent on art being a social barrier depends in large part on the observation that a barrier can be maintained only if taste is made to change quickly. The increased speed with which taste changes in modern society has brought the following condem-nation from one latter-day follower of Veblen:

Novelty, audacity and above all exclusiveness, the bright badge of social enterprise brings a fashion in, and when a hat or shoe has lost its social appeal, when everybody is wearing it, it dies of popularity. Such seems to be the fate of elitist art in our society, the social impulse that made it

fashionable with the few ends by making it vulgar with the many
whereupon the elite must look for something else (Quentin Bell, 1976,
p. 8).

The implication of this is, of course, that the bourgeoisie should not be
seen as the protector of culture in any sense at all.

This view serves as a starting-point for the recent work done by those
French followers of Louis Althusser concerned with the consumption
rather than (as in Eagleton) with the production of literature. This work
seeks to put flesh on Althusser's influential theory of 'ideological state
apparatuses' (1977). The core of this theory, that ideology 'interpellates
the subject', is, despite its superficial complexity, quite simple, and is
moreover already well known to followers of Max Weber: the argument
is that a social order is likely to seek legitimation through its
'apparatuses', whether religious or, latterly, educational. This concern
with the manner in which education, and particularly literature as an
element in education, legitimises society has been hailed as a new
departure by Pierre Macherey who regards it as a way of escaping the
interminable argument about literary quality that has traditionally
dogged Marxist sociologies of literature. The flavour of the approach
can be seen in an answer Macherey gave when asked whether this
approach would not 'reduce' literature entirely, and thus 'leave nothing
behind':

> Why do you want there to be something left? I take your question to
> mean that you fear that if one explains literature through the educational
> apparatus, then literature as such disappears. You see that as a
> reductionist explanation. I think that behind your objection lies the
> assumption of a hierarchical relationship between literary phenomena
> and educational phenomena: literature is something 'great', positive,
> something which endures, but education is very prosaic, something which
> one is obliged to go through which is not enjoyable, which one seeks to
> reject. You think that by analysing literature in terms of the school
> system, one diminishes it, one suppresses what is great in it. Perhaps,
> indeed, one does suppress something – one suppresses what Gorky called
> 'the religion of art'. Perhaps this explanation does strip art of the
> religious, mysterious, transcendental elements which one finds in it, or
> endows it with. But does one lose very much? Doesn't one gain
> something? You think that by explaining literature in terms of the
> educational apparatus, one diminishes it; I have the opposite impression,
> I think one enlarges its significance (1977, p. 5).

Mme Balibar has been the most successful in carrying out this
programme of simultaneously attacking the religion of art whilst
increasing its significance by showing its crucial role in supporting the
bourgeoisie. She begins her case by asserting that the French language
that was formally established in the revolutionary period proved of
service to class interests. The same point has been made by Raymond

Williams who has attacked the pretensions of 'standard' English thus:

> ... its naming as 'standard', with the implication no longer of a common but of a model language, represents the full coming to consciousness of a new concept of class speech: now no longer merely the functional convenience of a metropolitan class, but the means and emphasis of social distinction (Williams, 1971, p. 243).

Mme Balibar's argument about the French language is slightly more complicated and derives from the discovery that the model French of the revolutionary period was based on grammars of the old regime that were centred on the need to translate French into Latin. This was perhaps natural given the numbers of revolutionaries of legal background, but Mme Balibar insists that it was responsible for encouraging the development of different 'levels' of the French language: the higher level was, of course, only comprehensible to the highly educated. (Balibar and Laporte, 1974, *passim*). Her most interesting contribution is, however, the suggestion that the development of these levels depends in large part upon literature. Mme Balibar argues that the new national language encouraged an emphasis on style that can be seen at work in three ways. First, she argues that authors themselves were deeply affected by the new emphasis on style. George Sand, for example, spent much of her time in the early 1840s collecting examples of local speech; but none of this was included in the fictional treatment that she gave of the same rural workers in *La mare au diable* (Balibar, 1977). Much the same is true of Flaubert. Mme Balibar exerts great energies in analysing the styles of speech in *A Simple Heart* and interestingly notes that all, and especially the servant Félicité, speak perfect French. Mme Balibar is not one to shirk sweeping conclusions and concludes in this instance that the bourgeoisie was attempting to make the lower orders mute (1974, p. 159). Secondly, she considers that her examination of the manner in which literature came to be taught in French schools justifies her speaking of different levels of cultural comprehension; in the primary school literary passages are used for dictation and comprehension only, whereas in the secondary school the pupil is introduced to the author's work as a whole and trained to appreciate literary values. Mme Balibar, in other words, offers most interesting accounts of how a text becomes 'literature'. She suggests that the process involved amounts to 'sacralising the text' in a manner that removes it from the comprehension that can only ever result from placing it in its social context. This forms the basis of a third point which is made on the basis of empirical work on the schoolbooks of French children. She is able to show that books which do have radical intent (Zola's novels dealing with alcoholism are an example cited) tend to be 'misread' when they are used as school texts; the emphasis on style apparently replaces the obvious political message (Balibar, 1974, p. 45). In slight contrast, Raymond Williams seems to believe that it is the actual political content of books chosen for school that is important, rather than the more subtle argument of Mme Balibar as to levels of comprehension. Such at least seems to be the conclusion one should draw from his comment that the abstract pessimism of *Lord of the Flies* is 'endlessly prescribed in school examinations, to teach attitudes that rationalise an arbitrary and conventional world' (Williams, 1973, p. 119).

Mme Balibar's work is marked throughout by the feeling that bourgeois mentality is in fact hostile to any real spirit of enlightened culture. The logical consequences of this position have been drawn forcefully by John Berger. In his *Ways of Seeing*, Berger argues that classic genres of bourgeois art – portrait, landscape, and nude – are in large part meretricious; the glorification of power and position these genres are judged to contain is apparently so great as to vitiate their worth (1973). Art, in other words, suffers from too close an association with its social origin; in this case it suffers from the original sin of being a child of the bourgeoisie. Berger carries his position further by presuming that the abolition of the art of the few will help raise artistic standards. Thus he sees 'no reason to lament the passing of the portrait – the talent once involved in portrait painting can be used in some other way to serve a more urgent, modern function' (1972, p. 35). It is in no way surprising to find this position argued by a Marxist – albeit it does go against Marx's own appreciation of bourgeois culture and his belief that its glories would be accommodated in socialist society. For the character of Marxist belief is obviously such as to stress that the future will be an improvement on the past; abolition of an obstacle is surely justified given that human evolution is set on a beneficial, upward course.

Criticism of the theory of art as social control favoured by the bourgeoisie (and of those arguing for 'abolition' in particular) will concern us later. But two general characteristics of the argument as a whole may be noticed immediately. First, the very style of the argument is weak since it does not even attempt to offer a positive characterisation of precisely how non-bourgeois art will actually be better art. This type of argument has been dubbed by Gellner 'all-too-benign':

> What these approaches have in common is that they evade the
> requirement of a positive specification of truth, and pass the buck, with a
> more or less justificatory theory for so doing. They may naively claim
> that once the scales have fallen off our eyes, truth is there, ready to give
> herself; or they may be more guarded, and merely promise that no
> persistent deep obstacles will then remain; or the buck-passing may be
> complex, and they may merely say that the positive specification of
> difficult truths must be left to some other kind of agency ... (1974,
> p. 53).

Secondly, it is worth pointing out how peculiar this is as a Marxist theory. Gone it seems are the days when Marxism was a materialist theory; for we are here presented a highly 'idealist' argument presuming that social cohesion is guaranteed through belief – in this case the mistaken belief of the workers that the bourgeoisie are in fact cultured.

It seems that all those brute material forces that Marxists once discussed so avidly are held down by, of all things, art. This 'idealism with a vengeance' conjures up amusing thoughts of the leaders of the revolution, once aware of the theory described, marching with banners emblazoned with the call for the death of bourgeois high culture. This is an unlikely scenario. And these doubts may soon be much increased as new work on the British class structure seems poised to demonstrate that the privileged are not in fact able to control class recruitment with much success (Bourne, 1979).

The cultural contradictions of capitalism

It is not surprising to discover that the argument that culture supports capitalism is capable of neat reversal. When this is done we have the theory that, in the words of Daniel Bell its most prominent proponent, capitalism is suffering from a 'cultural contradiction'. The fact that the two theories are in contradiction (Bell is conservative and would favour what the Marxists hate, whilst they in turn would presumably favour what he loathes) should not hide the fact that both are united in their idealism: more precisely, both hold that a cultural factor is capable of creating or witholding social cohesion. And there is in fact even more resemblance between the two positions than this. Bell believes that culture did at one time serve as the vital cement for the capitalist order. His argument is that capitalism was able to work as a cultural, economic and political system only as long as the bourgeoisie remained religious. He is not always clear as to the exact benefits conferred by religion (albeit he waxes eloquent on the evil consequences of the decline of religion) but some of his hints in the matter are worth mentioning. Puritanism was important in creating an ethic that bound the three realms noted together. The puritan ethic was of obvious economic value. Bell hints that it was also of political service in encouraging people to make their own fates independent of the state; this was in part responsible for that pluralism of American politics that he feels was responsible for the diffusion of social conflict. But most important of all in Bell's eyes was the ability of religion to provide answers in the cultural realm to 'the existential questions that face all men'. The presence of such answers allowed for rational and restrained social behaviour.

Bell's argument is that the collapse of religion has led to the end of the cohesion of polity, economy and culture; these are now held to run on different principles (1976). The economy is concerned with ever-increasing growth, but is now troubled by excessive wage claims that cause inflation. The polity seeks to establish legitimacy, but is disrupted by insistent demands for participation. Bell, however, is untroubled by these difficulties which he feels could, in principle, be solved. But the image of feckless and instinctual human nature that we have already seen in his discussion of modernism worries him far more. The demonic in man is apparently released when he is no longer assured that life has meaning:

> ... religion ... was a way for people to cope with the problem of death.... When it was possible to believe, really believe, in heaven and hell, then some of the fear of death could be tempered or controlled.... It may well be that with the decline in religious *faith* in the past century and more, this fear of death as total annihilation, unconsciously expressed, has probably increased. One may hypothesize, in fact, that here is a cause of the breakthrough of the irrational, which is such a marked feature of the temper of our time. Fanaticism, violence, and cruelty are not, of course, unique in human history. But there was a time when such frenzies and mass emotions could be displaced, symbolised, drained away, and dispersed through religious devotion and practice. Now there is only this life, and the assertion of self becomes possible – for some even necessary – in the domination over others (1962, pp. 400–401).

The manner in which culture is responsible for releasing the demonic has already been demonstrated. Bell suggests that two processes are at work. On the one hand, modernism has investigated the character of instinct and desire, and has produced an anti-rational aesthetic of its own. But what scares him even more is the democratisation of such theories:

> Traditional modernism, no matter how daring, played out its impulses in the imagination, within the constraints of art. Whether demonic or murderous, the fantasies were expressed through the ordering principle of form. Art, therefore, even though subversive of society, still ranged itself on the side of order and, implicitly, of a rationality of form, if not of content. Post-modernism overflows the vessels of art. It tears down the boundaries and insists that acting out, rather than making distinctions, is the way to gain knowledge. The happening, the environment, the street and the scene, not the object or the stage, are the proper arena for life (1977b, p. 232).

Both Bell's account of modernism and his assumption that most popular literature is antinomian and demanding have already been extensively criticised. But if it be allowed for the sake of argument that there are cultural phenomena such as he describes, several further points can be made. It is not at all clear where Bell's analysis leads to. He offers the hope that:

> Despite the shambles of modern culture, some religious answers will surely be forthcoming, for religion is not (or no longer) a 'property' of society in the Durkheimian sense. It is a constitutive part of man's consciousness: the search for the pattern of the 'general order' of existence; the affective need to establish rituals and to make such conceptions sacred; the primordial need for relatedness to others, or to a set of meanings which will establish a transcendent response to the self

and the existential need to confront the finalities of suffering and death (1976, p. 169).

This seems far too hopeful given that Bell has suggested that nothing less than 'the demonic' has been released by modern culture. Consequently it comes as no surprise to find him contradicting these hopes in asserting that:

> ... the post-modern mood, touching deeper springs of human consciousness, and deeper, more restless longings than the overt political search for community, is only the first act of a drama that is still to be played out (1977b, p. 248).

The other difficulties about Bell's vision of a new religion stand out. The first is that Bell, like Durkheim before him, only considers the socially cohesive function of religion. Religion is in fact more than this, and it seems quite certain that converts are made on account of a new theology rather than because sociologists tell them that religion is good for them. Bell offers no account of the theology of his religious solution. Nor does he answer the nagging doubt occasioned by the comment of Brunschvicg to Aron that 'Nuremberg is religion according to Durkheim, society adoring itself', that the socially cohesive functions of religion may be bought at too great a price. And secondly, Bell's hope of grafting a new religion upon a society otherwise rationalised in Weberian terms is probably illusory. Once rationality is unfettered, it will criticise remorselessly, and such criticism effectively rules out religious answers. Gellner has explained why this is so: he demonstrates that our philosophy is based on an empirical vision (necessary above all for scientific knowledge) which encourages sensitivity to a boundary between fact and theory. As religious belief systems have gained much of their power from jumping back and forth across this boundary, this very injunction is sufficient to undermine their plausibility:

> ... the really important social impact of the ghost [i.e. empiricist] philosophy is the injunction 'Be sensitive to the boundary, and impose consistence with respect to it'; the secondary injunction, 'Down with the transcendent' (*Burn the books containing it* according to Hume, or *Call it technical nonsense* according to Ayer) does not matter much. If the first injunction is well observed and implemented, for all practical purposes the second is already performed and prejudged. In social contexts in which the first is well diffused and respected, it is perfectly possible to play down and, at a superficial level, ignore the second in the interests of courtesy, kindness, tact or antiquarianism. It hardly matters (Gellner, 1974, p. 122).

Bell's argument can be summarised by saying that he thinks Western societies are endangered by their cultures, the products of which he deems to be of uniformly low quality. At this point it is of some interest to note that Bell's own thesis is capable of radical formulation, as has recently been done by Jürgen Habermas in his *Legitimation Crisis*. Roughly speaking, Habermas agrees with Bell that capitalist societies at one time had a certain unity based on common values, and that this unity is now under question. However, as a neo-Marxist he welcomes the breakdown of this unity and consequently deems those cultural phenomena that he holds to contribute to it to be of significant quality. Habermas offers the following account of how the modernist art of the avant-garde came to question the character and life style of the bourgeois class:

> In the artistically beautiful, the bourgeoisie once could experience primarily its own ideals and the redemption, however fictive, of a promise of happiness that was merely suspended in everyday life. But in radicalised art, it soon had to recognise the negation rather than the complement of its social practice. In the aura of the bourgeois work of art – that is, in the cultist enjoyment of the already secularised, museum-like shrine – was mirrored a belief in the reality of the beautiful illusion. This belief crumbled along with the aura. The artistic independence of the formalist work of art *vis-à-vis* the art-enjoying public is the form of the new disbelief; and the gap between the avant-garde and the bourgeoise is its confirmation. Under the sign '*l'art pour l'art*', the autonomism of art is carried to the extreme. The truth thereby comes to light that in bourgeois society art expresses not the promise but the irretrievable sacrifice of bourgeois rationalisation ... (1976, p. 85).

Habermas's whole argument about the legitimation crisis of 'late capitalism' is highly complex and it is difficult to know how much weight to give to the cultural contradiction. But some weight must, in Habermas's eyes, be given, since avant-garde art 'strengthens the divergence between the values offered by the socio-cultural system and those demanded by the political and economic systems' (ibid., p. 86).

The unintended consequence of industrialism

Gellner has commented directly on Bell's thesis as to the cultural contradictions of capitalism. In a discussion of what he judges to be the superficial thought-systems characteristic of a schematised modern California, Gellner argues that:

> A really advanced industrial society does not any longer require cold rationality from its consumers; at most, it may demand it of its producers. But as it gets more advanced, the ratio both of personnel and of their time is tilted progressively more and more in favour of consumption, as against production. More consumers, fewer producers: less time at work, more at leisure. And in consumption, all tends towards ease and facility of manipulation rather than rigour and coldness. A modern piece of machinery may be a marvel of sustained, abstract rigorous

engineering thought; but its operating controls must be such that they can easily and rapidly be internalised by the average user, without arduousness or strain. So the user lives in a world in which most things have an air of easy, 'natural', 'spontaneous' manipulability. And why should not the world itself be conceived in this manner? (1975, p. 448)

Gellner shares Bell's dislike of what he considers facile thought-systems, but his argument is more sociologically traditional than Bell's in refusing to believe that the cultural realm somehow exists on its own, independent of the rest of society. More particularly, Gellner argues that there is a very close fit indeed between the character of 'super-affluent' societies and those cultural styles that Bell has dubbed 'pornotopia'. And an important addition may be made to Gellner's argument, namely that the conditions of super affluence seem to put the very habit of reading at a discount. But before more is said about this, the unintended consequence of industrialism needs to be considered.

The relationship between disciplined behaviour and industrialism is by now well known and fairly well accepted. Weber's sociology describes this connection ceaselessly, and his arguments have recently been taken up by historians (Thompson, 1967). It now seems quite clear that the process of development depends upon the breakdown of customary habits and the rise of abstract and routinised conduct. In a nutshell, the process of industrialism seems to consist in making the world cold, impersonal and rigorous where once it had been warm, human and idiosyncratic. It has been suggested already (in Chapter 7) that the rationalised disciplines necessary for industrialism are themselves the product of book learning. The other side of this coin is that industrialism placed a considerable and continuing emphasis on book culture. This can be seen most spectacularly in science; but for our purposes more important is the fact that an unintended consequence of such discipline was a vigorous literary culture. Some of the ways in which bourgeois literacy proved an enabling factor of importance for literary culture have been noted throughout this book, but can usefully be briefly recalled. Most obviously, this literary culture has been supported by the bourgeoisie, the standard-bearers of industrial civilisation. The bourgeoisie have traditionally formed the core of the reading public, and make fullest use of cultural institutions such as libraries and museums. Moreover, Peter Burke has argued that there is some general connection between cultural flowerings and periods of middle-class dominance. This connection seems particularly clear in fifteenth-century Italy as well as in the Netherlands; the connection receives interesting backing from the decline of Italian culture consequent on the 'refeudalisation' of the great merchant princes in the sixteenth century – as neo-aristrocrats such men seemed no longer able to create, however much they made use of, striking cultural achievements (Burke, 1974, pp. 336-7). In addition to this, it has been established that most authors and critics in English literary history came from educated bourgeois backgrounds. And this general view has also received suggestive support from the deliberations of Proust who was wont to tell his readers of his admiration for the bourgeois virtues of determination, intelligence and work. All of these qualities are contrasted unfavourably with the vain distractions that the aristocratic world (symbolised by Charlus) places in the way of an author; such distractions suffice to destroy the real promise of Swann's career, namely his projected critical monographs. In summary, then, it is being maintained that much of recent European literary culture has been significantly aided by the discipline and rigour of industrial society.

The bourgeois origins of readers and authors offer one line of support for the beneficial but unintended consequence of industrialism. Another line is offered by evidence suggesting that the demise of such discipline in conditions of super affluence seems to be unfavourable to literary culture. This evidence is provided by Gedin, whose *Literature in the Marketplace* argues that the Swedish experience of the effects of super affluence provides a pilot for what will happen elsewhere. Gedin demonstrates convincingly that the base of the literary culture, far from being extended in consequence of the social reforms that have marked Swedish social politics, has recently been seriously undermined. People read less, and it has become more difficult to publish original imaginative work, particularly first novels. Gedin offers two reasons additional to that offered by Gellner for what he, following Mrs Leavis, terms 'the disintegration of the reading public'. Firstly, the benefits of super affluences are such as to undermine the reading habit:

> Books are no longer a self-evident part of the way of life of a particular class, but represent only one of many possibilities. . . . Those who have a camera, fishing equipment, a dog, boat, piano, gramophone, have, of course, less time left to read books (Gedin, 1977, p. 58, 107).

In the case of Sweden, however, a more important factor seems to have been those political decisions on cultural policy undertaken on the basis of the realisation that the bourgeoisie alone makes full use of cultural institutions. Gedin notes that the discovery that larger numbers of people did not become more interested in culture as they became more affluent did not lead to the simple deduction that only smaller groups were interested in such matters. Nobody was apparently willing to accept this conclusion: 'instead they began to question the traditional definitions of culture' (Gedin, 1977, p. 137). In 1969 the Central Committee of the Social Democratic Party insisted that it was wrong to 'describe people who . . . go berry-picking, with a high degree of unity and interaction, as "culturally impoverished", without being guilty at the same time of a gross underestimation of the value of these people's lives' (ibid., p. 141). Whilst this is of course in one sense correct, Gedin suggests that its effect has been, not to consider 'high culture' as equal to other social activities, but to treat it, because it is the preserve of a few, as worse.

Gellner's general position may be further compared with that offered by the first two theories. The theory of art as social control seems more capable of destroying what is perhaps but a limited culture than of offering any guarantee that it will create anything better; Gellner's vision of a possible future, especially when backed up by Gedin's description of the Swedish experience, should make us very suspicious of this position. Gellner certainly has no love of new and facile cultural phenomena produced by super affluent societies, but his dislike differs from the hatred exhibited towards them by Bell in that it is based on a horror of the complete innocuousness of such styles. To some extent Bell is his own best critic in this matter when he remarks that:

> Today one finds asceticism in revolutionary movements and
> revolutionary regimes. Puritanism, in the psychological and sociological
> sense, is to be found in Communist China and in the regimes which fuse
> revolutionary sentiment with Koranic purposes, as in Algeria and Libya
> (1976, p. 82).

Bell fails to see that this admission undermines his whole argument as to the dangers implicit in modernism and its popularisation. Revolutions are indeed made or led by (probably necessarily) intolerant elites; it is hard to see the antinomian, sex-ridden and self-indulgent creatures who are the result, in Bell's eyes, of modern culture as capable of destroying anything. The reason for this is surely that our societies are legitimised in the last analysis by the 'material' factor of their ability to produce wealth. It is doubtful whether any societies cohere merely by virtue of belief, and almost certain that this is not the case with modern Western society – indeed, Michael Mann (1970) has argued convincingly that the stability of liberal democracies depends on the absence of any strongly held beliefs. This awareness distinguishes Gellner's position from the first two theories, and it thus allows him to consider the new 'pseudo cultures' as basically irrelevant to any larger questions of social stability. In a characteristic passage, he suggests that:

> The new pseudo-cultures continue to rely on this technology for a
> standard of living to which its members are accustomed and which they
> are certainly not seriously prepared to forego. These monks go out to an
> air conditioned wilderness. It is all rather like Tolstoy re-enacting
> peasant life in one part of his house and maintaining his habitual
> standards in another. So many Tolstoys these days . . . (1974, pp. 192–3).

The three theories considered can be summarised by means of the following diagram. Naturally the diagram loses some important details of the arguments, but is nevertheless useful in showing up basic differences. It should be noted that the terms 'super affluence' and 'industrial' are those used to describe Gellner's position. Bell would feel that 'post-industrial' and 'capitalist' capture his argument more accurately, whilst Habermas typically uses 'late capitalist' and 'capitalist' to describe his assessment of the change in Western society.

Finally, it can be seen from the diagram that no similar distinction applies to the first theory which, presumably, considers capitalist reality unchanged.

Table 8.1

	Impact of culture	Quality of culture	
		Industrial society	Super-affluence
Art as social control	Powerful support given to social order by mystifying masses	Weaker versions tend to regret benefits of literature not available for all, stronger versions consider culture of poor quality because only ever embraced for purposes of social distinction	
Cultural contradiction	In capitalist society supported social order, but now capable of playing a leading part in destruction of social order	Of high quality since Bell thinks highly of the ability of religion to join polity, economy and culture. Habermas agrees with diagnosis but as neo-Marxist dislikes the reality and so thinks of low quality	Bell loathes the release of demonic caused by 'pornotopia'. Habermas approves and judges the attack on capitalism to be of high quality
Unintended consequence	No very great impact at any time since societies gain legitimacy in more basic ways	Unintended consequence of discipline seen in rigorous and significant bourgeois literary culture	A low quality since facile; in this exactly suits the 'spontaneity' encouraged by super-affluence

Conclusion

The argument made in this chapter, and indeed to some extent throughout the book, is that bourgeois literacy helped to create a significant literary culture. This position is not usually upheld – indeed it is more usual to hear of the difficulties created by the bourgeois frame of mind. Undoubtedly these existed, and can be seen, for example, at work in an early entry in one of the greatest of puritan journals of self-examination, namely Beatrice Webb's diary:

> I have been haunted by the vulgar wish to create a novel. There is intense attractiveness in the comparative ease of descriptive writing. Compare it with work in which movements of commodities, percentages, depreciations, averages and all the ugly horrors of commerical facts are in the dominant place, and must remain so if the work is to be worthful

. . . (but) what have the whole lot of (novels) accomplished . . . (Beatrice Webb cited in Letwin, 1962, p. 354).

Such quotations can all too easily lead to the belief that the imagination is virtually socially unlocatable and that all we can do is to wait humbly for it to appear. It is indeed true and it has been admitted here that we know virtually nothing about the literary impulse, and it is also of course true that not every element of middle-class mentality favoured literature. Nor finally could it be maintained that bourgeois literary culture is the only one of distinction in history. But nevertheless the merits of discipline and the importance placed on the reading habit seem in the end important and too often neglected; if these factors perhaps destroyed Beatrice Webb's literary prospects, they certainly helped channel the imagination of George Eliot and, despite appearances, that of Dickens. Certainly the merits of 'Bourgeois Literacy' far outweigh the usual Marxist analysis of 'Bourgeois Literature' – although, as has been noted, Marx proves something of an exception to his followers in his own broad culture and in his insistence that the virtues of the bourgeoisie would be accommodated, and certainly not 'abolished', in socialism. If these general points are by now clear, the novelty of the argument being made perhaps justifies further consideration, and this can be given by comparing it with Raymond William's celebrated advocacy of a common culture.

The demand for a common culture has been something of a constant amongst the neo-populist strand in English thought that runs from Cobbett via Dickens, Chesterton and Tawney to Williams. Williams's own advocacy of the cause is extremely subtle and is, of course, part of a much wider social philosophy. Nevertheless, his attack on the ideas of 'bourgeois literature' at the end of his *Culture and Society* conveniently provides a point of comparison.

Williams attacks the concept of 'bourgeois literature' on the grounds that this description is both false and elitist:

> . . . it is important to remember that, in judging a culture, it is not enough to concentrate on habits which coincide with those of the observer. To the highly literate observer there is always a temptation to assume that reading plays as large a part in the lives of most people as it does in his own. . . . But, for good or ill, the majority of people do not yet give reading this importance in their lives; their ideas and feelings are, to a large extent, still moulded by a wider and more complex pattern of social and family life. There is an evident danger of delusion, to the highly literate person, if he supposes that he can judge the quality of general living by primary reference to the reading artefacts (1958, p. 297).

The last comment in this passage shows Williams preparing to introduce a distinction in the meaning of the word culture. His argument is that the working class have produced a culture (i.e. a way of life opposed and superior to the bourgeois ideal of individualism) but that they have spent less time producing 'culture' (in the sense of artistic artefacts). Williams makes his point thus:

> We may now see what is properly meant by 'working-class culture'. It is not proletarian art, or council houses, or a particular use of language; it is, rather, the basic collective idea, and the institutions, manners, habits of thought, and intentions which proceed from this. Bourgeois culture, similarly, is the basic individualist idea and the institutions, manners, habits of thought and intentions which proceed from that . . . The working class, because of its position, has not, since the Industrial Revolution, produced a culture in the narrower sense. The culture which it has produced, and which it is important to recognize, is the collective democratic institution, whether in the trade unions, the cooperative movement, or a political party (1958, p. 313).

The accuracy of Williams's portrait of the English working class as the carriers of this communitarian ideal does not really concern us. But the corollary to it – that when this ideal is institutionalised a common culture in both senses will be possible – does. But one last point should be noted. Williams claims that the stress on 'bourgeois culture' is politically unfortunate since:

> It can, for example, seriously mislead those who would now consider themselves as belonging to the dominant class. If they are encouraged, even by their opponents, to think of the existing culture (in the narrow sense) as their particular product and legacy, they will deceive themselves and others. For they will be encouraged to argue that, if their class position goes, the culture goes too . . . (1958, p. 308).

This last striking quotation necessitates asking whether the position advanced in this book is somehow necessarily elitist. An answer to this is perhaps more complex than Williams often allows.

For much of the argument that has been made here agrees with the very sensible points that Williams makes. In particular, it is indeed 'loutish' of the culturally privileged to refuse to encourage the spread of the ability to appreciate culture. This loutishness can often be seen in the glorification of unnecessary complexities of post-modernism and in the mistaken scorn poured, even by as intelligent a critic as Gedin, on popular literature. This limitation on the reading habit (about which the social control theory is surely correct) is particularly unfortunate, but it is a measure of the complexity of the situation that this limitation in part is the result of good intentions. This was certainly the case historically when the desire to force improving literature on the masses must have deadened the appeal of literature for many. And research done at Sheffield University suggests that 'limitation via good intentions' continues today. Peter Mann has discovered that forcing the 'classics' on teenagers when they are too young has counter-productive effects, and that lighter romantic literature is in itself no bar to the development of more mature tastes later (Mann, 1978). This drift away from reading in early teenage years seems quite widespread (Whitehead, 1977), and will only be avoided when these wise words of Dr Johnson are observed:

> I would let [a boy] at first read *any* English book which happens to engage his attention; because you have done a great deal when you have brought him to have entertainment from a book. He'll get better books afterwards (Dr Johnson cited in Altick, 1963, pp. 371–2).

All these points could be summed up by saying that there is nothing in the case made here for bourgeois literacy that goes against the desire for a greater spreading of the reading habit. And to this agreement with Williams on the matter of democracy can be added another. Whatever the value of literary achievement, it is doubtful whether the state of society should be judged with reference to this alone. Civilisation depends on virtues such as liberty and tolerance and a decent standard of living. If it is the case that Eastern Europe produces striking literary works by dissidents, this in no way makes up for its other deficiencies.

This last point could be put another way by saying that literature is not everything. But Williams's redefinition of culture (curiously similar to that of the Swedish Social Democratic Party in 1969) runs the danger of making literature almost nothing. The arguments in Chapter 7 concerning the 'uses of literacy' go against this. We would all, and perhaps especially sociologists, be disadvantaged if the 'freedom to investigate' characteristics of literature were diminished, however worthy the communitarian ideals created by the working class might be. Williams at times slides from dissatisfaction with an imperfect, because not generally shared, culture to something closer to dislike. This is combined with considerable optimism about the future in a manner which allows him to overlook the actual achievements of bourgeois culture. Although I share Williams's hopes for a situation in which the reading habit will be widespread, a certain scepticism about his optimism makes me much more appreciative of the achievements of bourgeois literacy, limited though these were. This scepticism comes from the realisation that the future may, if Gellner and Gedin are right, be worse rather than better. And this argument does not entail any of the unfortunate policy consequences in favour of class privileges that Williams abhors. For the possibility is that the bourgeoisie itself may lose its interest in literary culture. It is conceivable that the reading habit itself is on the wane. Some writers, notably McLuhan, have welcomed this and have argued that the move from the 'cold' age of print to the 'warm' age of electronic media will allow new and more democratic art forms to emerge. It is a measure of our ignorance that such theories are very hard to assess. Opinions can differ as to whether the artistic impulse is irrepressible, and whether it will suffer from the demise of bourgeois discipline or find new enabling factors of importance. Whatever the eventuality, however, the merits of the disciplined, rigorous and individualistic culture of industrial society should not be dismissed lightly or without understanding.

References

Abrams, P. (1976) 'Sociology and the unstatable', *New Universities Quarterly*, **31**.
Adorno, T. and **Horkheimer, M.** (1977) 'The culture industry', in Curran, J., Gurvitch, M., and Woollacott, J. (eds), *Mass Communication and Society*, Edward Arnold, London.
Albrecht, M. C. (1956) 'Does literature reflect common values?', *American Sociological Review*, **21**.
Althusser, L. (1977) *Lenin and Philosophy and Other Essays*, New Left Books, London.
Altick, R. D. (1962) 'The sociology of authorship', *New York Public Library Bulletin*.
Altick, R. D. (1963) *The English Common Reader*, University of Chicago Press, Chicago.
Alvarez, A. (1974) *The Savage God*, Penguin, Harmondsworth, originally published Weidenfeld and Nicolson, 1971.
Anant, V. (1976) 'A woman's own world', *New Society*, **35**.
Anderson, R. (1974) *The Purple Heart Throbs*, Hodder and Stoughton, London.
Arendt, H. (1968) *Antisemitism*, Viking Press, New York.
Auerbach, E. (1974) *Mimesis*, Princeton University Press, Princeton.
Balibar. R. (1974) *Les Français fictifs*, Hachette, Paris.
Balibar, R. (1977) 'Un cas de travail litéraire en France: La mare au diable de George Sand, 1846', Speech at Conference on Sociology of Literature, University of Essex.
Balibar, R. and **Laporte, D.** (1974) *Le Français national*, Hachette, Paris.
Baron, H. (1955) *The Crisis of the Early Italian Renaissance*, 2 vols, Princeton University Press.
Barthes, R. (1977a) *Image-Music-Text*, Fontana, London.
Barthes, R. (1977b) *Sade, Fourier and Loyola*, Jonathan Cape, London.
Bell, D. (1962) *The End of Ideology*, Collier Books, New York.
Bell, D. (1976) *The Cultural Contradictions of Capitalism*, Heinemann, London.
Bell, D. (1977a) 'The return of the sacred?', *British Journal of Sociology*, **28**.
Bell, D. (1977b) 'Beyond modernism, beyond self', in Anderson, Q., Donadio, S., and Marcus, S. (eds), *Art Politics and Will*, Basic Books, New York.
Bell, Q. (1976) *A Demotic Art*, University of Southampton Press, Southampton.
Bellow, S. (1975) *Humboldt's Gift*, Secker and Warburg, London.
Bellow, S. (1977) 'Writer and literature in American society', in Ben-David, J., and Clark, T. N. (eds), *Culture and Its Creators*, University of Chicago Press, Chicago.
Benjamin, W. (1973) *Charles Baudelaire*, New Left Books, London.
Berelson, B. and **Salter, P. J.** (1946) 'Majority and minority Americans: an analysis of magazine fiction', *Public Opinion Quarterly*, **10**.
Berger, J. (1972) *The Look of Things*, Penguin, Harmondsworth.
Berger, J. (1973) *Ways of Seeing*, Penguin, Harmondsworth.
Berger, J. (1976) 'Millet and a Third World', *New Society*, **35**.
Bergonzi, B. (1972) *The Situation of the Novel*, Penguin, Harmondsworth.
Bigsby, C. W. E. (ed.) (1976) *Approaches to Popular Culture*, Edward Arnold, London.
Billington, M. (1976) 'Article on censorship', *Guardian,* 17 Dec.
Blount, T. (1971) *Introduction to* David Copperfield (Dickens), Penguin, Harmondsworth.
Booth, W. (1966) *The Rhetoric of Fiction*, University of Chicago Press, Chicago.
Boswell, J. (1960) *Life of Johnson*, Oxford University Press, Oxford.
Bourdieu, P. (1968) 'Outline of a sociological theory of art perception', *International Social Science Journal*, **20**.

Bourdieu, P. and Darbel, A. (1969) *L'Amour de l'art*, Minuit, Paris.
Bourdieu P. and Passeron, C. (1977) *Reproduction*, Sage, London.
Bourne, R. (1979) 'The snakes and ladders of the British class system', *New Society*, **47**.
Bradbury, M. (1971) *The Social Context of Modern English Literature*, Blackwell, Oxford.
Bradbury, M. and McFarlane, J. (eds) (1976) *Modernism 1890–1930*, Penguin, London.
Bradbury, M. and Wilson, B. (1971) Introduction to Escarpit, R. (1971).
Brecht, B. (1974) 'Against Georg Lukács', *New Left Review*, **84**.
Bullock, A. (1976) 'The double image', in Bradbury, M. and McFarlane, J.
Burke, P. (1974) *Tradition and Innovation in Renaissance Italy*, Fontana, London.
Burns, E. and T. (eds) (1973) *The Sociology of Literature and Drama*, Penguin, Harmondsworth.
Caute, D. (1972) *The Illusion*, Panther, London.
Chesterton, G. K. (1905) *Heretics*, Watts, London.
Chesterton, G. K. (1913) *The Victorian Age in Literature*, John Lane, London.
Cruttwell, P. (1960) *The Shakespearean Moment*, Random House, New York.
Culler, J. (1975) *Structuralist Poetics*, Routledge and Kegan Paul, London.
Curtis, M. (1963), 'The alienated intellectuals of early Stuart England', *Past and Present*, **23**.
Deleuze, G. (1973), *Proust and Signs*, Allen Lane, London.
Derrida, J. (1976) *Of Grammatology*, translated from the French by G. C. Spivak, John Hopkins University Press, Baltimore.
Duvignaud, J. (1972) *The Sociology of Art*, Paladin, London.
Eagleton, T. (1970) *Exiles and Emigrés*, Chatto and Windus, London.
Eagleton, T. (1976a) *Criticism and Ideology*, New Left Books, London.
Eagleton, T. (1976b) *Marxism and the Literary Critic*, Methuen, London.
Escarpit, R. (1966) *The Book Revolution*, Harrap and UNESCO, London.
Escarpit, R. (1971) *The Sociology of Literature*, Cass, London.
Febvre, L. and Martin, H. (1976) *The Coming of the Book*, New Left Books, London.
Fiedler, L. (1965) 'The new mutants', *Partisan Review*, **32**.
Fiedler, L. (1969) *Love and Death in the American Novel*, Dell, New York.
Fiedler, L. (1972) *The Return of the Vanishing American*, Paladin, London.
Fiedler, L. (1974) 'Death and rebirth of the novel', in Halperin, J.
Filmer, P. (1969) 'The literary imagination and the explanation of socio cultural change in modern Britain', *European Journal of Sociology*, **10**.
Findlater, R. (1963) *What are Writers Worth?*, Society of Authors, London.
Findlater, R. (1966) *The Bookwriters, Who are They?*, Society of Authors, London.
Fletcher, J. and Bradbury, M. (1976) 'The introverted novel' in Bradbury, M., and McFarlane, J.
Ford, G. H. (1965) *Dickens and His Readers*, Norton Books, New York.
Gadamer, H. G. (1975) *Truth and Method*, Sheed and Ward, London.
Gans, H. (1974) *Popular Culture and High Culture*, Basic Books, New York.
Gedin, P. (1977) *Literature in the Marketplace*, Faber and Faber, London.
Gellner, E. (1964) *Thought and Change*, Weidenfeld and Nicolson, London.
Gellner, E. (1974) *Legitimation of Belief*, Cambridge University Press, Cambridge.
Gellner, E. (1975) 'Ethnomethodology: the reenchantment industry or the Californian way of subjectivity', *Philosophy of Social Science*, **5**.
Giddens, A. (1976) *New Rules of Sociological Method*, Hutchinson, London.
Goblot, E. (1973), 'Cultural education as a Middle Class Enclave', in Burns, E. and T.
Goldmann, L. (1970) *The Hidden God*, Routledge and Kegan Paul, London.
Goldmann, L. (1976) *Towards the Sociology of the Novel*, Tavistock, London.
Gombrich, E. (1963) *Art and Illusion*, Phaidon, London.
Gombrich, E. (1965) 'Visual discovery through art', *Arts Magazine*, **40**.
Gombrich, R. (1974) 'Huizinga and "Homo Ludens"', *Times Literary Supplement*, 4 Oct.
Goodlad, S. (1971) *A Sociology of Popular Drama*, Heinemann, London.
Goody, J. (ed.) (1977), 'Literacy, criticism and the growth of knowledge', in Ben-David, J. and Clark, T. N. (eds), *Culture and Its Creators*, University of Chicago Press, Chicago.
Green, M. (1977) *Children of the Sun*, Constable, London.

Greer, G. (1971) *The Female Eunuch*, Paladin, London.

Griest, G. (1970) *Mudie's Circulating Library and the Victorian Novel*, Indiana University Press, Indiana.

Gross, J. (1973) *The Rise and Fall of the Man of Letters*, Penguin, Harmondsworth, originally published Weidenfeld and Nicolson, 1969.

Habermas, J. (1976) *Legitimation Crisis*, Heinemann, London.

Hall, J. A. (1977) 'Politics and sincerity: the 'Existentialists' vs. Goffman and Proust', *Sociological Review*, **25**.

Hall, S. and **Whannel, P.** (1964) *The Popular Arts*, Hutchinson, London.

Halperin, J. (ed.) (1974) *The Theory of the Novel*, Oxford University Press, Oxford.

Hardy, B. (1975) *Tellers and Listeners*, Athlone Press, London.

Hegel, G. W. F. (1920) *Philosophy of Fine Art*, Allen and Unwin, London.

Heiserman, A. (1976) *The Novel Before the Novel*, University of Chicago Press, Chicago.

Hill, C. (1977) *Milton and the English Revolution*, Faber and Faber, London.

Hirsch, E. D. (1975) *Validity in Interpretation*, Yale University Press, New Haven.

Hobsbawm, E. (1964) *Labouring Men*, Weidenfeld and Nicolson, London.

Hoggart, R. (1973) *Speaking to Each Other*, 2 vols, Penguin, Harmondsworth, originally published Chatto and Windus, 1970.

James, L. (1963) *Fiction of the Working Man*, Oxford University Press, Oxford.

James, L. (ed.) (1976) *People into Print*, Allen Lane, London.

Jarvie, I. C. (1970) *Towards a Sociology of the Cinema*, Routledge and Kegan Paul, London.

Jay, M. (1973) *The Dialectical Imagination*, Heinemann, London.

Josipovici, G. (1973) *The World and the Book*, Paladin, London.

Kermode, F. (1967) *The Sense of an Ending*, Oxford University Press, Oxford.

Kermode, F. (1971) *Romantic Image*, Fontana, London.

Kermode, F. (1974) 'The novel and narrative', in Halperin, J.

Kermode, F. (1977) 'Can we say anything we like?', in Ben-David, J., and Clark, T. N. (eds), *Culture and Its Creators*, University of Chicago Press, Chicago.

Kramer, J. (1970) 'The social role of the literary critic', in Albrecht, M. C., Barnett, J. H., and Griff, M. (eds), *A Sociology of Art and Literature*, Duckworth, London.

Kristeva, J. (1976) *Le texte du Roman*, Mouton, Hague.

Lacan, J. (1977) *Ecrits: A Selection*, translated by Alan Sheridan, Tavistock, London.

Lacy, D. (1970) 'The economics of publishing, or Adam Smith and literature', in Albrecht, M. Barnett, J. H., and Griff, M. (eds), *A Sociology of Art and Literature*, Duckworth, London.

Lane, M. (1970a) 'Books and their Publishers' in Tunstall, J. (ed.), *Media Sociology*, Constable, London.

Lane, M. (1970b) 'Publishing house managers, publishing house organization and role conflict', *Sociology*, **4**.

Laslett, P. (1976) 'The wrong way through the telescope', *British Journal of Sociology*, **27**.

Laurenson, D. (1969) 'A sociological study of authorship', *British Journal of Sociology*, **20**.

Laurenson, D. and **Swingewood, A.** (1972) *The Sociology of Literature*, Paladin, London.

Lazarsfeld, P., Berelson, B. and **Gaudet, H.** (1944) *The People's Choice*, Duell, Sloan and Pearce, New York.

Leavis, F. R. (1930) *Mass Civilization and Minority Culture*, Minority Press, Cambridge.

Leavis, F. R. (1972) *The Great Tradition*, Penguin, Harmondsworth, originally published Chatto and Windus, 1948.

Leavis, F. R. (1975) *The Living Principle*, Chatto and Windus, London.

Leavis, Q. D. (1938) *Fiction and the Reading Public*, Chatto and Windus, London.

Lerner, L. (1977) 'The triumph of Scylla', *Encounter*, **49**.

Letwin, S. R. (1962) *The Pursuit of Certainty*, Cambridge University Press, Cambridge.

Lévi-Strauss, C. (1965) *Tristes Tropiques*, Viking Press, New York, Penguin, London (1976). First published 1955 in French.

Lodge, D. (1966) *The Language of Fiction*, Edward Arnold, London.

Lodge, D. (1976) 'The language of modernist fiction' in Bradbury, M., and McFarlane, J.

Lodge, D. (1977) *Modes of Modern Writing*, Edward Arnold, London.

Lopez, R. S. (1952) 'Hard Times and investment in culture', in W. K. Ferguson *et al The Renaissance*, Harper, New York.

Lowenthal, L. (1961) *Literature, Popular Culture and Society*, Prentice Hall, New Jersey.

Lowenthal, L. (1964) 'The reception of Dostoyevsky's work in Germany, 1880–1920', in Wilson, R. N. (ed.), *Arts in Society*, Prentice Hall, New Jersey.

Lucas, J. (ed.) (1971) *Literature and Politics in the Nineteenth Century*, Methuen, London.

Luckham B. (1971) *Library in Society*, Library Association, London.

Lukács, G. (1950) *Studies in European Realism*, Hillway, London.

Lukács, G. (1963) *The Meaning of Contemporary Realism*, Merlin, London.

Lukács, G. (1971) *The Theory of the Novel*, M. I. T. Press, Massachusetts.

Macherey, P. and Balibar, E. (1974) 'Presentation' in Balibar, R. (1974).

Macherey, P. (1968) *Pour une théorie de la production littéraire*, Maspero, Paris.

Macherey, P. (1977) Interview, *Red Letters*, 5.

MacDonald, J. R. (1965) *Rousseau and the French Revolution, 1762–1791*, Athlone Press, London.

MacKenzie H and J. (1973) *The Time Traveller*, Weidenfeld and Nicolson, London.

McQuail, D. (1970) 'The audience for television plays', in Tunstall, J. (ed.), *Media Sociology*, Constable, London.

McQuail, D. (1972) *Towards a Sociology of Mass Communications*, Collier Macmillan, London.

McQuail, D., Blumler, J. G. and Brown, J. R. (1972) 'The television audience: a revised perspective', in McQuail, D. (ed.), *Sociology of Mass Communications*, Penguin, Harmondsworth.

MacRae, D. G. (1970) 'Populism as an Ideology', in Gellner, E., and Ionescu, G. (eds), *Populism*, Weidenfeld and Nicolson, London.

Mann, P. (1966) 'Surveying a theatre audience: methodological problems', *British Journal of Sociology*, 17.

Mann, P. (1967) 'Surveying a theatre audience: findings', *British Journal of Sociology*, 18.

Mann, P. (1971) *Books, Borrowers and Buyers*, Andre Deutsch, London.

Mann, P. (1978) 'Teenage girls and fiction reading in rural and urban areas', *International Journal of Environmental Studies*, 11.

Martin, W. (1967) *The New Age under Orage*, Manchester University Press, Manchester.

Marx, K. and Engels, F. (1947) *Literature and Art*, International Publishers, New York.

Michels, R. (1949) *Political Parties*, Free Press, Glencoe, Illinois.

Noble, T. (1976) 'Sociology and literature' *British Journal of Sociology*, 27.

Orwell, G. (1970) *The Collected Essays, Journalism and Letters of George Orwell*, Penguin, Harmondsworth.

Painter, S. (1959, 1965) *Marcel Proust*, 2 vols, Chatto and Windus, London.

Pascal, R. (1977) 'The *Magic Mountain* and Adorno's critique of the traditional novel', in Bullivant, K. (ed.), *Culture and Society in the Weimar Republic*, Manchester University Press, Manchester.

Poggioli, R. (1968) *The Theory of the Avant-Garde*, Harvard University Press, Cambridge, Massachusetts.

Popper, K. R. (1972) *Objective Knowledge*, Oxford University Press, Oxford.

Potter, D. (1977) 'The Philistine Stigma', *Guardian*, 15 October.

Raab, F. (1964) *The English Face of Machiavelli*, Routledge and Kegan Paul, London.

Rank, O. (1968) *Art and Artist*, Agathon Press, New York.

Rockwell, J. (1974) *Fact in Fiction*, Routledge and Kegan Paul, London.

Rockwell, J. (1977) 'A Theory of Literature and Society', in Routh, J., and Wolff, J. (eds), *The Sociology of Literature: Theoretical Approaches*, Sociological Review Monograph Series, Keele.

Rougemont, D. de (1940) *Passion and Society*, Faber and Faber, London.

Sartre, J. P. (1963) *Search for a Method*, Vintage Books, New York.

Saunders, J. W. (1964) *The Profession of English Letters*, Routledge and Kegan Paul, London.

Schucking, L. L. (1960) *The Sociology of Literary Taste*, Routledge and Kegan Paul, London.

Schucking, L. L. (1970) *The Puritan Family*, Routledge and Kegan Paul, London.
Shattuck, R. (1964) *Proust's Binoculars*, Chatto and Windus, London.
Shattuck, R. (1970) *The Banquet Years*, Jonathan Cape, London.
Shattuck, R. (1974) *Proust*, Fontana, London.
Shearman, J. (1967) *Mannerism*, Penguin, Harmondsworth.
Shils, E. (1957) 'Daydreams and Nightmares: Reflections on the Criticisms of Mass Culture', *Sewanee Review*, 65.
Shils, E. (1972) *The Intellectuals and the Powers and Other Essays*, University of Chicago Press, Chicago.
Smith, A. (1976) *The Shadow in the Cave*, Quartet, London.
Spearman, D. (1966) *The Novel and Society*, Routledge and Kegan Paul, London.
Spearman, D. (1972) 'The social influence of fiction', *New Society*, 21.
Snow, C. P. (1959) *The Two Cultures and the Scientific Revolution*, Cambridge University Press, Cambridge.
Steiner, G. (1967) *Tolstoy or Dostoyevsky*, Penguin, Harmondsworth.
Steiner, G. (1969) *Language and Silence*, Penguin, Harmondsworth.
Steiner, G. (1972) *Extraterritorial*, Faber and Faber, London; Penguin, 1975.
Stern, F. (1965) *The Politics of Cultural Despair*, Anchor, New York.
Stone, L. (1964) 'The educational revolution in England, 1560–1640', *Past and Present*, 28.
Stone, L. (1969) 'Literacy and Education in England, 1640–1900' *Past and Present*, 42.
Swingewood, A. (1976) *The Novel and Revolution*, Macmillan, London.
Swingewood, A. (1977) *The Myth of Mass Culture*, Macmillan, London.
Sutherland, J. A. (1976) *Victorian Novels and Publishers*, Athlone Press, London.
Symons, J. (1974) *Bloody Murder*, Penguin, Harmondsworth.
Tawney, R. H. (1964) *Equality*, 4th edn., Allen and Unwin, London.
Thody, P. (1977) *Roland Barthes*, Macmillan, 1977.
Thomas, D. (1969) *A Long Time Burning*, Routledge and Kegan Paul, London.
Thompson E. P. (1967) 'Time, work–discipline and industrial capitalism' *Past and Present*, 38.
Trilling, L. (1950) *The Liberal Imagination*, Secker and Warburg, London.
Trilling, L. (1967) *Beyond Culture*, Penguin, Harmondsworth.
Trilling, L. (1973) *Sincerity and Authenticity*, Oxford University Press, Oxford.
Turnell, M. (1950) *The Novel in France*, Hamish Hamilton, London.
Vidal, G. (1977) *Matters of Fact and Fiction*, Heinemann, London.
Waples, D., Berelson, B. and Bradshaw, F. R. (1940) *What Reading does to People*, University of Chicago Press, Chicago.
Watson, G. (1973) *The Literary Critics*, Penguin, Harmondsworth, originally published Chatto and Windus, 1957.
Watt, I. (1963) *The Rise of the Novel*, Penguin, Harmondsworth.
Weatherby, W. O. (1977) 'Article on Publishing in New York', *Guardian*, 8 Oct.
Webb, R. K. (1950) 'Working class readers in Early Victorian England', *English Historical Review*, 65.
Weber, M. (1952) *Ancient Judaism*, Free Press, Glencoe, Illinois.
Weeks, R. P. (1954) 'Disentanglement as a theme in H. G. Wells' fiction', *Papers of the Michigan Academy of Science, Arts and Letters*.
Weitzmann, L. J., Eifler, D., Hakada, E. and Ross, C. (1971–2) 'Sex role socialization in picture books for preschool children', *American Journal of Sociology*, 77.
Whitehead, P. *et al.* (1977) *Children and their Books*, Macmillan, London.
Wilde, O. (1973) *De Profundis and Other Writings*, Penguin, Harmondswotth.
Williams, R. (1958) *Culture and Society*, Chatto and Windus, London; Penguin, 1971.
Williams, R. (1971) *The Long Revolution*, Penguin, Harmondsworth, originally published Chatto and Windus, 1961.
Williams, R. (1973) *The English Novel*, Paladin, London.
Williams, R. (1977) *Marxism and Literature*, Oxford University Press, Oxford.
Wimsatt, W. K. and Beardsley, M. C. (1946), 'The Intentional Fallacy', *Sewanee Review*, 54.
Wimsatt, W. K. and Beardsley, M. C. (1949) 'The Affective Fallacy', *Sewanee Review*, 57.

Wolff, J. (1975) *Hermeneutic Philosophy and the Sociology of Art*, Routledge and Kegan Paul, London.
Zeraffa, M. (1976) *Fictions*, Penguin, Harmondsworth.

Index